Fat and Beautiful

A Story of Love, Pain, and Courage

by Karen Harmon
with Linda Bonner

Tellwell Talent
www.tellwell.ca

ISBN
978-0-2288-5653-5 (Hardcover)
978-0-2288-5651-1 (Paperback)
978-0-2288-5652-8 (eBook)

I dedicate this book to my beautiful sister,
Linda Bonner. Her love for others
has inspired me and is an example for all to live by.

Many thanks to Sharon Bodner, my mentor,
extraordinary word master, and friend.

Special thanks to the fearless women whose stories
of love, pain, courage, and accomplishments
you will find at the back of this book:

Anne Fletcher Dion
Melena Mertens
Shahnaz Qayumi

TABLE OF CONTENTS

INTRODUCTION

1965, Dougie, Kenny, Karen and Linda

Looking Back

*"One can get in a car to see what man has made. One
must get on a horse to see what God has made."*

-Author Unknown

I am writing this book for my sister, about my sister, because she asked me to. Linda has had a remarkable life filled with drama, humour, adventure, and many difficult situations.

If you judge yourself and others based on size, if you were ever bullied or have been a bully yourself, then some of my sister's story might stir up feelings. However, on the other side of the coin, her biography may intrigue you and teach you some things about yourself that you are unaware of.

Her story is one of love, pain, and courage.

For many years, my sister Linda was a stranger to me. I knew that I loved her, but we were not close like typical sisters might be in a TV show or perhaps the well-known book *Little Women* by Louisa May Alcott.

Some of my memories are vague, and yet some are crystal clear. There is a thirteen-year age difference, which should explain my recollections or lack thereof. When I was born, she was a high school student with an entire life of her own. We were two sisters, with the same parents, but at vastly different stages of life. She left home at the age of eighteen. I was five, so of course, I stayed in the house our parents had built in North Vancouver.

Periodically, Linda came home from the Cariboo region of British Columbia, where she lived, to visit our family at Christmas. Occasionally, she would also pop in unexpectedly.

On these visits, we would sit together on her old bed, which she no longer needed, in an empty bedroom that she no longer slept in, as I was enlisted to help her wrap the family's Christmas presents. Grasping the tape dispenser, I would rip off strips of tape with my clumsy little fingers, careful not to let the tape stick to itself in the process. I would eagerly hand the varying lengths to my big sister to adhere to the festive packages.

Nestled onto Linda's lap in a big comfortable armchair, watching *I Love Lucy*, I would follow her lead to laugh at the funny parts. The mishaps between Lucy and Ethel became our shared sense of humour. I would wait patiently during the half-hour sitcom until Linda snickered, and then I would too.

Some nights, if we were lucky, we were allowed to get the TV trays out and eat dinner in front of the television. But only sometimes. Most nights, we sat at the dinner table, my father at one end and my mother at the other end, as she needed to sit closest to the kitchen for easy access and due to lots of getting up and down—a family of six, two boys, two girls, and a mom and dad in the 1960s. Throughout the meal, I pondered how Linda was somewhat of a guest or a newcomer to the setup. She fit in quite nicely, but it felt foreign. Here today, gone tomorrow, like a favourite auntie coming from a faraway land, home for the holidays briefly to tell stories, smile, laugh, and be on her way again.

When Linda was there, my mother prepared her favourite dishes, liver and onions with ketchup, mashed potatoes, mushrooms, and cauliflower. She liked them so much that she put ketchup on everything. My mother would give my brothers and me something else to eat on the nights she made our older sister her specialties. Linda never stayed long, so I did not mind her different menu plans.

It was during these times that memories of my sister were created.

Some parts of Linda's life stood out more than others, much like a glaring light. The switch would be turned on when she arrived and turned off when she left. What shone most brightly was how she referred to herself as fat, not as a complaint or in a looking for a compliment sort of way, but more as a statement. She often claimed that she was fat as if she liked being overweight. I would never have described her this way or any other way because I was young and did not know what people should or should not weigh.

I might not have noticed that she was of a larger body stature if she had not referred to us as Spaghetti Betty and Skinny Mini. A big sister and a little sister, one large and one small. Years later, a comic strip in the newspaper came out about two cartoon sisters, strangers to us, who were also called Spaghetti Betty and Skinny Mini. We had a good laugh about this because it was my sister who invented the nicknames. For the life of us, we could not figure out how two other sisters could be called the same names as we were.

Throughout my lifetime, it has come to be that the word Fat is wrong, just like the four-letter word that also begins with the letter F. Saying Fat is like a swear word. People frown or wince when they hear it. More times than once, I wondered if calling *yourself* fat was better than *someone else* calling you fat.

When Linda frequently said the F-word, "Fat," rather than saying nothing at all when referring to herself, other people in the room would squirm with discomfort and seem embarrassed. They did not know what to say or do or where to look. During the strained silence, Linda would throw her head back and laugh, like she had made a witty joke or read people's minds and caught them in the act of not being kind. Boom! The cat was let out of the bag. *I am fat, so there!*

She boasted that fat people were jolly. Like a club that the obese belonged to, it required its members to be a specific size. And only the joyful could be admitted. Skinny people would never understand and could never be allowed in. My sister said that a lot of thin people were grumpy because they were probably always hungry.

Food was a huge topic of conversation in our family. I remember my mother weighing food on a little scale because of a group my sister and mother belonged to called Weight Watchers. Food portions had to be just the right size, or they might not get enough points to pass.

Despite her size, Linda had lots of boyfriends, and because she was a cowgirl in a place called Clinton in the Cariboo, her male suitors were often cowboys. Bucking bronco types, these men rode the range, branded cattle, were proficient at building campfires, and loved beans right out of the tin.

Men who loved and preferred bigger women dated my sister. She was fun and always made plenty of jokes, like, "Why did the monkey throw the butter out of the window? Because he wanted to see a butterfly." Or "Why did the monkey throw the clock out of the window? Because he wanted to see time fly." She had many tricks up her sleeve that were always a lark. I laughed and always wanted to hear more.

At one point, Linda had a horse named Jack that was seventeen hands high. Jack was a white Appaloosa beauty and carried my sister's weight stoically. When riding the range or going on trail rides, Linda often exclaimed that she needed a bigger horse, one that could carry her safely and adequately. I think this observation was mostly for the horse's sake. Linda always rode Western, not English. There is a big difference, as riding Western is intended for cowboys who worked cattle from horseback. The Western saddle is made to distribute weight more evenly and is made comfortable for long hours of riding over rough terrain.

As a little sister, I looked up to my older sister and thought her to be beautiful. I admired how she dressed in the latest Western wear; embroidered roses adorned her denim blouses, and stretchy pants fit perfectly over her cowboy boots. Her earrings were little clip-on silver cowboy boots, and she wore a matching brooch that resembled a tiny cowboy hat. All her jewelry was pieced together thoughtfully to match every ensemble.

One time my sister dyed her brunette hair blonde and cut it short. Combined with her pink lipstick, Western attire, and red truck with white panels, heads would turn when she drove by.

Linda was different from other older sisters that I knew, and she did not behave or look like other women from the era. She was strong and independent. And yet, I had no idea how much she had struggled over the years with people's perception of her. I found out many years later just how cruelly she had been treated.

Perhaps the most defining moment of Linda's life occurred when she was pre-school age. Her mother had signed her up for swimming lessons at the seaside pool in Stanley Park. As they waited for the lesson to begin, another child ran up to Linda, stuck out their tongue, and called her Piggy-Pig, while snorting through their nose. Her mother was mortified and wanted to pop the bratty child between the eyes, as any mother would. Wisdom won, and she listened to the voice in her head that said not to do so.

Linda was somewhat oblivious to the incident at that time and began to test the cool salty water with her toes. As the group assembled, another child came along and pushed Linda so hard she smacked down on her bottom. He ran away, chanting, "Red alert, hippopotamus on the loose. Run for your lives!" Linda sat crying in the shallow water and refused the lessons.

Her mother was speechless and outraged by this unfair treatment of her daughter. Grabbing her by the hand, the two of them made their way to the concession stand for a Fudgesicle. While her mother tried to comfort her, Linda focused on her sweet chocolatey ice cream treat. Then something extraordinary caught her eye...

Two uniformed police officers were strolling by on their chestnut mares. They smiled and waved at five-year-old Linda. Leaping up from the park bench, she begged her mother for permission to pet the horses. She then pleaded for permission to bump the officer off the horse so that she herself could sit atop the magnificent animal and ride off into the sunset.

Regrettably, she had to settle for a friendly hello and stroking the horse's mane. When her mother lifted her precocious daughter to meet the horse's face, Linda completely ignored the officer and stared deeply into luminous brown, telepathic eyes—instantly falling in love.

In later years, my sister was greatly affected, like many other females, by the beautification industry, classism, sexism, trauma, and men's oppression. Her story is relatable and life-changing.

Above all else, Linda's life will inspire you.

Someone once told me, "Our struggles today are the good ole days tomorrow." As you read this book, I will let you decide if you agree.

CHAPTER ONE

And Baby Makes Three

*"The amazing thing about becoming a parent is that you
will never again be your own first priority."*

-Olivia Wilde

Vancouver is a major coastal city located in Western Canada, on
the west half of the Burrard Peninsula. It is bound to the north
by English Bay and the Burrard Inlet and to the south by the
Fraser River. The city has easy access to the Pacific Ocean and the
mountains of the Pacific Coast Range.

After the war in 1946, there was a crime wave across North
America. One gang broke out of an Ontario jail and got away
with $350,000 at Bath, Ontario, in the most significant bank
holdup on Canadian record. The robbers were chased across
four provinces before being cornered. Masked stick-up men
jumped into the headlines from coast to coast. Vancouver, British
Columbia, was no exception.

On August 25, 1947, almost nine months pregnant, Frances
Bonner, with her husband Vince, set out to do some errands before
enjoying a picnic at Spanish Banks Beach in Vancouver.

It was a warm morning, and Frances felt the strain to her lower
back from her sixty-pound pregnancy weight gain. Hot, tired, and

weary, her swollen ankles kept her in men's bedroom slippers, and she felt frustrated that she had outgrown her Woodward's loose-fitting house dresses. The only clothing articles that fit were her husband's boxer shorts beneath her mother's borrowed dress. Frances wondered if she would ever get her one-hundred-and-twenty-pound figure back. At five feet ten inches tall, people often referred to her as willowy thin, but on this day, she felt like a massive rhododendron. She was sure that her baby was never going to arrive and had taken up permanent residence in her belly, and therefore, forever a larger person she would be!

Thankfully, her husband Vince adored her just as she was. When he suggested they spend the afternoon at the beach in hopes of altering his wife's mood and discomfort, she delightfully accepted the invitation. Enjoying the beach's sights and sounds while sitting under a weeping willow tree with a cool ocean breeze could be just the thing on this hot summer day in Vancouver. Frances was not a complainer, and aside from feeling cumbersome, she was game for a few hours out and about.

Together they had prepared cucumber, onion, and cheese sandwiches on homemade white bread, and store-bought cookies, together with a thermos of instant coffee and no mugs, as Vince preferred drinking out of the accompanied lid from the insulated thermos. They did not mind sharing. Once ready, they walked to the nearest streetcar and planned to get out at the stop near their bank.

Frances was looking forward to sitting on the warm sand while leaning against a log to enjoy the cool ocean breeze and indulge in some french fries lightly sprinkled with salt and vinegar, in addition to their packed lunch. A small withdrawal from their joint chequing account was needed to cover the cost. She always did the bill paying and banking, and anything to do with money and household finances. But on this day, Vince accompanied her into the bank.

After entering the bank, they stood in a short line and waited for their turn and the bank teller's nod to proceed to her wicket.

The exchange was brief, with only the teller's comments about the weather and Frances's protruding belly. It was evident that Frances and Vince would be welcoming their long-awaited baby into the world any day. Thankfully, she was finally free from morning sickness with only a slight twinge of discomfort to her back and swollen ankles.

With the end of her pregnancy near, people rarely commented and mostly just tried to look the other way. A common occurrence would be raised eyebrows, blank stares or the odd wink, not to her but to her husband, as if they were visualizing how Frances got into that state in the first place.

Finishing up at the teller, Frances carefully placed the cash into the wallet in her handbag. As they made their way to the heavy glass doors to exit the bank, Vince firmly guided his wife with one arm wrapped around her waist while the other held open the door. He was especially feeling protective. Vince adored his pregnant wife and thought how cute she looked in his bedroom slippers, shuffling along in a public place.

As they were leaving, a masked man was entering. Vince's adrenaline and street smarts kicked in and propelled him forward, ensuring that his wife and precious cargo were at his side. Escorting Frances around the corner, the breathless Vince pulled his chatty wife into a shop.

Frances had not left the house in days, so she was happy and unusually talkative. She often held the position of captive audience, allowing Vince to be the relationship's talker and storyteller. However, excited about the beach, french fries, and her baby's arrival, Frances did not sense any danger or see the robber who had pushed past them.

Bewildered as to why Vince had taken her into a dry cleaner, Frances noticed a look of worry on her husband's face. When she asked him what was wrong, Vince realized that Frances was completely oblivious to the close call they'd just had at the bank. Staring into his wife's pale blue eyes, Vince hesitated to tell her that a masked gunman had entered the bank as they were leaving, and they had just made a narrow escape. He chose to make up a small fib.

He brushed off her questioning by telling her he thought he had seen a co-worker and was not in the mood to shoot the breeze—he just wanted to get to the beach.

There was no reason not to believe Vince, so Frances said, "Okay, the fellow you work with must be gone by now, so let's get going."

Vince nodded, and together they made their way back outside to the streetcar stop.

Climbing aboard was no easy feat. As Vince helped his wife from behind, the conductor noticed and scrambled to his feet to pull Frances up onto the trolley. All the pushing and pulling of Frances's expectant body caused her to burst out laughing. Old comedic routines that involved physical clumsiness, such as slipping on a banana peel, often gave her the giggles.

Once seated, the conductor exclaimed to Vince and Frances, "Hey, did you hear all the sirens? I guess the bank on the corner was just robbed at gunpoint."

With that news, Frances gasped and straight away fainted. When she came to, there was a flurry all around her. Vince was fanning her with a discarded newspaper, the streetcar driver was elevating her legs, and a mother of three crying children was hollering at someone to get an ambulance. Frances was in a daze, trying to wrap her head around what was going on. She still felt dizzy when coming to terms with the near escape of being in the middle of a bank robbery with bullets flying and hostages being taken. Frances imagined the worst-case scenario of giving birth in the bank's locked vault, making headline news. Visions of Bonnie and Clyde, John Dillinger, Babyface Nelson, and Pretty Boy Floyd, all deadly and widely known criminals, immediately came to Frances's mind.

Sitting up and noticing Vince at her side, she felt safe and protected. Almost instantly, she remembered why she fell in love with him in the first place. There was no denying that he was the most handsome man she had ever laid eyes on, comparable to the silver screen's movie actors. He could have been a movie matinee idol with his dark good looks, charm, wit, and adorable sense of humour—a complete package deal. But what struck her fancy the most was his desire to protect her, and she knew he would be a wonderful father.

Frances speculated that he could have used his striking good looks as a weapon or a tool to lure a damsel in distress. But instead, he wore it like a plate of armour, proud and gallant. Even to see him from across the room, anyone could tell that he was humble without an ounce of arrogance.

At the beginning of their courtship, she debated what made this man stand out from the rest. Was it his curly black hair and sun-drenched skin that other women would swoon over? Or perhaps it was his friendly green eyes that smiled in conjunction with his mouth when he frequently offered a wide, generous grin. Once the creases in the corner of his eyes took shape, a boisterous, contagious laugh would inevitably follow.

She concluded that she was reminded of a Greek statue or a Roman emperor with all his features combined, yet without royalty's hardened nobility.

Even though Frances would describe herself as plain and shy, opposite of what she thought would be the type of woman to snag a man like Vince, she did not have a jealous bone in her body. She knew without a shadow of a doubt that Vince was hers and hers alone.

She also never minded him paying attention to others. Frances could hear his voice, "Would you care to dance?"

"Why, yes," a most unsuspecting dance partner would respond. Vince gave his undivided attention for the entire duration of a song and dance number, which his partner eagerly received.

He had made it a habit to ask the wallflowers to be his dance partner at the many dances they attended. The name says it all, a beautiful flower that chooses to stand by the wall due to shyness, unpopularity, or lack of a partner. Vince's first choice was always the loners and not the obvious popular girls. In every aspect of the word, Vince Bonner was a gentleman through and through.

Frances's mind whirled back to the task at hand while she and Vince both waved off calling for an ambulance. They also chose not to go to the beach that day. After all the commotion, Vince decided to take Frances home.

Once there, they settled in to quietly eat their picnic on the wrap-around veranda in the home they shared with Frances's older sister Violet and her husband, Tommy.

Violet had been married twice before, and the whole family doubted that she would ever have a child. She often stated that children were for other people to have, and she was not about to sabotage her figure for the sake of a snotty-nosed brat. Secretly Frances and Vince would roll their eyes and utter under their breath, "Thank God for that."

Violet was considered "the pretty sister," while Frances was "the smart one." As sisters, they were complete opposites. Violet was a raven-haired outspoken beauty with a sharp tongue and a loud voice, often with a cocktail in hand. Frances was fair-skinned, blonde, and mild-mannered, often found quietly reading a book while sipping her coffee.

It was well-known to everyone in the family that Violet was insanely jealous of her pregnant sister. They speculated her often arrogant and rude comments were just another form of envy.

After their picnic supper and a few games of cards, Frances and Vince made an early night of it and went to bed. A few hours past midnight, Frances awoke, feeling like she had to go to the bathroom. She'd had similar feelings before over some seafood that had gone bad, but something told her that it was not food poisoning this time.

She nudged Vince awake and whispered, "I think it's time," at which he flew out of bed knowing what he needed to do. Helping Frances on with his men's slippers and overcoat, they proceeded out to the car, grabbing on the way the suitcase that had been sitting by the door for weeks.

During the car ride, Frances felt completely unprepared, a feeling that dated back to her childhood when any conversation regarding her time of the month, let alone having a baby or how the baby was conceived, was utterly unheard of. Even now, she felt just as naive and wished she could take it all back—the marriage, pregnancy, and baby that would be arriving soon. At one point during her childhood, she thought that she might like to become a Catholic nun. The thought of intimacy with another had made her cringe.

Built in 1927, The Salvation Army Grace Hospital stood at Heather Street and 26th Avenue in Vancouver. When it officially opened, it was proudly equipped with fifty beds and bassinets. By 1947 the hospital was modern and upscale, with a new wing for nurses in training.

Vince was not allowed into the delivery room, as was the custom and protocol in those days. Instead, he was ushered out to the waiting room by one of the nurses and told to sit tight. Lighting up a cigarette, he sat close to the nearest ashtray, knowing it would undoubtedly be a long night. He was pleased that Frances refused to drink or smoke during her pregnancy, not that he thought it mattered, but because she said it sickened her to do either.

To ease his mind, he let himself daydream and remember the first day he had laid eyes on Frances. It was a blind date, which is the worst kind of date imaginable. But this one was different and what made it so unique was that both Frances and Vince had been paired up with different people and had not intended to be with each other.

While seated at a table for four, it was Frances who caught his eye. She was tall, blonde, and willowy thin. Vince was intrigued by Frances's shyness but also by her ability to laugh. Some might have called her plain, but Vince felt her beauty was arresting, and he knew right away that she was just his type.

Perhaps there is such a thing as love at first sight, he thought.

However, Vince was with someone else that evening, a petite brunette who never stopped talking. He was struggling to remember her name. Madge? Martha? Marilyn? No matter how he tried, he could not get it right. Each time Vince fumbled over her name, she would scowl and curtly correct him that it was Mary. Apologizing, Vince bowed his head in embarrassment.

Vince thought the name Frances was glamorous and memorable. He knew that it would be etched in his mind forever. He gathered that Frances felt the same way about him because, over dinner, their hands lightly grazed each other when coincidently reaching for their cutlery at the same time. An electric jolt surged through Vince's hand. He had hoped that the same thing had happened to Frances.

As a rule, even though Vince was outgoing, he was not overly forward with showing physical affection towards his dates. On this night, however, Vince fought his usual shyness and boldly took it upon himself to reach for Frances's hand under the table. He was immediately pleased to find that it was right there waiting for him.

With a smile on his face, Vince snapped back to the present, sensing that someone was standing over him. Leaping to his feet, he came face to face with a nurse telling him that his baby daughter had been born. The nurse stated that he could see his wife and baby shortly. Given the room number and told to stay in the waiting room so mother and baby could rest, Vince spent the next forty-five minutes calling family and friends from the only pay telephone in the vicinity to announce the news that their daughter had arrived early on the morning of August 26, 1947.

He called Frances's mother first, followed by a hesitant call to Violet. Vince was pleased that both women were happy with the news. As a rule, Violet's jealousy was uncontainable. He hoped that she would not cause trouble. Violet secretly hoped that there would be problems for her younger sister with the new baby. She seethed at the very thought of all the attention Frances would soon be getting. Although she assumed her thoughts and feelings were contained, her envy was as apparent as the nose on her face. Everyone in the family knew.

Frances had made it clear to Vince that she did not have any experience or earth-shattering drive to be a mother. Of course, she always knew that she would dutifully eventually have a baby, but her own relationship with her mother was not something she was proud of. She did not want to bungle raising a child as she felt her mother had done with her.

In retrospect, Frances had felt closer to her father. Her mother's antics and mood swings were almost unbearable to Frances, as it was a common practice that her mom locked herself in her bedroom for days, leaving it up to her husband, Joe, to take care of their two daughters. On top of all of that, Frances was aware that her mother also had several affairs.

During the 1930s Depression-era, people often knocked at their door looking for work and handouts. Because her father was a station agent, they lived above the train station. Therefore, many transient people were coming and going. Her father was kind and generous, periodically taking in drifters in exchange for work around the terminal. Unfortunately, Frances's mother, unbeknownst to her father, was also generous but in a different manner. Very early on, Frances came to understand the term, "What goes on behind closed doors stays behind closed doors."

The very thought of her mother's indiscretions made her mind feel stretched and warped, so she had taken to blocking out what seemed indecent and wrong and did not speak about it to anyone, even Vince.

In 1946, a song came out on the radio called "Linda." It became very popular and was frequently played. Performed by Buddy Clark, the song was written in 1942 by Jack Lawrence when Lawrence was in the service in World War II. The song title was taken from the name Linda, given to the one-year-old daughter of his attorney, Lee Eastman. (Linda Eastman would eventually become the wife of Paul McCartney from the Beatles singing group.)

The song first reached the Billboard Magazine charts on March 28, 1947, and remained there for nine weeks. Therefore, many babies in the following year, and many years after, were given the name of Linda.

Choosing the perfect name for his beloved baby girl was crucial to Vince because growing up on the prairies in the 1920s, he had been teased mercilessly because of his name. His mother had abandoned him at the age of five. She had fled with his sisters due to immense poverty, leaving Vince and his older brother Hank to fend for themselves, alone with a drunken father and cantankerous uncles to raise them. Vince moped around, bewildered and heartbroken, seeking attention, acceptance, and love.

Sadly, there did not seem to be a lot of compassion in the Depression-era, especially by an alcoholic father and uncles helplessly trying to raise Vince and his older brother, all seemingly lacking know-how. Coping during desperate times of poverty and no foreseeable work meant focusing on putting food on the table rather than nurturing two little boys.

Vincent Alphonse Bonner was a name that was easy to make fun of. *Innocent Vinocent* and *Alphonse the Elephant* were just a couple of the configurations other children came up with regarding Vince's name.

With his upbringing, such as it was, Vince had made it known to Frances that his desire and mission in life was to break the cycle of abuse and family dysfunction he was born into. To this, Frances wholeheartedly agreed.

Into the wee hours of the night, they would spend hours talking about their pasts. Frances's story was different from Vince's but had its fair share of family neglect as well.

Raised by a mother with a personality disorder, before there was a label or therapy for such a thing, and having a sister who often despised her, Frances knew she wanted her children to be brought up differently. She was thankful for her loving father. The latter often made up for the shortcomings and disabilities in the family home.

Frances and Vince vowed to one another not to argue in front of their children, nor to spank or lay a hand on them even though the doctors and child specialists said otherwise—"Spare the rod and spoil the child." They both disagreed with this outdated statement and method of raising children.

Before their first baby entered this world, they had decided to pick a name that could not be made fun of, which was crucial to Vince. After hearing the sweet sound of Buddy Clark's voice churning out the famous song by Linda's name, Vince suggested they call their daughter the same.

Impossibly, they could not foresee the future. It was not until six years later that their firstborn girl would come running home from school in tears because she had been made fun of, having been called Linda Pinda. Both parents would immediately feel at a loss.

Frances had been a tomboy and a bit of a bully herself in school, so she enthusiastically reacted to Linda's plight with a zealous "Why don't you give those bullies a knuckle sandwich the next time they call you names?"

"Sometimes, that's just how life is," Frances said to her daughter's wide-eyed tear-stained face.

Grandpa Joe and baby Linda

Grandma and baby Linda

Frances with Linda

Vince with Linda

Grandma, Vince and new baby Linda

New proud parents

The family home, 5th and Bayswater, Vancouver B.C.

CHAPTER TWO

Off to the Races

"I love little people, and it is not a slight thing when
they, who are so fresh from God, love us."

–Charles Dickens

Linda was the apple of her parents' eyes and apple pie alamode to her grandparents'.

Frances allowed her mother and husband to hold, coddle, change, and play with baby Linda as often and as freely as possible. She was not an overly protective or doting mother, and she appreciated all the help she could get.

Violet, on the other hand, only paid attention to the baby when they had company over. She was the perfect auntie, oohing and awing for all to see. But when she was home alone with her husband, Tommy, her disdainful, slurred comments could be heard throughout the house.

"Why does that baby need so much attention from our mother?"

"They are spoiling that child, and they'll be sorry."

"I wish that kid would shut up!"

"I do not envy Frances in the least. She'll regret the day that baby was ever born when she loses her figure and her husband!"

On and on, she would lament. Everyone tried to ignore her and look the other way, but it was hard to block out her droning voice. Violet's negativity was taking a toll on everyone in the household.

Vince was employed in construction, and upon returning from a trying day's work, after jumping in the shower and getting cleaned up, baby Linda was his main priority. Frances adored this side of her husband, and she had speculated that this would be the case even before they got engaged and inevitably married.

For the early part of her life, at least until she started school, Linda was raised around adults—grownups who did not speak baby talk or tickle her under her chin just to witness a giggle. Even before Linda could formulate words, they undoubtedly expected her to understand them as they went about their day-to-day activities, discussing current events, the weather, and completing daily household chores. They treated her like one of them, and she responded accordingly.

Assisting in setting the table when she could barely walk, offering to light her grandmother's cigarettes, and standing on a stool to feed various clothing items through the wringer washing machine were all tasks that Linda wanted to do. She begged to help and be just like a grownup.

Unfortunately, as small and uncoordinated as she was, household duties were never without incident. Periodically Linda broke a dish carrying one too many plates to the kitchen table. More than once, she burned her stubby little fingers on a match, standing on tippy toes with arms outstretched to the puckered mouth to failingly light her grandmother's cigarette.

But worst of all was getting her hand caught in the rollers while trying to guide a wet shirt sleeve through the washing machine. An old wringer washer's defining feature is the tub, with an agitator to move the suds through the laundry, dislodge dirt and grime, and rinse it out. The laundry needs to then be fed through the wringer to squeeze out the water.

On a mild spring morning, mother and daughter set out onto the back porch of their Kitsilano, Vancouver home to hang out the wash. The washing machine was situated on the back porch for convenience purposes near the clothesline. One of Linda's favourite activities was to hand her mother wet clothes to peg them on the line.

With chapped red hands, she would feed the clothes through the machine, and as they came out the other side, she would hand the freshly laundered clothes to her mother, a fun and rewarding process for both of them.

On this particular day, while she eagerly guided her father's work shirt through the cleaning device, she somehow did not let go in time, and her little hand proceeded to remain attached to the cuff. As it was pulled in and trapped midway between the rollers with forearm encased, she screamed her head off, and Frances, who was overseeing everything, froze. Upon hearing his little girl's cries, Vince ran outside to the back porch and, with super-human strength, managed to pry apart the arm-eating contraption before it reached little Linda's elbow. All was well, and after a few bounces on father's knee, her tears ceased, and she begged to continue with the half-finished wash.

Regularly, Linda accompanied her family to the horse races at the Pacific National Exhibition. It was a family outing, with Frances and Vince, Edith and Joe, and Violet and Tommy, all hopping onto the streetcar with toddler Linda in tow.

Linda's grandparents, Frances's parents Edith and Joe, were impeccable dressers. Joe never left the house unless he was wearing a three-piece suit, including a vest, pocket watch, and derby hat. Edith, like Joe, always wore a hat. But unlike Joe, she would spend hours getting ready, administering a full face of makeup, a snug-fitting girdle, support hose, buckle-up shoes, and a proper dress that never fell above the knee.

Frances was far less concerned about fashion and often settled for a simple dress, low-heeled pumps, and no makeup, aside from a bright shade of lipstick adorning her pale complexion. On the other hand, Violet loved going out and, taking after their mother, would spend hours getting ready. Every event was marked as a reason to celebrate, therefore accompanying Violet's outfit was a flask of bourbon or gin tucked neatly inside her handbag.

Mink stoles were the going trend, and Violet owned at least four in varying shades. Depending on the season, Violet chose a suitable fur and style that made its mark around her broad shoulders. In contrast, Frances was content wearing one of Vince's oversized sweaters, or if the weather unexpectantly turned, she enjoyed his comfortable, strong arm gently wrapped around her slim frame to keep warm.

In contrast to all the fuss, Tommy and Vince wore their usual suits, white-collar dress shirts, and thin, black ties.

These six family members were the main characters who set an example and played a role in influencing Linda during her early formative years: Linda's doting mother and father, her volatile aunt and docile uncle, and her unbalanced grandmother and adoring grandfather. Eccentricities and drama were, therefore, commonplace.

The Vancouver Racecourse is situated at the north end of the Pacific National Exhibition. In 1888 the provincial government granted 160 acres of land for recreational use in a place referred to as Hastings Park, and in 1892, horse racing made its debut.

In 1926, Happyland opened (the predecessor to Playland) for the delight of young and old alike. The grounds featured a merry-go-round, Ferris wheel, and the Big Dipper Roller Coaster, along with treats such as cotton candy and candied apples. Bingo, the 4H Club, and arcade games rounded out the activities.

By the 1930s, Hastings Street on race day was equivalent to the Granville strip on a Saturday night. It was a grand event and a hub for politicians, dignitaries, socialites, and the well-to-do. Folks would dress up in their most acceptable attire and spend the day at the Hastings Racecourse.

Tragically, in early 1942, before Frances and Vince met, over 8,000 Japanese Canadians were incarcerated at Hastings Park before being sent to internment work camps in the BC Interior or elsewhere across Canada. This was due to the fear ignited by the

Japanese involvement in the Second World War. They were given only a twenty-four-hour warning and only allowed two suitcases each. Many lost most of their possessions as they were forcibly relocated and interned in the name of national security. The majority of these were Canadian citizens by birth.

Confiscated cars and trucks were parked in the middle of the Hastings Park Racecourse. The Custodian of Enemy Property sold these vehicles and all other properties at auction without the owners' knowledge or consent.

After the war, the 1950s brought an expansion to the racetrack that consisted of five-eighths of a mile, and occasionally Frances and Vince would take the streetcar to the racetrack to bet on a few horses. Shortly after Linda's birth, it became a regular weekly family outing.

In her bonnet and frilly dresses, Linda enjoyed standing on her father's knees to cheer on the jockeys and their acclaimed steeds. As the crowd roared and applauded, Linda did the same. When the commentator narrated the neck-and-neck race to the finish line, so did Linda. She hollered at the top of her lungs in unison. The family and anyone else in earshot laughed at Linda's antics, which encouraged her to continue.

After the races, when things were wrapping up, Linda begged to be introduced to the thoroughbreds, as they appeared for all to see in the winner's circle. She wanted to know the horses who were competing to win, place, or show.

Thus began Linda's passion and, to some, her obsession with horses.

In 1950, at three years old, Linda was outgoing and friendly to all, not shy in the least, and she talked a mile a minute. Some would say she was three going on thirty. In those years, kids watched *Howdy Doody*, while teenagers watched *Bonanza*, and young and old alike tuned in to *Ed Sullivan*, *The Jack Benny Program*, *Jackie Gleason*, and *Gene Autry*.

It was also the year that Frances, Vince, and his brother Hank decided to drive to Minneapolis, Minnesota. Their particular destination was the historic town of Sauk Centre, Minnesota, where Vince and Hank's mother lived. The land is understood to be Sioux Dakota land, ceded in the treaty of 1846. Many place names in the region bear reference to the Sauk people.

Incidentally, Sauk Centre is also the location of the boyhood home of Sinclair Lewis, novelist and winner of the Nobel Prize in Literature. It served as the inspiration for Gopher Prairie, Lewis's fictional setting for his 1920 novel *Main Street*.

Thirteen years prior, Vince had rekindled his relationship with his mother. He had spent many years searching for her, writing letters to various places where he hoped to find her, which turned out to be a painful task. Letters emblazoned with "Return to Sender" on the front of the envelope would wind up back in Vince's care months later.

Eventually, at the age of twenty-one, he did find her. One of his heartfelt letters arrived in his long-lost mother's mailbox. They reunited and promised to remain in touch.

Back in 1921 in Saskatchewan, Canada, when Vince was five years old, times were tough, and for his mother, married to an alcoholic and with four children, the living conditions were impossible. Poverty and one too many arguments engulfed his young mother in hopelessness. Neither of Vince's parents could withstand their hardships any longer. The last thing Vince could remember was his mother hitting his father over the head with a cast-iron frying pan. Thinking she had killed him, she fled.

Loading up the wagon, she took the two girls and left her two sons behind in the care of her husband's brothers Chuck and Earl.

The straw that had broken the camel's back was a late night of drinking and card playing. Earl came home three sheets to the wind, drunker than a skunk. With no money for food, Martha was livid that with four children under the age of six, Earl would once again drink up all their money. Waiting in hiding with a cast iron frying pan behind her back as he came through the door of their clapboard shack, she clobbered unsuspecting drunken Earl senseless.

This was a considerably easy feat for Martha, as she stood five feet ten inches and carried her larger body stature well. Earl, on the other hand, was five feet seven inches, never sober, and as the story goes, weighed one hundred and twenty pounds soaking wet.

Fearful that she had killed Earl, Martha headed straight across the Canadian-US border to North Dakota.

North Dakota's geography consists of three regions. In the east is the Red River Valley. West of this is the Missouri Plateau, and the southwestern part of North Dakota is covered by the Great Plains, accentuated by the Badlands. Years later, Gene Autry would sing and record his claim-to-fame song, "Red River Valley," which often reminded Vince of his mother.

Martha was familiar with the area because before moving to Saskatchewan as a young bride, she had been raised by an American soldier who had married a beautiful Aboriginal woman from the Blackfoot Nation.

She relished her simple childhood and missed the wide-open plains and how her mother referred to her as Mika, which means "Intelligent Racoon." Simultaneously, her father liked to call her Nina, telling Martha the pet name meant "Strong."

In 1921 when Martha returned to her birthplace, her parents had since passed, but she felt safe and at home in North Dakota. While her daughters (Vince's sisters) Bonnie and Geneva were still young, Martha remarried and had more children. Unfortunately, she married another alcoholic, and history was to repeat itself.

However, in 1950 all Martha's children were grown up, and her two boys, brothers in their thirties, took turns driving from Vancouver, British Columbia, to the Midwest of the United States to see her. She could not have been happier to have all four of her adult children together.

Vince could hardly wait to introduce his beautiful wife and daughter to his mother. He was achingly proud of them both. With this imminent family reunion, soon Linda would be meeting more eclectic relatives, particularly two aunties who could hold their own in fashion, conversation, dramatic storytelling, and humorous anecdotes.

Upon their arrival, bear-hold hugs and wet kisses were had by all. They were a family of loud, animated talkers and little Linda fit right in. Frances, on the other hand, was quiet and found the beauty and vitality of Vince's sisters overwhelming. She admired them but preferred to watch from a distance, enjoying all the merriment and goings-on.

Vince's younger sister Bonnie was petite, trim, and stylish. Her hair was thick dark curls just like his, and her stories were of trials and tribulations working as a cocktail waitress in Chicago, complete with tales of mobsters and colourful escapades with the men she had dated.

Linda listened intently to her auntie's recollections of late nights, parties, and dance hall girls. When Auntie Bonnie went into her rendition of the can-can dance, Linda stood up alongside her, flipping up her skirt at the end of the number to show off her little girl panties. Frances was horrified while the other family members all laughed in unison at Vince's big-little girl.

Unlike Bonnie, Vince's older sister Geneva was tall and statuesque, living in Florida where the sun shone brightly on a daily basis, and oranges grew in every yard. Her home there was a ranch style, complete with swimming pool, cabana, and pool boy. She was also stylishly dressed, and her jet-black hair hung down her back in a thick, shiny braid.

Geneva, warmly referred to as Auntie GiGi, told a different story to that of Bonnie. Her recollections were similar to Vince's memories of the dirt floor in their childhood clapboard home. She remembered their parents' last violent argument and then being torn away from her brothers to travel by horse and buggy to another place of poverty. Shortly after arriving, her mother married an abusive man, and they had more children.

Geneva went on to share more tragic tales of a stepdad that would line the children up with an unloaded shotgun pointed at them, threatening them if they did not behave, followed by a loud belly laugh. Bowed heads followed the narrative as the now-adult siblings sat silently, not knowing what to say or do.

The play-by-play of unfortunate events spilled out like a pent-up dam with no regard to consequences if it were to burst. Finally, when Auntie GiGi stopped talking, and the room fell silent, she made a complete about-face and changed the subject to happy stories of travel in far-off lands, the Native American jewelry she handcrafted, and her successful husband and beautiful children. She finished up by inviting everyone to her luxurious home in sun-drenched Florida, the Sunshine State of palm trees and citrus fruit, and the boating capital of the world.

That was that. The full account of her traumatic childhood horror story was swept under the carpet and never brought up or spoken of again.

Meanwhile, little Linda's eyes were round as saucers as she tried to take in the account of family violence and trauma, and the story unfolded before her like a roller coaster, climbing the steep tracks with fear and anticipation, and then free falling down the other side at breakneck speeds into exuberant laughter.

Both women had intriguing and vivid recollections and narratives of their lives, causing every listener to be on the edge of their seat. They always stood up to speak, and their hands were mesmerizing, moving in unison with their animated faces while delivering a detailed run-down of days gone by.

Aside from her shyness, Frances was captivated. She could see where her husband got all his antics, realizing that it must run in the family, and her quick-witted, three-year-old little girl was following in her father's and aunties' footsteps, especially with dramatics and humour. She noted, thankfully, that Linda's upbringing was much happier and healthier than that which Vince, Hank, Bonnie, and Geneva had endured.

Linda's parents and the other grownups around her were never quite sure if Linda's behaviour was attention-seeking, naughty, or just looking for a laugh. Still, she shocked everyone in the vicinity with her actions and demeanour on more than one occasion.

While visiting and taking driving tours around Minneapolis, Linda grabbed her newly introduced grandmother's hat and threw it out the window of the back seat while travelling down the freeway. She also found a box of matches and thought it would be fun to light them one at a time and throw them out the window too. Before any throwing could take place, Linda dropped a lit match between her bare legs. Frances was able to intercept and confiscate the whole matchbox, and thankfully no one was hurt. Especially little Linda.

Instead, she carried on jabbering to no one in particular. Linda would often sing at the top of her lungs and recite the horse race commentator's description of a race to the finish line. This usually gave whoever was listening something funny to laugh about, wondering why on earth a young child would know such a thing.

Aside from her seemingly cheeky behaviour, Linda was loved by all. She was confident, determined, and always had an opinion of her own. Shortly after returning home from their cross-country road trip, Linda developed a small habit. To phrase it politely, she liked to collect souvenirs.

Frances and Vince were social. They enjoyed card games, dinner parties, and visits with friends. They noticed that Linda liked to bring a purse whenever they went on outings. Her bag was always empty when they left their home, but upon returning home, Linda's purse would be full of all sorts of things.

When Frances and Vince asked her where she got all her items from, she boldly stated, "I like to collect souvenirs from the houses we visit." Upon going through Linda's handbag, they would pull out bars of soap, nail files, salt and pepper shakers, decks of cards, and once even a toothbrush.

It was calmly explained to Linda that one must not take things from people's homes, and the name for it was called stealing. Stealing was against the law. It was not kind, and people just might not invite her back if she became a kleptomaniac. From then on, Linda was frisked at the door before leaving people's homes. She did get away with it one last time when her parents forgot to check under her hat.

Linda and her Grandpa Joe (Frances's father) had a unique relationship. He teased her, and she teased back. He nicknamed her his little movie star. Sometimes he would call her Doris Day or Dale Evans, whoever was popular at the time.

Linda would put on her mother's high heel shoes and dance around like Carmen Miranda, minus the bowl of fruit on her head. Grandfather would applaud and encourage her. On one of her performances, she did a high kick, and her high heel shoe (obviously too big) landed directly in her grandpa's teacup. Laughter was heard all around, renewing Linda's lust for entertaining, no matter how silly.

Practical jokes have been going on since the beginning of time, and the 1950s were no exception. "Nicky, Nicky Nine Doors" was the practise of knocking on a door or ringing a doorbell and running away before it was answered. Another joke was loosening the saltshaker in a restaurant so the next unsuspecting customer would be shocked and dismayed when their entire meal was doused in salt. Yet another old trick was taking an empty snuff tin, filling it with flour, attaching an elastic band and a paper clip and then offering up some snuff (chewing tobacco) to an innocent victim. When they opened the lid, the elastic band would unwind, spinning the paper clip and causing the flour to fly into the face of whoever was lifting the lid.

Vince was clever at fixing up such gimmicks and jokes. "Back in the Depression-era in a one-room schoolhouse, kids were forced to be creative," he could often be heard saying.

Being around grownups, Linda was privy to the goings-on and somehow came into possession of some itching powder. Not knowing when enough was enough, she snuck into Grandpa's bedroom, opened a chest of drawers, and poured itching powder into Grandpa's long johns. He wore his long johns every day since moving from the prairies, as he said the damp Vancouver weather caused him to be cold right down to his bones. On the day of the itching powder fiasco, he went the whole day thinking that something was terribly wrong.

When they figured out who the culprit was and what she had done, Linda was sent to her room by perplexed parents, with a cheeky grin on her face behind their backs. Grandpa, of course, forgave his little granddaughter, whom he was sure would become the next Shirley Temple or part of *The Three Stooges* gang, a vaudeville and comedy act show that he delighted in. Dating back to 1922, they starred in short films by Columbia Pictures. Their claim to fame was physical humour, slapstick, and practical jokes.

By the time Linda was four years old, she had pleaded, wished, and prayed for Santa Claus to leave a full-grown horse for her under the Christmas tree. Upon waking early Christmas morning, she had an inconsolable temper tantrum at the absence of her long-awaited, hoped-for mare. Instead, she received a shiny red bicycle and hated it the moment she laid eyes on it. Linda ran to her bedroom in a fit of tears, never to place her bottom on the resented bicycle seat.

From there on in, picture books depicting horses were purchased, and the conversation around the dinner table revolved around horses. Trips were made to dude ranches in the Okanagan, and together with her dad, Linda's wishes of learning how to ride a horse were fulfilled.

Aside from horses, Frances had hoped that her daughter would enjoy other interests as well. Having not known how to swim growing up, Frances felt that she had missed out on a lot of fun. Therefore, she insisted that her children needed to learn how to swim. They would be allowed to learn and would enjoy the fantastic exercise and the pastime of pool parties and beaches, all the while being safe. Frances herself was fearful around water.

By 1932, there were two seaside saltwater pools in Stanley Park, one at Second Beach and one at Lumberman's Arch. Frances had spent wonderful afternoons during her courtship with Vince walking the paths and trails, picnicking at the beach, and longing to learn how to swim.

Unfortunately, due to a bad childhood experience of being thrown in the water with the expectation that she would automatically know how to swim, Frances almost drowned. She made the decision right then that she would never become a swimmer!

In 1951 Frances decided that proper swimming lessons would be just the ticket for their daughter. She wanted her to grow up knowing what to do if she was ever unexpectedly tossed into the water at a moment's notice like she herself had been.

Both of the outdoor seaside pools at Stanley Park were referred to as "draw and fill" pools, which meant the pools used sun-warmed water from the ocean. Once a week, the pool gates were opened at low tide to release the water back into the sea before the next high tide of clean water. The following day of this procedure was reserved for swimming lessons.

Wearing sundresses over their bathing suits, buckle-up sandals on their feet, wide-brimmed sun hats on their heads and cat-rimmed sunglasses, mother and daughter rode the streetcar over the Burrard Street Bridge and walked the rest of the way to Second Beach.

Being hot and tired upon their arrival, Frances was dismayed when a child ran up to Linda, stuck out their tongue, and called her Piggy-Pig while snorting through their nose. Her mother was mortified and wanted to pop the bratty child right between the eyes, as any mother would. Wisdom won, and she listened to the voice in her head that advised her not to do so.

Oblivious to her swimming lesson classmate, Linda began to put her toes in the cool salty water. As her group assembled, another child came along and pushed Linda so hard she smacked down on her bottom. As he ran away, he chanted, "Red alert, hippopotamus on the loose. Run for your lives!" While Linda sat crying in two-inch deep water, she refused the lessons.

Frances was speechless and outraged at how her daughter had been treated. Grabbing Linda by the hand, they left the confines of the overcrowded, child-infested water. Settling in for Fudgesicles from the nearby concession stand, her mother tried to comfort her. "There, there. I don't know how to swim either. It's not what it's all cracked up to be anyway, so never mind."

Even though Linda sensed something was not right, and the boys were being nasty, she focused on her sweet chocolate ice cream treat that had begun to drip down her arm and soon forgot about the abruptness of their departure from the swimming pool.

In 1908, the first Vancouver Police Mounted Squad was formed. They were assigned to patrol Stanley Park's 1,000 acres of public recreational lands. During the unrest of the 1920s and '30s, the officers roamed the streets, enforcing the law and protecting the citizens. They have been a fixture in the area ever since.

It was on this specific day, in the midst of her swimming pool trauma, that Linda would have a most important encounter that would shape her future. Something extraordinary was about to catch her eye...

Two uniformed police officers were strolling by on their chestnut mares. They smiled and waved at five-year-old Linda. Leaping up from the park bench, she begged her mother for permission to pet the horses. She then pleaded for permission to bump the officer off the magnificent horse so she could take over the reins and ride off into the sunset.

Regrettably, she had to settle for a friendly hello and stroking the horse's mane. When Frances lifted her precocious daughter up to meet the horse's face, Linda completely ignored the officer and stared deeply into luminous brown, telepathic eyes—instantly falling in love.

On the long walk back to the streetcar, Linda told her mother that she would be making a profession as a horseback riding police officer long before women would ever be inducted into the police force.

On this eventful day, Linda decided she would never learn how to swim and refused ever to wear a bathing suit again. She also met her first horse face to face, falling irrevocably in love. As if that were not enough, she suddenly came to the conclusion that she preferred the name Murphy over Linda and proceeded to tell her parents' friends and her grandparents to please refer to her as "Murphy" in the future. Although the name and the choosing of it made no sense, the family obligingly accommodated Linda's request.

Frances and Vince had been busy building their dream home in North Vancouver. They were tired of Violet's jealousy and were ready to move their little family of three to their new home. With that came a neighbourhood full of children for Linda to play with. No longer would she be a child living among adults, acting like an adult, and she would soon be attending school with her peers.

Frances had loved school and everything about learning and was always with her nose in a book. She delighted in history, social studies, political science, and English. Although her dream of becoming a writer, a newspaper reporter, or a private detective was traded in for a wedding ring and a baby carriage, she now had her daughter's upcoming education to live through vicariously.

Vince, on the other hand, disliked school and could only remember the bad times. As a child, he was desperately poor and hungry all the time. And the bullies were insurmountable. The teacher forced him to write with a hand that did not feel natural. He kept trying to switch to his left hand but got his knuckles whacked, therefore changing to his right. Chicken scratches were how his teacher described his penmanship.

His small hometown school only went to Grade 7, and shortly after completing his seventh year, Vince had run away. In 1929 he rode the rails to Northern BC and was happy to have left his desolate prairie school behind him, in addition to his dysfunctional upbringing.

As excited as Frances was for Linda's first day of school, Vince could multiply by ten his wife's excitement with his silent worry. He was determined to protect his daughter from what he was sure would be on the horizon—mean teachers, bullies, and endless visits to the principal's office.

His thoughts and feelings were kept a secret, even to Frances. He surely did not want to squelch her joy and enthusiasm for their daughter's education.

Not only that, but Frances was also pregnant with their second child. By May of the next year, they would be adding to their family, and Vince's dream of more children would become a reality.

Frances and Vince

Frances and Vince dressed up

Frances wearing Vince's suit jacket

Ready for a day at the races

Joe and Edith

Edith, Tommy and Violet

Edith and Violet all dolled up

Frances and Vince

Frances

Linda, always happy

Auntie Bonnie and Uncle Hank

Auntie Gigi and Uncle Hank

Mommy and Linda

Daddy, Linda & Mommy

CHAPTER THREE

Names Will Never Hurt Me

*"My pain may be the reason for somebody's laugh. But my
laugh must never be the reason for somebody's pain."*

– Charlie Chaplin

By Linda's sixth birthday, without any warnings, everything in her
world was about to change.

Before long, she would be saying goodbye to her grandma and
grandpa, hello to a new home and an unwanted school, and receive
the shocking delivery of a baby brother by an unknown stork.
Linda was beside herself and not looking forward to complying
with any changes coming her way.

Vince, on the other hand, was finally getting his wish after
waiting five years. Frances was expecting their second child, and
he could not be happier. Their brand new house was completed,
and they were ready to move. The address would be 509 East
Eighteenth Street in North Vancouver, a beautifully wooded area
near the streetcar on Grand Boulevard. Frances was good with
money and very frugal, saving portions of Vince's paycheques from
the time they had first been married on December 15, 1945. Now
seven years later, they were ready to make it on their own.

North Vancouver extends from the Capilano River on the west, and on the east, to Deep Cove on the Indian Arm. Back then, it was connected to downtown Vancouver at the First Narrows, by the Lion's Gate Bridge, which at the time was relatively new. Construction began in March 1937, and it opened in November 1938. The name Lions Gate Bridge was chosen in honour of the Two Sisters Mountains, a beautiful pair of mountain peaks located north of North Vancouver. When driving north on the bridge, one can see them directly ahead.

The First Nations legend of "The Two Sisters" tells the story of two daughters who requested peace between all First Nations tribes. The mountain range represents the chief's daughters who have stood for thousands of years guarding and requesting peace for the Pacific Coast and the Capilano Canyon's quiet protected forest and waters. Later, early explorers renamed them "The Lions," after the Landseer Lions in Trafalgar Square, England. They can be seen wrapped in the sun, the snow, and the stars of all seasons.

A pair of cast concrete lions, designed by sculptor Charles Marega, were placed on either side on the south of the Lions Gate Bridge in January 1939. A toll of twenty-five cents was charged for each car or horse and carriage. Five cents was the toll for pedestrians or bicycles.

Months into Frances's second pregnancy, Violet decided to tell Linda about the menacing stork dropping off a special delivery. Knowing that Frances and Vince would be moving, Violet decided that it was time she got to know her niece and what better way to develop a relationship with the child than to read her bedtime stories?

After observing her sister's marriage from a close vantage point, Violet decided she and Tommy were not suitable for one another. All they did was sit around drinking, playing cards, and using up all of Tommy's money. She failed to acknowledge the endless arguments, and if the thought did cross her mind, Tommy was to blame for everything because Violet always knew that she was still right and won every disagreement.

Realizing that she did not want to be alone, Violet decided to make some changes. First and foremost, she had to get rid of Tommy. Her next move was to take up with the helicopter pilot she was already having an affair with. With her impending divorce, Violet felt a little lighter. Plus, her man on the side was giving her self-confidence a much-needed boost. She was happy.

Frances and Vince were somewhat saddened by Tommy and Violet's forthcoming divorce, as they both loved him. However, they were delighted at the turnaround they were witnessing in Violet. She seemed calmer, was drinking less and therefore was more self-contained. They were thrilled that another family member was on board with loving and spending time with their daughter.

Linda enjoyed her auntie's mannerisms and sometimes pretended to be just like Violet by prancing around in her mother's pumps and oversized dresses. As she sauntered around the house with her nose in the air imitating Violet's haughty behaviour, the other adults in the house would be in stitches. Even Violet smirked with approval.

A story often told to young children to avoid the truth or awkward question of "Where do babies come from?" was the folklore tale about the long-legged stork. According to the legend, the stork flies over rooftops bringing a newborn baby in a white cloth bundle to its new, unsuspecting parents. The fable of the stork distributing babies goes back as far as ancient Greece. Many cultures around the world have stories linking storks with babies. Egypt, the Middle East, China, India, Israel, and First Nations cultures all have colourful versions of the same story.

Every night after Linda's bedtime snack with Grandma and a bubble bath overseen by Daddy, it was off to the big armchair by the front room window for stories with Auntie Vi. Snuggling in with her stuffed animal horse next to her aunt, Linda listened intently to the fables. "The Three Little Pigs and the Big Bad Wolf," "Hansel and Gretel," and lastly, the one about the giant white stork that was bringing a baby brother in its beak to drop off on their doorstep.

Auntie Vi's added rendition was that after dropping the baby off, the stork would scoop Linda up in its oversized beak and take her away. "So, you better be good or else the stork will take you away!" laughed Auntie Vi before turning off the light.

Just before falling asleep, Linda would have visions of little pigs being chased by wolves, herself getting locked up in a candy cane house by an evil witch, and worst of all, a giant stork snatching her out of her bed just after delivering her baby brother on the doorstep.

Linda never told her mommy and daddy why she wanted to sleep with the lights on and her bedroom door open or why she was desperate for the stork *not* to come. Instead, she hoped that the giant stork would not find their new address because they were moving.

At the end of World War ll, the days of being frugal and families just making do were quickly becoming a thing of the past. The 1950s brought prosperity and perfection. Employment and wages were up, and the economy was getting stronger by the day. Considering the toll on families during the Great Depression, World War l experts expected a decline in births. Instead, after World War ll, the Baby Boom was sweeping the nation.

After years of wartime rationing, the 1950s saw Canadian families hungry for fatty and sugary snacks. Parents began to splurge on impulse food, buying indulgences for children like ice cream, bubble gum, and pop. Supermarkets picked up on this trend, and shelves were filled with baked goods and candies.

While most of the 1940s had been spent saving sugar rations for special occasions like weddings or birthdays, new ad campaigns in the '50s suggested mothers feed their children meals they liked. Mothers were told that sugar was a valuable food source of energy for children.

With television programs, a new popular trend was catchy television commercials that came on before, during, and after every program. The television viewing audience came to love the memorable jingles that went with them.

The best example of the 1950s sugar trend was breakfast cereal, from "Snap, Crackle, Pop Rice Krispies" to "They're Grrreat—Tony the Tiger Frosted Flakes." The packaging had bright, appealing colours and cartoon characters that appealed to children.

Inside the cereal boxes were sugar-coated cereal and collectable toys and comics. Some of the favourite treasures were Tarzan comic books, Hanging Monkeys, Sky King statues and an actual land deed to be found in every box of Quaker Oats. These deeds were part of a launch for a new television show called *Sgt. Preston of the Yukon*. The deeds were of no value, but children did not know that, as they begged and pleaded for their parents to buy box after box, mesmerized by the idea of owning one full inch of land in the Yukon.

Just a few of the advertising slogans quipped by every young child were these: "If I were an Oscar Meyer Weiner, everyone would be in love with me;" "Ay, Yi, Yi, I am the Frito Bandito;" "Fifty million times a day at work or play, there is nothing like an ice-cold Coca Cola;" "It's the Pepsi Generation."

Everybody loved the Pillsbury Dough Boy and wanted to poke his belly. From Kraft Dinner to products like Swanson TV Dinners, these were (thought to be) nutritional snacks and meals just like Mom made—food options to give Mom a break for a family on the go. Duncan Hines and Betty Crocker were collectively in on the convenience foods gravy train.

Health-conscious doctors, dentists, and psychologists were ridiculed for trying to persuade parents otherwise. Advertising campaigns boasted that sugar was harmless and a valuable source of a child's nutritional needs.

Frances was pulled in hook, line, and sinker because she had always loved sweets. She was ready to embrace the sugar trend. Since the day she was born, she professed to have had a sweet tooth, never giving it a second thought to have a thick slab of chocolate cake for breakfast with her morning coffee. Her mother had always been in on the sugar bandwagon, too, and had a waistline to prove it.

As for Vince, having been raised early on in the Depression-era, food had become a cherished substance that one must value and treasure for fear that it could all disappear without a moment's notice. He could be referred to as "a big eater" with a "healthy appetite" and was a lover of all condiments, especially ketchup and seasoning salt, so much so that Linda used to call it "Dad's Salt," as in "pass the Dad's Salt please." For many years, well into adulthood, Linda was unaware of the correct name of the flavourful spice. Eventually, she was quite disappointed when she discovered its correct name. She insisted on calling it Dad's salt anyway.

After Frances, Vince, and Linda were settled in their new home, Grandma offered to take Linda shopping for a new school outfit one week before school. Linda was to take the bus and meet her grandmother at the Hudson's Bay Department store on Georgia and Granville Street. The first Hudson's Bay Department store in Vancouver, BC, was built in 1893. Refurbished and added onto in 1927, the cream and terra cotta building with Corinthian columns was the hub and place to shop for clothes, shoes, household items, and furniture. The last additions to the store were made in 1949.

Going on the city bus alone was not a new occurrence and had become a favourite adventure for Linda ever since moving across the water to North Vancouver. Completely legal and not frowned upon at that time, children rode the bus without a parent or guardian's help all the time, travelling from A to B and then home again.

On the scheduled day for school clothes shopping with Grandma, everything went as planned. When Frances put her daughter on the bus, she explained to the driver when to let her out. When the bus pulled up to Granville and Georgia's corner, there was Grandma, all smiles, waiting for Linda, her one and only granddaughter.

As the bus ground to a halt, Linda knew what to do. Saying, "Thank you, have a nice day and goodbye," to the driver, she greeted her grandmother waiting on the sidewalk with laughter and squeals. It wasn't every day that Linda got a new outfit.

First, it was an ice cream soda and donut from Scott's Café, and then the little girl's dress department at The Bay. Linda was a chatterbox, and Grandma enjoyed listening to her ramble on about current events, the new house, the mailman, the milkman, and all the goings-on in the new neighbourhood.

Once inside The Bay's big glass doors, taking the escalator up to the third floor, Linda started jumping up and down when she saw all the latest little girl's fashions—frilly dresses with ruffles, checks, plaids, and stripes.

When the salesgirl came over to check in on them, she took one look at Linda and then commented that they might not have any sizes large enough to fit her. She then suggested they go over to the Junior Miss section for teenagers.

Grandmother was flabbergasted while Linda was devastated.

Heading home alone on the bus, Linda stared out the window as her six-year-old legs dangled back and forth. She was hugely disappointed that she had to settle for a light blue, plain dress that was "all the rage with the older girls," as the clerk so enthusiastically stated.

She could still hear her grandmother whisper under her breath, "That Frances is feeding you far too many sweets!" In reality, Linda was also aware of her grandmother's many homemade treats and desserts that Linda had become accustomed to on her visits to their house. She especially loved the six-layer chocolate cake and trips to the ice cream parlour with her grandfather. Sometimes her tummy ached from fullness all the way home on the bus.

Even at six years old, Linda was tall for her age, and as the lady in the teen dress department at The Bay said, "Such a pretty girl, and there is nothing wrong with being big-boned."

Linda had no concept of what the term big-boned even meant. All she knew was that she felt awkward and did not look like the other little girls her age. *I do indeed seem to have strangely large bones,* she thought.

The night before Linda's first day of school, she had a bath, and her mother carefully put pin curls in her hair. In the morning, she reluctantly put on her new dress and, looking down at her stomach, she placed her hands on her small protruding belly and said, "Mommy, am I going to have a baby too?"

Frances did not know what to say but told Linda, "Don't be silly. That's just baby fat."

Which made absolutely no sense to Linda because she knew without a shadow of a doubt that she was no longer a baby.

Half-heartedly walking to school with her mother, Linda pleaded that she was not ready for school, and when that did not work, she brought up her enormous bones, which Frances had no idea what her daughter was talking about.

Brushing off Linda's stalling, Frances proceeded on the ten-block walk to Ridgeway Elementary with Linda in tow. Lining up outside with other children and their doting mothers, Linda felt tears sting her eyes, but she knew it was no use. Her mother appeared to be so happy, and she did not want to disappoint her.

When the loud shrill of the school bell rang, mothers kissed their children, and the students trekked inside like dutiful little soldiers—single file, one by one.

Finding a desk, Linda sat down and stared straight ahead at the Queen of England's portrait. For some reason, she felt comforted by the ruby-red lipsticked woman, who looked more like a princess than a queen. And what made Linda feel even better was that she thought Her Royal Highness had a remarkable resemblance to her mother.

Shortly after the roll call, Linda decided that her teacher was unusually tiny, thinking that her bones must be abnormally small, not like her own extraordinary large ones. She was careful not to make accidental eye contact but could not help noticing her teacher's little feet and pointy shoes. She was dressed in a long, pleated skirt and white, collared blouse, held together at the throat by a brooch in the shape of a flower. Her hair was grey and severely pulled back into a small bun. Her eyes were small and perfectly round like black marbles, Linda thought.

Linda summed up her teacher's appearance as a duplicate of one of the evil fairy tale characters Linda's Auntie Vi read about, the ones who gave her nightmares.

As she began to settle in, Linda was taken off guard when her impish storybook teacher smacked a long ruler on a desk in the front row. The sound was deafening. Every child in the room covered their ears and sat up straighter. Terror gripped them, and all the students sat in dead silence. After the slap of the ruler on the desk, the teacher said, "Everyone quiet, *now*!" and proceeded to recite the alphabet, with all of the students obediently, robotically repeating after their feared teacher.

When the children were sent outside at recess, Linda noticed a group of girls gathering by the swings. All were dressed in the frilly dresses from the little girl's section of The Bay, the same styles Linda had hoped for when shopping with her grandmother.

Always friendly and never at a loss for words, Linda approached her classmates to ask them their names and see if they wanted to play hopscotch.

Before any of them spoke, one girl moved towards Linda and said, "Oh, here comes Linda Pinda, Linda Pinda, Linda Pinda, you sure do *not* look like a pin!"

All the nearby children erupted into giggles.

Linda was initially surprised at the sing-song rhyming of her name. At a loss for how to react, she slunk off in the other direction. She scanned the schoolyard looking for an adult to run to, but none could be seen.

Linda's disdain for going to school began on that first day of Grade 1. After school that day, Linda pleaded with her mother not to send her back, stating that all the kids were mean, and her teacher was straight out of an evil fairy tale.

Not only had Frances been a tomboy and a bit of a bully herself in school, but as a parent, she also knew that school was mandatory. She mustered up the best advice she could by saying, "Why don't you give those bullies a knuckle sandwich the next time they call you names?" She followed by stating, "Sometimes, that's just how life is." Together they set the table for dinner as Linda silently wept, without letting her mother see her tears.

Without realizing she was doing so, Frances continued to treat Linda nothing like a little girl at all. Instead of explaining and teaching, she dished out jobs and duties without realizing the need to address the possible consequences of the bullying, which could be impacting Linda as a victim. Always wanting to please and to be a grown-up before her time, Linda gladly and willingly accepted the duties assigned to her.

One Saturday morning, instead of playing outside, Linda chose to defrost the icebox upon her mother's suggestion. Unexpectedly, Linda's pint-sized hand got stuck to the interior surface of accumulated ice crystals. She tried to free her fingers, but they were stuck like glue. Her cries went unnoticed because, at the kitchen table, Frances had her nose in a book. Once again, Daddy came to the rescue, having just come in from outdoors. For fear of ripping the skin, Vince poured warm water over Linda's attached fingers, gently prying them loose from the ice.

Frances had a ritual of ironing clothes while watching her favourite soap opera called *Love of Life*, an ironic title, since loving life while keeping house turned out to be Frances's most loathed activity. She did love her family, though, and did the best she could. However, one day another housekeeping incident found Linda fainting at the ironing board. She had chosen to help her mother, and while standing on a chair, she diligently pressed the hot appliance, swiping up and down, back and forth. Her father's dress shirts were tricky. As she maneuvered the buttons, starched collar, and long sleeve, six-year-old Linda complained of feeling tired. Before her mother could take note, Linda was stumbling off the chair in a heap on the floor at her mother's feet. Hearing the commotion, her father once again came to the aid of his precious firstborn daughter.

Aside from Linda's disappointment with school, the new neighbourhood was wonderful. The new house was a modest and practical home and a delight for Frances, Vince, and Linda. They got to know the neighbours and soon figured out who they meshed with.

Behind them, across the back lane, were Astrid and Tom, a childless couple. They speculated that she weighed at least three hundred pounds, while Tom was just a little bit of a man, hardly weighing anything at all. Frances and Vince marvelled at how outwardly in love they were. Tom adored the ground that Astrid walked on.

Directly next door were Ingrid and Tommy Stephen, with their two children, Carol and baby Kenny. Ingrid was a petite gal with curly hair and glasses, always dressed in the latest fashions. Tommy was a bigger jovial man with perpetually rosy cheeks and a constant ear-to-ear smile. Frances and Vince took to this couple, and Vince soon began planning fishing trips with Tommy. At the same time, Ingrid and Frances chatted from their back porches over their clotheslines, smoking cigarettes and relaying the latest events on their favourite soap opera, *Love of Life*.

Having been raised in an adult world, Linda relished this new selection of grown-ups to imitate and learn from. She was always in on the conversation and never held back, throwing in her two cents worth of comments regarding which neighbours she liked best, who she thought to be pretty, who wore the nicest cologne, who had the most charming back yards, and who had the most obnoxious children.

On the other side of their home lived Vera and Marvin. She was drop-dead gorgeous with platinum blonde hair, a tiny waistline, and a Marilyn Monroe essence. She did not connect very well with the other women, while the men in the neighbourhood delighted in her. Marvin was a sailor and was thought to be much younger than Vera, with qualities reminiscent of a teenage boy. He was handsome and kind and simply head over heels in love with Vera.

Over time, people noticed that while Marvin was away in the Navy, Vera was entertaining gentlemen callers. When Marvin returned, their arguing could be heard two blocks away, followed by slamming doors and crying children.

For the sake of not being rude, the other wives invited Vera to tea periodically but noticed some of their things were missing after she left—jewelry, hats, money, and various other items. Eventually, they confronted Vera, only to receive a flustered denial in her low, sweetly breathless voice—"Pardon me? Oh my, I would never do such a thing! For heaven's sake, your accusations are simply atrocious!"

Memories of Linda's souvenir gathering came to mind, leaving Frances with a soft spot for Vera. The other neighbours were not so understanding. Deciding to set a trap, they caught Vera red-handed with a few one-dollar bills and a container of shaving cream. The enticement worked. All they did was leave the money and shaving cream as bait on the vanity in the bathroom. The women stood outside the bathroom door like Perry Mason and Della Street, accosting Vera as she exited the bathroom. The whole shakedown was awkward and embarrassing, especially for Frances.

Vera and Marvin eventually moved away and did not leave a forwarding address. One day some of the neighbours stuck up a sign on their door that said *Vera can no longer be found at this address.* The frequent visiting men stopped calling.

Linda missed Vera and her movie star qualities but was excited to see who was going to move into their house next. She hoped it would be another couple without children because, so far, Linda found other children to be mean-spirited and not nearly as much fun as grown-ups.

Much to her parents' relief, eventually, Linda managed to make a few friends when the neighbours gathered for Christmas parties, block parties, card games, PTA meetings, and fishing trips. Family-oriented events soon filled up the space and time of a perfect suburban lifestyle. Everyone loved her parents, Frances and Vince, so Linda felt loved too.

Charles Woodward established Woodward's Department Store at the corner of Main and Georgia Streets in Vancouver in 1892. By 1902, the store was incorporated, and a new store was built on the corner of Hastings and Abbott Streets.

The chain was different from other department stores because they included a supermarket known as "The Food Floor." There were five floors to choose from at the Vancouver location, with an attendant-operated elevator to take you to each one. Pressing the button and waiting for the elevator to arrive, the attendant would slide the accordion-like gate open and firmly ask, "Which floor, please?" Sitting upon a small stool, the elevator operator proceeded to take the shoppers to their desired floor.

Many Canadians remember Woodward's famous jingle, "Dollar 49 Day, Tuesday," held on the first Tuesday of every month. Frances was sure to meet her mother there every week to get the best deals they could find.

Every December, a visit to Santa Claus and Christmas shopping at Woodward's Department Store had become Linda's most treasured activity. Listening to such radio shows as *Gunsmoke*, *The Lone Ranger*, and *The Cisco Kid* were also among her favoured activities. *Gunsmoke* was an American Western drama series first airing on the radio in 1949. The stories took place in and around Dodge City, Kansas, during the American West's thriving cattle days and settlement in the 1870s. The main character was Marshal Matt Dillion, played by William Conrad on the radio and later James Arness on television.

Linda relished anything Western and everything to do with cowboys and horses. For the third year in a row for Christmas that year, Linda again requested a real horse to be left under the tree but decided to set her sights a little lower, as it had become evident the real horse was out of the question.

When the day arrived to sit on Santa's knee at Woodward's Department Store, Linda could hardly contain herself. She had memorized and rehearsed her wish list to be recited at a moment's notice. Waiting patiently in line with her blossoming pregnant mother, Linda silently repeated what she was going to say.

When it was her turn, before being helped up onto Santa's knee by one of his elves, the helper looked to Frances and said, "You'll need to help me, ma'am. This is a bigger child than I am used to lifting." Without batting an eye, Linda allowed her fully pregnant mother to lift her onto Santa's lap.

Looking into Santa's weary face, Linda politely said, "Hello, Santa. I know you must be tired and sick of all these pestering, greedy children, so I will make this quick. All I want for Christmas is a baby doll, but not a regular white one. I would like a black dolly, please."

With raised eyebrows, Santa was at a loss for words and suggested that Linda pick something else.

Reacting cordially, Linda said, "No, thank you. The only other thing I want is a horse, which is far too big to get down the chimney, I am assuming."

Her reason for the request was that in their neighbourhood, at the end of her street, there was a family of colour with a son named Harry Jerome. Linda was completely taken by this boy and absolutely adored him. Harry, in later years, went on to win an Olympic bronze medal in track in Tokyo. He also finished fourth in the 200m in that same Olympic challenge of 1964.

When Christmas morning rolled around, Linda was up before dawn but was told by her parents to wait for Grandma, Grandpa, Auntie Vi, and her new boyfriend to arrive before opening her presents.

In the meantime, Linda was allowed to open her Christmas stocking. A fun tradition had developed over the years where Frances would take a few of Vince's wool work socks, and using a ring from the shower curtain, hang the stockings from the fireplace. Deep in the toe would be a Mandarin orange and a bag of Licorice Allsorts candies, with a few shelled nuts sprinkled in for good measure.

By lunchtime, the relatives had arrived, and each one was allowed to open one gift at a time, taking turns and going around the room. Linda went first. Opening her hoped-for dolly with great care and exuberance, she threw it on the floor with disdain the second she opened the package, bursting into tears.

Her dad exclaimed, "But on your list, you asked for just this kind of doll!"

Linda responded through her sobs with, "Yes, but I wanted her to be a black dolly!"

In the spring of 1954, when Linda was almost finished Grade 1, her brother Douglas was born. He had beautiful alabaster skin, big dark eyes, a mischievous grin and immediately became the family's new joy, especially for Grandfather and Daddy. Much to Linda's dismay, she was no longer the centre of attention, and on top of that disaster, through no fault of her own, she had also become addicted to sugar.

Frances and Linda on the steps of the new home

Happy times horseback riding

A portrait of Linda

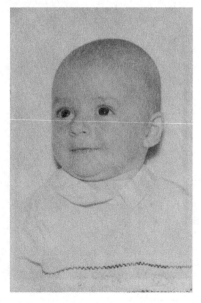

Beautiful Baby Douglas

Linda dressed as Murphy in her souvenir collecting hat

Sweet little Linda

Daddy, Linda, Grandma and Grandpa having a picnic

Joe and Edith in front of their house, always dressed up

Baby Douglas, Linda and Grandma on the steps of the new house

Linda always happy and laughing

Linda and Grandma enjoying each others company

509 east 18th street in North Vancouver, the Bonner's new home

CHAPTER FOUR

Horse Sense

"Horses change lives. They give our young people confidence and self-esteem.
They provide peace and tranquility to troubled souls—they give us hope."

–Toni Robinson

As Linda's obsession with horses was increasingly on the rise, her parents thought it would be the perfect opportunity to send her away for two weeks to a horseback riding summer camp. With the completion of her terrible first year of school and the new addition of a baby brother, Linda's passion could be fulfilled with a fun experience and would be just what the doctor ordered.

Besides, after the summer holidays, Linda would be entering Grade 2, and Frances and Vince anticipated that it would go more smoothly than Grade 1. A busy child is a happy child, was the hope of both parents.

Just before Linda's seventh birthday, Frances signed her up for horse camp. Along with the application and where to send the cheque came a list of what to bring. To Frances's alarm, this required some shopping:

- six white dress shirts
- cowboy boots, penny loafers, saddle shoes, sandals, and sneakers

- sleeping bag
- pillow
- flashlight
- notebook, pen, and eraser
- rainwear
- bathing suit and towel
- blue jeans, slacks, and a party dress
- various sweaters, a raincoat, and a winter parka

Both Frances and Vince thought the extensive list was ridiculous but decided that perhaps the abundance of what to bring meant the camp would be top-notch. So, they bit the bullet and purchased all of the necessary items.

In 1954, The Canadian Pacific Railway operated the British Columbia Coast Steamship Service to various ports in Washington State, Northern BC, and Vancouver Island.

This summer camp was located on Vancouver Island, so Frances and Vince drove Linda downtown to the Vancouver Harbour to meet the camp counsellors and fellow campers. They would all board the Steamship Ferry together, leaving Frances, Vince, and baby Douglas waving goodbye at the dock.

When they arrived at the terminal an hour early, Frances realized they had forgotten Linda's shoe bag, with five pairs of varying shoes and boots purchased as mandatory footwear. Vince jumped in the car, raced home across the Lions Gate Bridge, grabbed the forgotten bag and made it back to the ferry just in time.

Linda was excited, anticipating the meeting of new friends and the horse that would become hers for the length of the two-week summer camp adventure. She was not nervous or anxious in the least.

Even though she was only almost seven years old, she was well seasoned in horseback riding. Ever since her big disappointment of not getting a horse under the Christmas tree at four years old, her mom and dad were instrumental in giving her horseback riding lessons and experience from that day forward. On trips to the Cariboo, the Okanagan, and Kamloops, Vince was always able to find a stable or dude ranch to take his four, five, six, and almost seven-year-old daughter horseback riding.

Frances often sat in the car or stayed back at the motel with her stack of books and newspapers, as reading was her most treasured activity. Vince and Linda persuaded her to join them on one or two occasions, but not being a horse enthusiast, Frances was often given an old plug (the name reserved for a slower, older horse). Frances found the whole activity quite dull. She was not a nature lover and would find herself dozing off and almost slipping right off the saddle onto the side of the trail. This, of course, caused laughter all around, and Frances, being a good sport, would chuckle right along with everyone else.

Eventually, and collectively deciding that the money would be better spent elsewhere, Frances opted out of the experience altogether. Leaving Vince to be Linda's riding companion, Frances went back to sitting on the sidelines with a book in hand.

Summer camp at a horse ranch was the perfect activity for horse-loving Linda. She was well experienced in mucking the stalls—a term that means to scoop the horse's manure out of the stall where a horse is contained—and in brushing the horses. Using a footstool, she even knew how to put on and take off a saddle.

Much to Linda's dismay, everything was to come crashing down, and she would be filled with disappointment only hours after arriving at camp.

An old, dilapidated bus was waiting at the ferry dock to pick everyone up. Once there, the campers were assigned their lodging and then taken to the barns and introduced to their horse. With unbridled excitement, Linda could barely contain herself. She chatted with other campers and counsellors about how she had been looking forward to summer camp all year—especially meeting the horse assigned to her.

She imagined an Appaloosa or perhaps a spotted mare, maybe a black stallion or a chestnut quarter horse. The options were endless, and in the end, Linda knew that she would love any horse that was meant in the stars to be hers, if only for fourteen days. She secretly vowed to faithfully and willingly take care of her horse to the very best of her ability, maybe even better than all the other campers. She daydreamed that her daddy would let her bring the filly home with her when all was said and done. Wishful thinking, she knew, but Linda was always proud of her high hopes.

There were all ages and capabilities at the camp, so they started with the eldest, which the camp counsellors assumed were the most experienced riders. With Linda being the youngest one at camp, it was speculated that she would be the most inexperienced rider. Therefore, she was chosen to go last.

After the older children had each been assigned a horse, Linda, being the youngest, was appointed a donkey—jackass, burro, otherwise known as a mule—because there were no more horses left.

Not only was she hugely disappointed, but she was also irate. She refused to accept the donkey and tried to explain that she was an intermediate rider. Unfortunately, no one would believe her. After her complaining and fussing, she was labelled a troublemaker.

Instead of crying or slinking off, Linda demanded to call her parents, but the camp rule was no phone calls home for the first week, with no exceptions.

Hugely disappointed, Linda cried silently into her pillow that night. Through her tears, she took out her pencil and paper and began a letter home...

> Dear Mommy and Daddy,
>
> If you have any feelings for me or love in your heart, you will pick me up this instant. My time at this godforsaken camp is not working out very well at all. You may notice the tear stains on this letter because I am crying right now.
>
> Love from your only daughter,
>
> Linda

P.S. Some kids are singing, "Fatty, fatty two-by-four, can't fit through the bathroom door," and I think they are singing it about me.

P.P.S. they keep wanting me to wear the dumb bathing suit you packed for me, and I absoloutly (sic) refuse. They say I am the most disagreeable child they have ever seen.

P.P.P.S. I demand that you come and get me now, or I will simply perish!

Unfortunately, the mail was only picked up once a week, and then delivery took another week. On the last day of camp, Linda's first letter arrived at home just as Frances and Vince were coming to pick her up. A new letter was delivered every day thereafter for thirteen days after the camp had ended when Linda was back at home—each letter becoming more dramatic and desperate.

When Linda had again demanded to use the camp telephone, this time she was told that it was out of order.

So Linda endured her first camp experience with Chico the donkey and took loving care of him. As donkeys are notorious for being stubborn, Linda could barely get this one to move, therefore missing most trail rides. Never once was she given a turn on one of the horses. The white starched shirts itched, and there was no need for all the pairs of shoes after all. Refusing to swim during free time, Linda became an outcast. Trying to look on the bright side, she had made a friend in Chico.

Shortly after returning home from horseback (donkey) riding camp, Linda turned seven years old and was ready to begin Grade 2. Speculating, as both of her parents had done, that Grade 2 would be much better than Grade 1, Linda was looking forward to a break from baby Douglas and was desperate to grow up. Linda could not deny that the baby was adorable, but he was a serious baby and did not do much other than eat and sleep, so she concluded that her baby brother was boring. She had started to grow fond of him but not as much as everyone else had.

In the meantime, Vince was busy at work on the North Shore, driving a bulldozer for a man named Ernie Livesey. He had become skilled and was an extremely hard worker. His days were long, up early but home by 5:00 p.m. for supper. Frances was paying the bills, cooking, cleaning, and taking care of the baby and her always chatty and precocious daughter, Linda.

In 1954, the economy was continuing to grow. Movie tickets were seventy cents. *On The Waterfront,* with Marlon Brando, was a box office success, and *Father Knows Best* was the television show that everyone watched. Elvis Presley cut his first album, and Bill Haley and the Comets were singing "Rock Around the Clock." *The Tonight Show* was first aired with Steve Allan, and Marilyn Monroe had just married Joe DiMaggio. Popular books were edgy and modern—*Live and Let Die* by Ian Fleming and *Lord of The Flies* by William Golding. Dwight Eisenhower was President of the United States, and Louis St. Laurent was the Prime Minister of Canada.

All was well in the Bonner household until the first day of Grade 2 for Linda, when all hell broke loose. Once again, having gone back-to-school clothes shopping with her grandmother, Linda was happy with their purchases and loved her new black-and-white saddle shoes.

Instead of her mother walking her to school, Linda went by herself, feeling proud and independent. Baby Douglas was a late sleeper, and Vince always brought Frances breakfast in bed, so the whole family encouraged Linda to make it to school independently.

About two blocks before arriving at school, an older boy, at least in Grade 5, hollered in Linda's direction, "Hey, where are you going, Tub-O-Lard?"

Linda instinctively looked behind her, and no one was there. Spinning back around, she came face to face with the meanest bully at school and the most despised fifth-grader. She immediately realized the big bully was speaking to her. Thus began the torture of another year of school.

Holding her nose high, as it always seemed to work for Auntie Vi, Linda strode the rest of the way to school as if she did not have a care in the world. Deep down inside, she feared the worst and wondered how on earth she could endure another year of taunting and name-calling.

Linda's new Grade 2 teacher at Ridgeway Elementary, Mrs. Alison, had soft auburn curls and wore a bright yellow dress. She dressed in pretty, colourful dresses every day, just like out of the Eaton's catalogue, Linda thought. She could not help but be pleased with how becoming and pleasant her new teacher appeared.

Being teased for her weight did not stop, and no matter how many people she told, nothing was ever done. Her walks to school were almost unbearable; "Fatso," "Lardo," and "Two-Ton-Tessie" were common names that Linda was ridiculed with. She learned early on to hold her head up high and walk with confidence. She tried to block out the comments by reciting all her favourite TV shows, what day of the week they aired, and at what time.

However, Linda managed to make a few friends her age who liked her for who she was. They also shared her love of horses. Together at recess time, they would prance around playing horses. They talked about the movie *National Velvet* with Elizabeth Taylor and the book *Black Beauty* and how they were all going to own a horse someday. They shared their love for Hopalong Cassidy and his horse, Trooper.

Linda had her own Hopalong Cassidy lunch kit and liked to order Hopalong's favourite drink called sarsaparilla. She wasn't interested in the guns but loved anything else to do with the Old West and horses.

Every Sunday afternoon, Linda would lose herself in *The Roy Rogers Show*, a half-hour Western drama. All the kids in the neighbourhood would play outside immediately afterward, pretending to be Roy Roger's famous horse, Trigger. They would gallop up and down the back lane, clicking their tongues, saying "giddy-up" and smacking their rear ends, acting as horse and rider.

Linda and her friends chanted "Hi-ho, Silver! Away!" as they galloped and trotted throughout her neighbourhood streets. *The*

Lone Ranger captivated young and old alike as an American Western drama TV series, which aired from 1949-1957. Clayton Moore was in the starring role, and Jay Silverheels, a member of the Mohawk First Nations people in Canada, played Tonto, the Lone Ranger's companion.

The fictional storyline began after six Texas Rangers were massacred, with only one member surviving. After that, the "lone" survivor disguised himself with a black mask and travelled with Tonto to assist those challenged by the lawless elements.

At the end of every episode, after the Lone Ranger and Tonto left, someone asked the sheriff, "Who was that masked man?" The person responding said, "That was the Lone Ranger." The last scene was always the Lone Ranger and Tonto riding off into the sunset, yelling, "Hi-ho, Silver! Away!"

When not impersonating horses, Linda plodded along, waiting for second grade to end.

Aside from the name-calling, she had also grown to exceedingly despise Mrs. Alison. Mostly because she repeatedly got after Linda for not writing correctly, frequently complaining in a raised voice, "Stop scribbling! I cannot read your writing. What a mess!" She eventually determined that Linda was a lost cause and should never try handwriting again, as she was useless. Linda became more and more frustrated, and with each negative remark, she became more reluctant to try. Ultimately, just before the end of Grade 2, Mrs. Alison insisted that Linda print for the rest of the school year.

Another form of discipline, if the children were not measuring up, was to stand them in the corner. Every day, three or four students could be seen standing in all four corners of the classroom. Linda was always one of them. Her year-end report card stated that Linda was a failure at perfecting the art of handwriting.

Crestfallen and embarrassed with Grade 2, Linda quickly changed gears and was happy that she had another school year under her belt. She anticipated the upcoming summer holidays when she would be turning eight. Her dad had even suggested they might buy her a horse.

A day of horseback riding, Linda and Daddy

Linda and baby Douglas

New business, Vince Bonner Bulldozing, Daddy,
baby Kenneth, Linda and Douglas

Linda and Douglas

Linda and Douglas, beside daddy's new work truck

Frances and Linda in front of Vince's bulldozer

Merry Christmas Linda

CHAPTER FIVE

High Expectations

"Courage is being scared to death but saddling up anyway."

-John Wayne

Summer, glorious summer! At last, unlimited Western shows on TV, camping trips, and horseback riding, block parties for families in the neighbourhood, and friends to play horses with. Linda would be free from the teasing and bullying for two whole months! She was elated.

Vince loved his family, work, and friends, but he wanted his little girl to be happy more than anything. Thus began his search for a horse. They figured with all the dude ranches and lessons they were giving Linda, that she would benefit, and so would their pocketbook, if she had a horse of her own.

For years they discussed Linda's obsession with horses. Was it just a passing fancy or indeed their daughter's life-long joy? However, they always concluded that they were happy she had an activity she enjoyed. As long as she showed an interest in such a magnificent creature, they would support it, whether it was just a hobby or an eventual profession. They were acknowledging that perhaps the academics did not matter so much.

Frances and Vince were also thrilled that another school year had come to a close. Aware of the name-calling but with no idea as to the extent, they believed Linda to be on the dramatic side and were never sure if she was exaggerating as to how bad it really was. Either way, both parents were happy that it was now summer holidays, and the teasing would subside for a time and maybe even stop altogether.

On the first day of summer vacation, Vince realized that "his little girl" was ready for a horse of her own. He found a beautiful bay mare in the Vancouver Sun classified ads. However, the horse was located way up in the North Thompson area just outside of Kamloops. Vince's friend also found a mare at the same place for his daughter, so both fathers were thrilled.

They had each wired seventy-five dollars to secure the sale, and while they were planning to trailer the horses to North Vancouver, a telephone call came that the horses had been stolen. Both fathers speculated that they had been conned, as neither got their money back. Frances was furious because she had noticed over the years that money and her husband did not get along too well. Or rather, Vince had a knack for getting taken advantage of.

Linda was naturally heartbroken but rallied when her dad arranged for her to participate at the prestigious Laura Lynn Riding Stables in North Vancouver. The stables were created by John and Evy Donovan in 1953.

John's father, George Lucas Donovan, came from Ireland in 1908 to Ontario, and in 1912, moved the family to Vancouver to start an office equipment business on Hastings Street. On June 6, 1938, his son John married an employee of the family business, a beautiful woman named Evelynn. In 1950, John purchased a twenty-four-acre estate from the District of North Vancouver. His desire was to preserve the acreage. In honour of his wife Evelynn and his mother Laura, he named the property Laura Lynn. In January 1951, John and Evy moved out of the city with their six children to the property located in Lynn Valley.

The acreage had many natural, forested trails meandering to the peak of Grouse Mountain. The Donovans felt that a riding club and community centre would be an excellent use of the beautiful property for all those in the region. They built the Laura Lynn Equestrian Centre in 1953 and contracted with a Norwegian family from West Vancouver to construct Scandinavian-style guest cabins.

Their next project was the building of Laura Lynn Lodge. The lodge served as a social centre for visitors, family friends, and riding club members. Western-style and English-style riding shows were a common occurrence at the club. All of the family were involved with keeping up the property, and in 1959, John created a romantic heart-shaped lake, fully stocked with fish, as an anniversary present to his wife Evy. He appropriately named his creation Evelynn Lake. To this day, even though the area has been somewhat developed, great care has been taken to preserve the natural beauty of the property. It is a cherished treasure to the City of North Vancouver, enjoyed by all.

Working in the bulldozing business, Vince spent most of his time clearing lots in North and West Vancouver, meeting many residents in the process. Consequently, he knew of the Donovan family and the beautiful spread they were developing in Lynn Valley. As they were on a fixed income, Frances suggested that Vince look into Linda doing some volunteer work at Laura Lynn in exchange for a ride here and there.

A couple of days after the botched horse purchase, Vince drove her to the stable, made arrangements, and right then and there, Linda began mucking the stalls and grooming horses in exchange for free rides whenever a horse was made available to her. She quickly grew to love the hard work. She revelled in the fresh air mixed with the comforting, earthy smell of leather, manure, and sweaty horses.

Linda was a faithful volunteer and loved the ranch life so much that she never fretted if she did not ride one of the horses on certain days. She enjoyed her duties, breathing in the leather saddle smell, joking around with the other stable hands, and feeling like an honest-to-goodness rancher.

Linda was big for her age and looked older than all of her friends. Due to the physical labour and fun she had riding horses, she excelled. She was doing what she liked and loved what she was doing.

After spending the summer days at the riding stable, she came straight home to watch one of her many favourite Western shows, one of which was based in the ninteenth century.

Rifleman, starring Chuck Connors, was about a widower raising his son as a single dad. The two had a strong father-son bond. Set in the 1880s, the father taught his son the value of courage, honesty, and tolerance. In each episode, a reference was made to the Bible. Sometimes the son also taught the father a lesson or two.

Another all-time family favourite was a show called *Gunsmoke*, centred around the character of Matt Dillon, a US marshal who maintained law and order in a frontier town. The supporting characters were Miss Kitty, owner of the Long Branch Saloon, which doubled as a bordello; Doc Adams, the town doctor; and Deputy Marshal Chester Goode, Dillon's loyal sidekick. Later, this character was replaced by Festus Hagen.

Much of the series featured Dillon and his allies battling bandits, robbers, or other threats that blew in like the prairie winds. The show was famous for its shootouts but also for its psychological drama and tense situations, which were frequently resolved with moral integrity.

Throughout the neighbourhood, Linda and her friends played a *Gunsmoke* game, not so much interested in the shootouts, mostly just riding the range and pretending to be Miss Kitty on horseback.

Eventually, all good things come to an end, and with only a few weeks left of summer, Linda knew that the inevitable was just around the corner. She was not looking forward to Grade 3. She wondered if the bullies would be out in full force and if she would be victim to another mean teacher.

Regarding her education, Linda felt wholly misunderstood, as it seemed she had a reputation of being a tattletale. Her teachers did not seem to understand she was trying to protect herself from the world's tormentors and ruffians.

Of course I am a tattletale, she thought. *What else can I be? How else can I protect myself?*

Linda wished her Laura Lynn days and Western show nights would last forever. For some reason, her uncertainty about going back to school was making her exceptionally hungry. Bewildered, she noticed that the closer the first day of school was, the more she wanted to eat. She never understood why but felt accepted by her grandma, who always supported her granddaughter's "healthy appetite." On the other hand, her mother occasionally commented how overeating would make her fat.

Four days before the start of school, Linda took the bus to meet grandma across town. They met at their usual spot, had lunch, and then went back-to-school dress shopping at The Bay. Linda had come to accept that she was destined to find her clothes in the teen department, and her dreams of frilly little girl dresses were over.

With her Hopalong Cassidy lunch kit, new dress, and shoes, she was off to a fresh start at a new school. Only two blocks from Linda's home, she was registered for Grade 3 at Queensbury Elementary.

Officially eight years old, Linda chose to be optimistic that she had left the bullies behind at her old school, Ridgeway Elementary. Unfortunately, she allowed herself to become too optimistic, and on her first day of school, she heard, "Hey, horse shit lover," hollered from across the playing field.

Linda guessed that each school had its fair share of bullies. These meanies somehow knew that she was cleaning the stalls at Laura Lynn over the summer. Holding back the tears, she was determined not to be a tattle this time. Spotting some of her friends on the playground from the previous year at Ridgeway, Linda ran over to be with them. But something had changed—her friends looked the same, but she stood at least two feet taller than them. Ignoring her, they ran off.

Linda stood for a moment, a split-second, feeling at a loss. Why was she always rejected? She could not understand it, but, once again, she was determined not to let the bad behaviour of others get the better of her.

When the bell rang, Linda took her time and sauntered inside her brand-new state-of-the-art classroom. Sizing up her new teacher, Linda noticed a tall, plain-looking woman standing just below the familiar Queen's portrait. Naturally, Linda gravitated towards the pretty teachers, but this one was different. She was not as outwardly appealing, but she smiled and had a calm presence. Linda liked her immediately.

After singing "God Save the Queen" and reciting "The Lord's Prayer," the class was told to take out their writing scribblers.

Linda raised her hand and said, "I do not know how to write, and I am unteachable." The other students laughed.

But her new teacher silenced them and said, "Linda, everyone in my class must try, and I will be the judge of who is teachable and who is unteachable. I have the feeling that you could very well be the cleverest girl I have had the pleasure of meeting."

Smiling inwardly, Linda followed the teacher's instructions, and with a little extra guidance, Linda was writing beautifully within weeks. She wished she could show her pessimistic second-grade teacher from the year before how her chicken scratch had turned into an eloquent script, praised by her new and improved Grade 3 teacher.

Besides the continuous bullying before and after school she endured, Linda loved her teacher. But every day, she could hardly wait to run home at 3:00 p.m. to watch her shows. Some days after school, her dad drove her to Laura Lynn, where she volunteered until suppertime. And every Saturday and Sunday, Linda was at the stable from sunrise to sunset.

Throughout the year, her mom tried to get her interested in swimming lessons, ice skating lessons, tap dancing, and baton. Linda mostly refused only after failing miserably. There would always be an argument. Linda hated wearing a bathing suit, girl's pretty white ice skates were not made big enough, and she was not about to wear bigger boy's ugly black skates, tapdancing made her feel uncoordinated and awkward, and she got kicked out of baton for almost knocking the teacher's eye out. She even disliked the childhood game of hopscotch because it hurt her knees. Besides, all that hopping was boring and monotonous.

The straw that broke the camel's back for Linda trying anything other than horseback riding was the occasion when she was invited to a roller-skating birthday party.

During the 1950s and '60s, the art deco Building F on the PNE grounds was also known as Rollerland, a popular hangout for roller-skating on the weekends. Linda was excited to have a party to attend. She took the ferry at the bottom of Lonsdale to the foot of Columbia Street. Once there, she knew what bus to take to the Pacific National Exhibition and Rollerland.

Unbeknownst to Linda, all the girls at the birthday already knew how to skate. Left to her own devices after making more than one attempt, Linda could not stay up. Instead of getting helped up when she fell, the girls' older brothers and friends called her a dummy and too fat to learn.

Linda was tired of bearing witness to her failures and exclaimed to her entire family, "Horses and Western television shows are my only interest, so please stop trying to turn me into something I am not." She felt proud and quite sure of herself for making the bold statement and pleased that nobody argued the point.

The summer between Grades 3 and 4, Linda's parents decided to let her stay two weeks at Laura Lynn because she begged not to go on the family's usual trip to Kelowna to see relatives. Linda argued to both parents that her grandpa and everyone else there was old and stodgy. With baby Douglas being the centre of attention, in her mind, she speculated that she would be ignored and have nothing to do. Frances had to agree.

"Besides," Linda lamented, "I will be nine years old soon. I am practically a teenager!"

Feeling grown up and looking much older, along with her keen horse knowledge, Linda would be responsible for taking riders on trail rides at Laura Lynn. After summing up the pros and cons, her parents could not refuse, and Linda was allowed to stay back at Laura Lynn Riding Stables. It proved to be the best two weeks of her life.

Every night when she went to sleep, Linda would dream about her future. She was already counting the days until high school graduation. She planned to move out as soon as possible and move up to the Cariboo, get a horse of her own, and a job on a ranch.

Linda's father was familiar with the Cariboo. He had settled there as a young man in Barkerville, the Cariboo Gold Rush capital. Linda enjoyed the stories her father told of the old days, riding the rails and panning for gold in the Cariboo.

Since then, Barkerville had been turned into a heritage town, boasting of the Old West, allowing tourists to pan for gold, and was completely set up with dance hall girls, cowboys, and horses tied to hitching posts. Gift shops sold sundries, peppermint sticks, postcards, calendars, placemats, ornaments, and all things depicting the Old West.

Vince had long since explained that the name for the Cariboo region came from the abundance of caribou that roamed the lands when settlers first arrived in 1861—stretching from the Fraser Canyon to the Cariboo Mountains.

Eventually, just like every other year, the summer holidays ended way too soon for Linda. The two-block walk up the hill to Queensbury Elementary was off to a better start than previous years. At the beginning of Grade 4, Linda had made an observation that the bullies backed off when she was around other children, so she made a point of walking to school with some of her neighbourhood friends. Even though she had lost touch due to most of her time being spent at Laura Lynn, she had enough sense to rekindle her relationships with the kids living next door.

Bringing forth her charismatic personality when she wanted to, Linda could turn on her charm and be polite and friendly at just the right times. When seeking out friends, she copied her dad's personality and natural skill to be comical. Combined with the added responsibility at Laura Lynn, Linda's self-confidence had grown immeasurably.

An excellent pastime, and one of her favourite ways to entertain her friends, was to play the backwards game. During the Depression-era, with no television, toys, or money, her dad explained how he used to make up games. The backwards game went like this...

You simply ask your friends to say their first and last names backwards. For example, Vince Bonner would be Ecniv Rennob, Linda Bonner – Adnil Rennob, Frances Bonner – Secnarf Rennob, Douglas Bonner – Salguod Rennob, and so on. The game was sure to get a laugh and was a great way to get a conversation going.

Linda coasted. She was chatting up friends and new acquaintances, following her teacher's demands, and daydreaming when no expectations were being made on her. Everything was hunky-dory until a new mandatory program was instilled into the regular classroom curriculum. It was called choir practice.

Linda hated singing, primarily because she felt she could not carry a tune. She also did not like standing up in front of people. She was still self-conscience about her weight and traumatized by the names she had been called for most of her school years.

When complaining to her mom about her inability to carry a tune and how she despised choir, Frances waved her hand in the air and said, "Just move your mouth to the words, and no one will be the wiser."

The next day at choir practice, in the middle of singing "Waltzing Matilda," Linda's teacher caught her moving her mouth with no words coming out. She was made to get up in front of her class and sing the song alone, and being off-key, the kids laughed and pointed, beginning an altogether new reason for Linda to be made fun of.

Frances was called into the principal's office, and when it was explained that Linda had defied her teacher by moving her lips during choir, Frances was annoyed. Stating that she supported her daughter, she replied in a stern voice, "I am the one who told Linda to move her lips instead of singing." To Linda's delight, the teasing about her singing voice eventually stopped, and she continued to just mouth the words to all the songs for the remainder of the year. She could not help but boast and feel proud of her mother, who could not carry a tune either.

Frances and Vince were expecting another baby to be born sometime in October 1956. Linda hoped for a baby sister. She prayed and prayed for it to be a girl.

Since learning "The Lord's Prayer" at the start of Grade 1, Linda was fascinated with the morning ritual of reciting "Our Father Who Art in Heaven." She had also noticed churches around her city and wondered what went on inside of them.

Always outspoken, she asked her mother if they could go to church sometime. Some people from a local church had come into the school, handing out brochures. This made Linda even more curious. Having been raised a Catholic, Frances denounced her religion when she first moved to Vancouver at nineteen. She'd had a few bad experiences as a young girl at the Catholic girl's school she attended, and due to having been forced to go, she gladly left it all behind on the godforsaken prairies many years earlier.

As a little boy, Vince had wondered why a loving god would not come to rescue him from years of poverty and abuse, so he agreed with Frances, and he was in no uncertain terms in need of religion. He did find peace, love, and tranquillity in nature and thought if there were a god, he would at least give him credit for creating such a beautiful place to dwell in.

Being an avid reader, Frances researched the information on the brochure that Linda had brought home and found that the church was the furthest religion from the Catholic faith, so she decided that Linda could try her luck there. She liked the idea that the Pentecostal belief was referred to as spirit-filled, which sounded lighter and more appealing than kneeling inside a dark confession box repeating Hail Marys and recounting one's sins.

Shortly after Linda's request and her mother's research, one Sunday, Linda was dropped off at the closest Pentecostal church her mother could find.

Upon her arrival, Linda was impressed with the long wooden benches known as pews until she actually sat on one. She then admired the congregation's friendliness until the music started, and they all began speaking in tongues and rolling around on the floor. Before much more could happen, Linda was convinced she had been dropped off in the looney bin, so she high-tailed it out of there before she could fall victim to her feet being washed or demons being cast out of her body. She speculated that she might have a few of those lingering about within but thought it best to keep them. She waited outside for her parents to pick her up and never asked to go to church again.

Occasionally as a family, minus father, Frances would take the kids to Saint Andrew's Anglican Church. It was often a battle, as everyone complained how boring it was. Because of the fight to get everyone ready and out the door, Frances eventually gave up. She settled on a once-a-year visit every Easter.

Linda would soon be entering Grade 5. Houses were being sold for $10-15,000. The average monthly rent was $88.00, the average yearly wage was $4,500, and gasoline was twenty-two cents a gallon. Everyone was listening to "Heartbreak Hotel" by the one and only Elvis Presley, who was now being referred to as "Elvis the Pelvis."

Families were tuning in to *The Price is Right*, a new television game show hosted by Bill Cullen. The widely popular *Ten Commandments* movie with Charlton Heston as Moses was a box office success despite being the most expensive film ever made, having also been nominated for seven academy awards. *My Fair Lady* opened on Broadway, starring Julie Andrews as Eliza Doolittle. The musical comedy became a smash-hit. Movie actress Grace Kelly married Prince Rainer, and she became Princess Grace of Monaco.

IBM released its first computer with a hard drive, the IBM 305 RAMAC. The machine weighed about one tonne and measured five megabytes of data. In the United States, the US Supreme Court ruled on the *Browder vs Gayle* case. The ruling stated that racial segregation on buses was unconstitutional.

With a new baby arriving that year, Vince had grown tired of his two-bit wages working for other people and the peer pressure to go to the beer parlour every night after work. On a few occasions, Vince got caught up in the camaraderie of having one too many beers after work, returning home later than usual with a changed personality that Frances did not recognize.

Reminiscent of his childhood with a drunken father in cahoots with his two uncles, only to have his mother abandon him, Vince was able to take heed when Frances reminded him of his past. By no means was she going to be his partner in crime or be a wife sitting outside the beer parlour in a car full of kids.

Vince adored, respected, and valued Frances's opinion, so he cut ties with some of his drinking buddies because, as Frances put it, bicycles and vacations for the kids should come first.

There can be advantages and disadvantages to looking older than you are, and it can be commonplace to be given more responsibility. Linda was quickly learning that looking more mature than other girls her age could bring her distinct disadvantages. Teachers, parents, classmates, and strangers seemed to have higher expectations of her.

She felt it all started at The Bay department store when instructed to purchase clothes from the Miss Teen section. Her Grade 2 teacher had expected her to automatically know how to write because she looked far more advanced. The bullies who had called her names assumed she could take it because she looked older and walked with confidence.

At six, seven, and eight years old, Linda could not always replicate older people's actions and often could not understand what was appropriate. Subsequently, she had fears related to her performance. To Linda, it always seemed she was a little girl trapped in a young woman's body.

It has been documented and well-known that children often tease other children who are different in some way. Bullying can be worse in preteens and teenagers, as self-esteem is at its most vulnerable. Linda was plagued, as far back as she could remember, with never looking like her friends. It seemed expectations were always higher for her from most adults in her life—teachers, relatives, neighbours, and family.

In Grade 5, Linda's peers were still little girls, whereas Linda was fully developed and unexpectedly got her period, to her dismay and horror. She ran to her teacher from the playground, screaming for an ambulance and stating that she was bleeding to death. Her peers, with their mouths agape, pointed at her with unease.

She was sent to the nurse's office. The on-site school nurse explained the whole emergence into womanhood, and Linda was sent home with appropriate sanitary napkins in a paper bag and a perceived death sentence in her heart. Putting colour into her nightmares, she ran home from school and screamed for her mother as she slammed the front door. Frances was embarrassed and had no idea how to deal with Linda's sudden leap into being a full-fledged woman.

The female body, puberty, and getting one's period were not discussed when Frances was coming of age. She had been unprepared, and therefore, did not prepare Linda, especially since Frances had been fifteen when it happened to her and was referred to as a late bloomer.

Linda was ten years old. To Frances, as mature as her daughter appeared to be, she was still a little girl, and she thought there was more time—at least three more years—before she would have to face the facts and explain to her daughter the uncomfortable transformation into womanhood.

Linda was not ready. She still pranced around the yard and played out episodes of *Gunsmoke*. Now, much to her dismay, she had turned entirely into Miss Kitty overnight and did not like it one little bit. Linda prayed that acquiring a bordello would not be the next event!

She knew that she would never get used to what the nurse called "her time of the month." The whole scenario made her blush. And then came "the cramps!" The worst part of having a monthly visitor was everything that went with it, Linda thought. She soon discovered the secret code and how taboo menstruating was, never talked about and considered shameful—the Curse.

On one occasion, she was taken off guard while she was at Laura Lynn and sought out an older woman who had the appropriate "time of the month paraphernalia." She discretely gave Linda some pads and a plastic bag.

Not having gained the experience of worldly discretion, Linda removed her undergarments and placed them in the appointed plastic bag. She threw them in a nearby garbage can next to the barn. One of Linda's friends, a boy named Peter, just happened to be looking for a discarded plastic bag to carry his belongings home in. He saw what he thought was an empty plastic bag in the trash and was devastated when he opened it and saw the contents. Seeing the shock on Peter's face, Linda yelled at him that there had been an accident and that he had happened upon the bloody bandages and to stop being a blockhead!

Thinking fast on her feet had become Linda's saviour on more than one occasion, and in the years to come, it would be a proven skill to get her out of numerous tricky situations.

Linda shopping downtown Vancouver with Grandma

Douglas, baby Kenneth and big sister Linda

A road trip and a horseback ride for Linda

Fun times horseback riding

Grandma, Douglas, and Linda at Stanly Park, Vancouver

Linda loving her brothers Kenny and Dougie

Linda and daddy's bulldozer

Grade three, second row from the top, five
students over from the right, Linda

CHAPTER SIX

A Grownup Decision

"Someday, you will be old enough to start reading fairy tales again."

-C.S. Lewis

Westerns became so popular that they dominated television viewing. From 1949 to the late '60s, there were over 100 Western series that aired on networks. Viewers escaped their humdrum lives to watch their favourite heroes overcome all adversaries. It was good versus bad, hero versus villain in the nineteenth-century Old West.

Parents liked how most Westerns taught good values of honesty and integrity, hard work, racial tolerance, determination to succeed, and justice. At the end of the shows, moral lessons had been taught and learned.

Wagon Train was one of the most popular Western shows of the '50s and '60s, from 1957-1962. This American Western series followed TV characters Major Seth Adams and his scout Flint McCullough as they engaged in adventures, leaving post-Civil War behind and navigating their way to the Wild West of California on a wagon train. Travelling through the plains, deserts, and the Rocky Mountains, encountering gunfights and cowboys, "wagons-ho" became the catchphrase for all the kids watching.

Even though she lived in a family of five, Linda was the only one who relished watching Western shows on television. She never minded making her way downstairs to the TV room, with snacks in one hand and a diet soda in the other, to watch her coveted shows alone.

The first diet soda was sugar-free ginger ale, made by the Kirsch Bottling Company in Brooklyn, for diabetic patients at a Jewish sanatorium. It was called No-Cal. With Linda becoming more self-conscious of her size, she decided to cut down by consuming the latest craze, diet soda. She did not understand any caloric or dieting concepts, but the commercials stated that drinking diet soda could keep the weight off.

After Kenneth, or Kenny, was born, the Bonner family was complete. Frances and Vince had decided initially on two children, and having had a girl and a boy, they figured they were done. Kenny was an unexpected tow-headed, blue-eyed cherub. Frances thought that an angel had been gifted to her from the heavens above.

Of course, she loved all three of her children equally, but there was something audacious about this one. She could not put her finger on it but felt a kindred spirit to the cheeky grin and the fair-complexioned baby boy.

The summer after Kenny's birth, Vince had a grand idea. Every year, he and his buddies went fishing, and this year they had decided on Watch Lake. Vince researched that there was a stable and horse ranch at the Watch Lake Lodge and Guest Ranch. A win-win, fishing for him and horseback riding for his very horsey daughter. Watch Lake is located at the south end of the Cariboo at 70 Mile House, only a six-hour drive from Vancouver, where the highway meets the horse.

The year was 1959, and by the end of summer, Linda would be turning twelve years old. Unbeknownst to Linda, her father had made arrangements with the lodge to allow his daughter to stay for free, in exchange for the lodge owner's daughter travelling back to North Vancouver with Vince and Linda, so she could attend the Pacific National Exhibition, mostly for the livestock and, in particular, the horses.

Dimps was to become Linda's new best friend. Never before had she met a more horse-orientated girl than herself. Dimps was the ultimate cowgirl, a real tomboy, very hardy, and she knew her stuff around horses. She was the same age as Linda and was of average size but built strong, with short, dark hair, freckles, and sparkling brown eyes. They were a perfect match.

Every day together for the extent of Linda's seven-day stay, they groomed horses, worked the ranch, and went for endless horseback rides. Dimps's mother, being a bit of a worrywart, insisted the girls ride bareback. Her thoughts were that if anything should happen out in the wild blue yonder, they could get hung up on the saddle or stirrups and get dragged. This was a fear that plagued her.

As a seasoned rider, Linda did not care one iota how she had to ride. All she cared about was riding in any way, shape, or form. And now, she splendidly had a friend who was perhaps even more seasoned than she was.

Just like the Wrigley's Doublemint Chewing Gum ads, together, Linda and Dimps had "double strength" and were fearless and unstoppable when it came to horseback riding. They often joked around, calling themselves the "Doublemint Twins," just like the newspaper and television ad campaign.

Everything was "out of sight" and "super-duper" until Linda's horse, known as Fly, stepped in a hornet's nest. Poor Fly turned into a bucking bronco as the hornets began stinging. Without the saddle horn or stirrups to hold onto, Linda was thrown from the horse's back. Much to her dismay, she, too, was repeatedly stung.

With no one to blame, Linda did not cry. Nature is nature, only doing its thing, not like the deliberate bullies back at school. Instead, she worried about Fly as he took off running back to the barn. Linda jumped up behind Dimps on her horse and was doubled back to the lodge.

Both horse and rider healed, and Linda would forever have gold-dappled memories of her time at the Watch Lake Lodge, her friend Dimps, and Fly. As the orange sun sunk low on the horizon, the week was up, and soon Dimps would be accompanying Linda to a few days at the PNE.

Linda did not want to leave the ranch, and Dimps could hardly wait to attend the fair she had heard about and longed to be a part of her whole life up until then. As they drove back to North Vancouver, Linda cried as Dimps rejoiced.

For three summers in a row, Linda had taken to staying at Laura Lynn while her parents took the boys camping to the Okanagan. They always stopped in Osoyoos for the still, dry heat, which was perfect for camping, fishing, and swimming. Their trips included stops in Kelowna to visit Vince's dad and uncles and then to Enderby to see his brother Hank with his wife and children. Their tradition was to purchase orchard fruit at various fruit stands along the way to be canned, pickled, and stewed when they got home.

Just before Linda's twelfth birthday, she made a grown-up decision that would first shock, then annoy her parents, and eventually came to be thought of as an unexpected yet somewhat expected turn of events.

During Linda's two-week stay that summer at Laura Lynn, the owners brought some new horses in. One, in particular, was a beautiful dapple grey mare, which was malnourished and thin, having been mistreated. She had been rescued with other horses from a wayward, bankrupt riding stable in the Cariboo.

Unfortunately, the horse would not let anyone get near her. She reared and snorted, kicked and bucked, and no one could do anything with her. Even the most experienced men who worked and cared for all the animals could not tame this beast.

All except for Linda. She secretly named the horse Tosca, and it was love at first sight for both of them. Linda later found out that all the horses had come from the Interior and had been neglected and that Tosca's new baby colt had died during birth. For Linda, this was exceptionally painful.

For some reason, the skittish, untrained, and maimed horse felt akin to Linda. They shared the same feelings of being misunderstood and fearful of those who could overtake them and be less than kind. In knowing this, Linda could get close enough to whisper into the horse's ear, "No wonder you are so hard to handle; you are heartbroken." While gently stroking the horse's neck, she went on to say, "Of course you are mad and upset. You have every right to be."

After biting, kicking, and scaring off one too many stable hands, the owners reluctantly decided to send the horse away. When Linda got wind that her beloved Tosca was going to be sent to the horse meat factory and end up as dog food, she was devastated.

Linda cried and begged for the Donovans to keep her. Over the years, the family had gotten to know Linda well, and she was one of their favourites. While valuing her hard work and dedication, it was apparent that she also had a unique connection with the otherwise unruly horse. They offered Linda a deal that she could not refuse, suggesting she purchase the horse for the tune of $75.00, which could be paid off in volunteer work. She gladly accepted the offer.

When Frances and Vince got home from their trip and Linda broke the news, they were initially upset. After that, realizing that their little girl was growing up, they acknowledged they had always known that the world of horses and anything pertaining to them would be an integral part of her life. Besides, they admired Linda's ability to swing such a great deal.

Now the proud owner of her horse, Linda realized that her acquired independence and moxie came to her through no fault of her own. The circumstances of being treated like a grown-up from the day she was born, maneuvering around bullies, her father's charismatic sense of humour, and finding love and a connection from a majestic beast would one day turn out to be her saving grace.

Linda barely noticed the year of Grade 7 because it flew by quickly. She also did not pay much attention to her little brothers. She thought they were cute and all but relished in her own life at the stables and her new best friend, Tosca.

When the summer holidays rolled around, just after Grade 7, her family announced another trip to the Okanogan, and

Linda assumed that she would be staying at Laura Lynn again. Unfortunately, because of increased popularity in the riding club, they were unable to house Linda this time, and on the verge of turning thirteen, she pleaded with her parents to allow her to stay home alone.

Frances almost said yes, but was fearful that anything could go wrong. With her obsession with murder mystery novels and keeping up on all current events, Frances could not bear the thought of her daughter left alone with possible unsavoury characters lurking about.

Disappointed, Linda agreed to a babysitter. When the day arrived, and the family was off, Linda met the eighteen-year-old teenager supervising her. Initially, Linda thought that the young woman might work out. They both shared the same love of Westerns and junk food, and after a day at Laura Lynn, they began a routine of Swanson TV frozen dinner entrees in front of the television every evening. Linda thought she had made a friend as they popped popcorn and chatted about their obsession with horses and anything Western.

At the start of the weekend, the young caregiver informed Linda that "they" had a date. Utterly not interested in boys and unbeknownst to her family, Linda had already had her fair share of passes.

Looking many years her senior, Linda still received comments about her weight and size from her peers, but more frequent were the lewd comments and propositions from much older boys. They felt it their right to ogle and comment about Linda's ample bosom. She generally brushed them off and, once in a while, exclaimed, "I am only a child, so back off!" Her stern remark usually did the trick, so Linda felt no need to tell anyone.

When Saturday rolled around, the teenage babysitter started to read Linda the riot act, which consisted of how she expected Linda to behave. She began by telling Linda how important the date was to her and indicated that she needed Linda to pretend that she was eighteen.

After an hour of applying makeup and loaning her seductive clothes, twelve-year-old Linda thought of the date as one would think about playing dress-up and pretending to be Miss Kitty from *Gunsmoke*.

She did not realize that the young woman responsible for her would wind up in the back seat, making out with her boyfriend, leaving Linda to fend for herself in the front seat with the boyfriend's buddy. Initially paralyzed with fright, Linda had the sink or swim mentality and proceeded to talk. She talked and talked and talked.

The much older male enjoyed Linda's recollections of *The Lone Ranger, Wagon Train,* and how her mother took her to meet Roy Rogers, Dale Evans, and Trigger the horse when they came to town for publicity purposes. She explained about caring for her horse named Tosca and her eventual future of becoming a cowgirl and ranch hand in British Columbia's Interior.

Fortunately, Linda came home from the date unharmed and relieved but exhausted. Deciding that whatever her babysitter was doing in the back seat was disgusting, Linda chalked it up to another event to add to the list of what *not* to tell her parents.

Linda had an epiphany that night—not only was she not ready to date, but she also decided that she did not need a man. Nor did she want a *Leave it to Beaver* future complete with a white picket fence, businessman husband, and wifely duties that went with it. She was a cowgirl, and all she wanted was a horse and the wide-open range.

With her brothers rapidly growing up, they had very little in common with their big sister. However, one thing that brought them together was tuning in to a show called *Bonanza*, airing from 1959 onward.

Gathering in front of the television, the siblings thought it was a spectacular sight to see one of the first series to be filmed in colour, with picturesque scenes of Lake Tahoe, Nevada. RCA, the manufacturer of colour television sets, was the primary sponsor during its first two seasons. By season three, *Bonanza* soared in the ratings.

The show revolved around the Cartwrights, a fictional all-male family of ranchers living in the mid-1800s near Virginia City, Nevada. Heading the family was Ben (Lorne Greene), three times a widower, with a son from each marriage; Adam (Pernell Roberts) was the eldest, serious and responsible; Hoss (Dan Blocker) was the middle son, gregarious and oafish; Little Joe (Michael Landon), the youngest, was handsome and romantic.

The plot often developed from personality conflicts between the brothers and eventually turned toward mining and managing the Cartwright ranch, called The Ponderosa. Often the family was called to deal with unruly outsiders and to restore peace. Rather than settle disputes with typical cowboy gun-slinging, the Cartwrights employed diplomacy and dialogue. Linda instantly fell in love with Hoss, thinking that she might consider marriage if her husband-to-be was anything like the handsome, gentle giant.

Vince and Frances were frugal, as were most who experienced and lived through the Depression-era. Their spendthrift ways were reflected in the modest house they chose to build. There was no view, even though they lived on a hill and could have implemented one. The house came with five bedrooms and two bathrooms, and the required kitchen, dining, and living room. The furnace room, fruit cupboard, and TV room were in the basement, and of course, there was a front and back yard. A clothesline for Frances graced the back porch, helping to save on the heating bill all year long, and there were enough trees left in the backyard for a rope swing. To Vince, both were a must.

Frances only purchased meat on sale, and Vince enjoyed gardening. He grew potatoes at the side of the house, planting green beans and tomatoes that he watched make their way up the back of their home. The backyard fruit trees supplied them with cherries and pears for canning, and they both enjoyed making pickles and pickling beets. The succulent peaches and nectarines from their Okanagan summer trips could be enjoyed all year round due to their diligent canning sprees. Down in the basement of their 1940s North Vancouver home was the room they called "the fruit cupboard," a cold, dark room with wooden shelves, stored jars, and jars of home-canned goods that would take the family through the winter and spring.

Rarely did they go out for dinner, but on occasion, a special treat for the whole family would be a splurge of fried chicken from the White Spot. White Spot is a Canadian restaurant chain based in Vancouver, British Columbia, best known for its hamburgers, Pirate Pack children's meal, triple-o sauce, and milkshakes.

In the 1920s, Nat Bailey operated a travelling lunch counter out of a 1918 Model T Ford. He sold hotdogs for a dime and ice cream for a nickel. In 1928, Nat Bailey founded the first White Spot restaurant in BC. Initially, he had planned on calling it the Granville Barbecue. However, he changed his mind when a friend suggested he name it after a popular restaurant on Wilshire Boulevard in Los Angeles, California, in part because the name sounded spotless and clean.

One evening while picking up White Spot chicken for the family dinner, Vince made a joke with Nat Bailey. He said, "You should put a sign outside your restaurant that says, 'Have Chicken, Will Travel.'" Both men erupted into fits of laughter. Vince grabbed his chicken and headed home to set up the TV trays in the living room for the family to watch *Have Gun, Will Travel*. This TV series followed the adventures of a man called Paladin. He was a gentleman investigator gunfighter who travelled around the Old West, working as a mercenary for people who hired him to solve their problems.

The very next day, a new sign was posted outside of the local White Spot Restaurant, coining the phrase suggested by Vince Bonner... "Have Chicken, Will Travel," it stated for all to see.

At the end of the summer, just before Linda was to begin Grade 8, Frances and Vince wanted to take the family to Harrison Hot Springs, a beautiful hotel out past Mission, BC, that boasted natural hot springs, healing whirlpools, and a wonderful vacation only two hours east of North Vancouver.

Linda begged not to go. She hated swimming and only wanted to be with horses. Besides, she had just gotten a job working with a veterinarian and did not want to miss work and tending to Tosca. Once again, she requested to stay home alone.

The tricky part with Linda is that she still appeared so much older than she was. Standing five feet eight inches tall, with a voluptuous figure and a mature attitude, Frances and Vince were torn. Although she would be thirteen years old in only a few weeks, she was still technically twelve. They thought it best if they got another sitter.

Having not told her mom and dad of the last close call, Linda felt that she could not plead any further, even though she was fearful of another mishap occurring. The next caregiver was someone Frances found in the newspaper, a woman in her twenties who came with good references.

The weekend went well for Frances, Vince, Dougie, and Kenny. They swam, ate in the Copper Room, and walked the trails. Frances did not swim or walk, so she read her mystery novels contentedly and enjoyed soaking in the whirlpool.

Arriving home Sunday afternoon, they came into an empty house, realizing that Linda was probably at the stable feeding Tosca and would be arriving home soon. Shortly after dark, Vince started to worry, so he jumped in the truck and headed up to Laura Lynn.

A couple of things had gone on that weekend, and Linda figured she would be in trouble for both of them.

On Saturday morning before work, Linda decided to take a bath to get ready. At twelve years old, as any little girl would do, she ran the water, poured in the bubbles, undressed, and as she lowered herself into the tub, she noticed that the door had become ajar. Linda figured she could quickly finish up but was startled when she spotted her babysitter spying on her.

Two unrecognizable eyes—an older woman, a supposed caregiver—disrespectfully held her gaze and peered at Linda through the crack in the door.

Alarmed, Linda demanded the young woman close the door, but she refused and continued to watch. The only thing Linda could do was find her towel, hurry up and get out of the tub, run to her room to dress, and leave the house.

She was embarrassed and bewildered as to what the heck the woman was doing. Pushing it out of her mind, she hurriedly walked to the veterinary clinic.

Arriving hours too early for work, she pretended to have missed the animals and made up a story to stay past her shift until the place closed. When she got home, Linda locked herself in her bedroom.

She brought some snacks home to eat in her room and spent the time reading her book *My Friend Flicka,* and was thankful for the lock on her bedroom door. Linda stayed silent when she heard a light knocking and ignored the woman entirely.

Upon waking up, she went directly to Laura Lynn.

The whole next day was spent reflecting on that alarming event, and she could not understand for the life of her why a twenty-something-year-old woman would want to do what she did. As they were short-staffed that day, Linda was asked to take a new rider's group on an all-day trail ride. She was alarmed to see her dad waiting for her when the ride ended. She would have notified her parents that it would be after dark by the time she returned, but she had no way to tell them.

When the family arrived home to a messy house, cold bath water still in the tub, and the house empty, void of sitter and daughter, they were worried out of their minds. It was pure instinct that sent Vince to the riding stable.

Even though it was not Vince's parenting style, he yelled at Linda to get in the car after the horses had been tended to. Arriving home, Linda dissolved into a heap of tears and explained the two damaging caregivers and how at the stables she was asked to take a group out on a ride. While Vince comforted her, Frances was livid at the strangers who were supposed to be caring for their daughter.

Overeating may not always be from a dramatic event such as witnessing a death, suffering a sexual assault, experiencing a severe car accident, or being deployed in combat. It could be caused by having a family pet die, losing a job, being forgotten at school, or going through a divorce or difficult breakup.

All can have the same effects—an increase in anxiety and frustration and, in some cases, post-traumatic stress disorder with its disassociation and avoidance.

By the time Linda was thirteen years old, she had endured years of name-calling, an emergence into womanhood way before her time, and two incidences of sexual misconduct. She found comfort in food and believed that she was destined to be a larger person. Whenever she caught a glimpse of herself in the mirror, she was reminded of The Bay's saleswoman, who referred to her as big-boned and abnormally large when she was only six years old.

She was undoubtedly loved and nurtured by her parents, but the hush-hush mentality of not discussing one's hurts and disappointments was a common practice. In other words, it was best to cry behind closed doors and remain unemotional when faced with adversity. One must never explain in public how deeply they have been hurt or mistreated—at least this had become Linda's regular train of thought, and nobody explained otherwise.

Therefore, when Linda decided to try smoking at the age of thirteen, and her mother found out, Frances's reaction was supportive and kind. She felt her daughter had been through so much already. That surprised a young teenager who was testing the waters.

Being in high school, Linda desperately wanted to fit in. She was tired of the bullies. She also felt grown-up, mature, and ready to be classified as someone other than Linda Pinda and Fatty-fatty-two-by-four.

Shortly after beginning Grade 8, one fall Saturday afternoon, Linda asked her mom if she could go to the Cedar V movie theatre in Lynn Valley, having been invited by some of her new high school friends. Frances gladly agreed and offered her the money. Casually, Frances opened Linda's purse to put the cash inside. Initially shocked and dismayed, she found nestled next to Linda's wallet a pack of cigarettes.

During World War 1, it was a widespread practice to send tobacco overseas to soldiers as an act of patriotism. Many soldiers returned home from the war, touting the benefits of smoking. This, coupled with the increase in tobacco product advertising, led to a rise in cigarette use, especially among women.

In Canada in the 1920s, 2.4 billion cigarettes were consumed compared to 87 million in 1896. Celebrities endorsed certain cigarette brands, tobacco companies sponsored parades and events like the first Canadian Football League radio broadcasts, and tobacco product packaging became more innovative and attractive. Cigarettes were given as gifts on occasions such as Christmas and Father's Day.

During World War ll, cigarettes again were offered to soldiers as gifts and symbols of support from back home. As smoking gained popularity, it became acceptable to smoke in more public places.

By the 1950s, however, doctors and scientists were sharing concerns about the harmful effects of smoking and tobacco use on people's health. Articles were published in well-known magazines and journals. In 1954 the Canadian Government decided to conduct its own study on smoking and its health effects.

On June 17, 1963, when approximately fifty percent of Canadians smoked, Canada's Minister of National Health and Welfare, Judy LaMarsh, declared in parliament for the first time, "There is scientific evidence that cigarette smoking is a contributory cause of lung cancer. It may also be associated with chronic bronchitis and coronary heart disease."

When she spotted the cigarettes in Linda's purse, Frances was at first surprised, especially since she herself had only started smoking when she was twenty-five. Having been raised in a strict home, she had her every move watched and commented on. Consequently, she decided to take a different approach with her eldest child. She asked Linda if she was smoking. When Linda defiantly answered yes, Frances said, "I really wish you wouldn't smoke, but if you must, could you please only smoke at home and not in public?"

Taken aback, Linda chose to throw her cigarettes away that day and never smoke again. She did not like the taste anyway, and because her mother was preventing her from having to sneak around, Linda also decided never to drink alcohol. "What's the point?" Linda concluded.

In reality, she had only wanted to appear cool, with-it, and grown up to her new friends. Trying to break free from what her reputation had become need not involve adding two nasty habits, Linda concluded.

Meanwhile, baby number four was to arrive, and Vince was thrilled but decidedly in need of a vasectomy. This was not a common practice in Canada, so Vince crossed the United States border to have the simple procedure and thus prevent more surprises.

At thirteen years old, Linda was the eldest sister to three younger siblings. Dougie was six, Kenny was four, and the new baby required her parents' attention much more than Linda did. She spent most of her time at Laura Lynn and her veterinary job, trying to spend as little time at school as possible. Her occasional downtime was spent engrossed in her many Western shows on television.

Rawhide, an American Western TV series starring Clint Eastwood, aired 1959–1965. Set in the 1860s, *Rawhide* portrayed the challenges faced by the drovers of a cattle drive. Most episodes revolved around crooked townspeople or lawless politicians, from which the main characters had to rescue people. Often set in parched plains, the common themes involved ghostly riders, wolves raiding cattle, bandits, murderers, and other desperate situations requiring a rescue. There was a constant need to find water for the cattle. What made the show unique is that it frequently dealt with controversial topics. In one episode, Robert Culp played an ex-soldier on the drive who had become addicted to morphine. Another drover, Jesus from Mexico, was faced with racism at times from those outside of the crew.

Television shows would encourage Linda. Her father would teach her love and empathy, and her mother's secret would soon be revealed, although Linda would not understand it for many years to come.

Linda with other Laura Lynn riders in the PNE parade

Dougie, Linda and Kenny all dressed up

Grandma, Linda, Dougie, Kenny and Mother

Happy with baby Kenneth

CHAPTER SEVEN

Mountain Shadows

"The earth has music for those who listen."

-unknown

The 1960s was the era of peace, love, civil rights, and fast-food franchises. Places like McDonald's, A & W, and Dairy Queen began to open chains across the country, and Coke dominated every menu. Coke's status as the soda industry leader, combined with its advertising power, made it the go-to soft drink. Canadians associated the ultimate fun food, a hamburger and french fries, with a Coke. Advertising also positioned the popular beverage as a multicultural drink that appealed to open-minded young people concerned about the Vietnam war, civil rights, and the environment.

In 1960, a new house cost approximately $13,000, the average income was around $5,500 per year, gasoline was twenty-five cents a gallon, and the average price of a new car was $2,500–3,000.

New products that consumers were buying up like hotcakes in the 1960s included things like Barbie Dolls, Troll Dolls, Chatty Cathy, colour televisions, Mix Masters, ant farms, Etch-a-Sketch, electric toothbrushes, Coppertone suntanning lotion, Clairol hair dye and electric blankets.

Another event to add to the list of what was happening in the '60s was the birth of Linda's baby sister, Karen. It went almost completely unnoticed by Linda because she was busy doing life. She was thirteen, her mother was nearly forty, and her dad was forty-five. The baby was just that, the baby of the family and loved by all. Linda overheard her parents say this would be the last one, and she wondered how they would possibly manage.

By the time she turned fourteen, Linda was neither a hippy nor an activist. She had long since finished playing with dolls and never liked playing children's games unless it involved horses. She still had her sights set on a career in ranching. With her drive and ambition more vital than ever, in 1961, just before her fourteenth birthday, her parents said she could take a job for the summer in Kelowna at a dude ranch.

The Mountain Shadows riding stable in Kelowna, British Columbia, was a Western-themed, dusty place of horses, trail rides, one or two stable hands, and a wonderful family that ran the whole business. In other words, a dream come true for horse-driven Linda. There she felt vibrant, skilled, and respected. Whenever Linda was surrounded by one horse or more and her Western counterparts, the bullies, tormentors, predators, and naysayers were obscured in her memory.

Her accommodations at the ranch were on the back porch of the main house—simple and cozy. The morning sun made an entrance through the mesh windows, waking Linda each morning to the sounds of chirping birds, clucking chickens, and the wonderful aroma of bacon and coffee. The sunsets and deep black night sky illuminated millions of stars through the screened-in windows, inviting Linda to slip off into a deep sleep each night. Linda was especially loved by the family at Mountain Shadows.

Vince, however, was not so sure that his firstborn daughter would excel. Or rather, he was worried about how Linda would be treated. So it was decided the whole family would pop in to visit and check up on Linda. Shortly after Linda arrived at the stables,

Vince, Frances, Douglas, Kenny, and baby Karen set off for the Mountain Shadows.

Arriving in the late afternoon, Vince and Frances were happy to see that all was well. Linda seemed to have settled in quite nicely. Vince booked a trail ride with his daughter for the entire family to enjoy. Even baby Karen sat in front of Vince on the saddle. In turn, Linda was happy that everyone at the Mountain Shadows could meet her family, especially her handsome father. After only a few days, the family left to do their usual Okanagan summer festivities.

Linda was not afraid of hard work. Her duties were no different than at Laura Lynn, all of which she was highly seasoned and skilled at completing—grooming horses, cleaning stalls, and taking the guests on horseback riding trails.

Meandering through the Okanagan pine forests was where Linda wanted to be. She never gave a second thought to her family back home or to school. She imagined if she were to die right then and there, her life would be complete.

It was on the peaceful, passive trail rides that Linda allowed her mind to wander occasionally. She remembered how just a few years back, she made a conscious decision not to be sad. Sadness resulted in tears, which resulted in more name-calling: "Don't be a baby," or "Cry baby, cry baby." The taunters' remarks were ceaseless. If not about her weight, then it would be about the tears that followed. Therefore, she forced only acceptable emotions to grace her persona, causing all other feelings to be pushed down— anger, disappointment, fear...the list could go on and on. In Linda's mind, avoiding sadness at all costs was a weapon against the bullies.

Put on a brave face, show a stiff upper lip, and when all else fails, smile in the face of adversity, Linda told herself.

Linda idolized her dad and admired his sense of humour. She liked to believe all her positivity and ability to block out the painful name-calling was handed down from him. When faced with a tricky situation, she immediately whispered to herself, *What would my father do?*

Halfway through her summer job at Mountain Shadows, Linda woke up like any other day. She washed her face, brushed her teeth, threw on her work clothes and cowboy boots, and then headed straight out to the barns to check on the horses.

The morning felt fresh, and Linda was looking forward to the day's events. After a hearty breakfast of hotcakes, bacon, eggs, and hash browns, it would be back to the barns to saddle up the horses for an all-day trail ride. Soon she would be enjoying nature at its finest, meandering through alpine meadows with spectacular wildflowers while leading eight to ten intermediate riders.

Linda liked the unpredictability of how alpine foliage all bloomed at different times, creating a continually changing wave of colour across the high-altitude hills. It was helpful as a guide to learn the names and varieties of such flora and fauna that sprawled across the mountain meadows.

Linda's favourite was the bright red Indian Paintbrush that grew on top of a straight, hairy stem. And if one could dislike a flower, it was the Hawkweed that bloomed all summer long that Linda was not fond of. Even though it bloomed in a pretty bright yellow, it grew like a weed, often invading other perennials and taking over, reminding Linda of the bullies back at home. When the horses trampled down flowers in their path, Linda secretly pretended that each flower represented her nameless tormentors' faces.

Sizing up all the new riders, Linda figured it would be an easy day. Seasoned riders, tame, well-fed and rested horses, and a gorgeous sunny day stretched out before them.

After walking, trotting, and galloping on a few straightaways, the morning turned into the afternoon, so Linda and the other guide decided to stop the group for lunch.

They tied the horses to trees in a pleasant meadow to allow them to graze. Linda found some perfect tufts, mounds of dirt for herself and the group to settle in on, open their packs, and chow down on sandwiches, cookies, and bottles of Coke. A rancher's life was never disturbed by a bit of dirt; it only added to the experience, especially for the paying customers.

Within minutes she and others began shifting around in their seats. Many jumped up, some squealed in discomfort, and others ran for the trees, stripping down right out of their pants! They realized they had set up their picnic right in the middle of several anthills.

Once an ant invades your pants, they pinch and bite and fight with whatever it is that has invaded *them*. In this case, at least a dozen bottoms were bitten in their snug, sweaty blue jeans.

Making a quick get-away, the trail riders cut their day short. Upon returning, it was straight to the showers for all the riders. Aside from the discomfort, the whole afternoon escapade made for many laughs around the supper table that night in retelling the "ants in the pants" story.

Near the end of summer, Linda got word that Auntie Vi and her new husband, Pete, wanted to stop at the ranch to visit her. It had been quite a few years since Linda's eccentric aunt had moved from Vancouver to Vernon, which was only a thirty-minute drive from Mountain Shadows just outside of Kelowna—a lovely outing for Violet and a visitor for Linda.

Violet had married the helicopter pilot she left Tommy for, and she had opened a chain of laundromats in Vernon. She had become a well-known businesswoman and a closet alcoholic. Violet could drink any man under the table, including her husband.

Long past the age of having children, Violet had no regrets. Occasionally she wondered what it would have been like to have a doe-eyed infant to call her own, but she valued her gin, independence, and undivided attention of Pete far too much to be bothered with any child-rearing misgivings.

Of Frances's four children, Violet felt closest to Linda. She had lived with the toddler for a time and could remember Linda's precocious personality. Violet liked to think they were kindred spirits and often smiled at the thought of it.

The visit was set for a Sunday afternoon. Linda was scheduled to take out a group on the same day but planned to be back by noon. It was an early morning ride, so up before dawn, Linda had the horses saddled and ready to go. It was barely daylight as the ride began. The temperature made for a cooler morning, but as soon as they saw the sun begin to rise, they stopped for a break to rest and take in the stunning glow set against the cornflower blue sky.

All the riders remained perched on their horses as they took in the breathtaking view, picture-perfect meadows, and wildflowers encased in a dewy sunrise. The other leader passed around a thermos of strong camp coffee and cowboy-style tin cups, accompanied by biscuits slathered with apricot preserves for the riders' enjoyment.

Linda disliked coffee and tea, cigarettes and liquor. She did not like the taste, so why bother? Everyone at the stable seemed to partake in all four. Linda was proud and stood firm in her beliefs, refusing to fall victim to the peer pressure of taking a sip from the flasks when they were passed around at home, and pretty much everywhere else Linda went.

To Linda, the coffee everyone raved about tasted like thick, bitter mud, and the booze had a harsh, biting flavour. She only needed to taste it once to realize the beverage, like coffee, was not for her. Both her mother and father smoked, and she was relieved when her mother gave her permission a few years back to join them. She gladly refused because sneaking around was the fun part.

Lost in her thoughts, Linda did not notice the blazing heat begin to surface with the rising sun.

After the coffee and biscuits were consumed, the riders were ready to continue. The horses proceeded on with a gentle nudge of heels to the lead horse's sides and a soft clicking of the tongue with the usual command of "giddy-up" from the guides.

In the meantime, the hot sunshine brought out the rattlesnakes. Like other reptiles, rattlesnakes are "cold-blooded" or ectothermic, relying essentially on outside heat sources rather than an internal metabolism to maintain their body temperature. They typically function most effectively at temperatures between seventy and nintey degrees Fahrenheit. Morning and evening are their favoured activity time.

It is well known in the horse community that horses are nervous about strange movements. Creepy, wiggly snakes, without a doubt, fall into that category. The terms skittish or spooked are standard, often used to describe a horse that has been startled.

Linda, like her four-hoofed friends, hated snakes. She had a bad experience only a few years ago when some of the boys that hung out at Laura Lynn had tried putting a harmless garden snake down the front of her shirt.

It was not just the snake that traumatized Linda. The boys' mean action of aggressively touching her and pinning her down caused Linda the most harm. From that day forward, she was petrified of snakes and people who said they were "only teasing."

As horses and riders rounded a corner, they came across some rocks and boulders on the side of the trail—a perfect place for rattlesnakes to sun themselves. The reptiles were just as spooked and surprised as the horses were, immediately slithering back under their stone haven, therefore startling horse and rider alike.

Blindsided because of the bend in the path, the rustling and quick movement caused Linda's horse to rear, kick its back legs out, and buck her off. Unprepared, Linda flew from her horse onto the boulders and nesting rattlers.

Aside from being terrified of the snakes, Linda could not move. She lay there with her body contorted in agonizing pain. Much to the dismay of the other riders, they assumed she had broken her back. Naturally, the riders immediately dismounted and offered to help.

More than fearing the worst about her back, Linda feared that her weight would prevent anyone from lifting her.

Instead, she used her quick wit and beat them to the punch by saying, "This fat girl may have broken her back, but if you try to lift her, you will all have broken backs too!" The response was an awkward silence, and after a few brief seconds, the dead air erupted into the sound of laughter.

In Linda's mind, she had won, never once thinking about self-deprecating humour. In fact, at almost fourteen, all she cared about was relieving the awkward silence, speaking aloud the collective unspoken thoughts, and getting a laugh.

Bingo! She had cracked the code by calling herself *Fat* before anyone else could. No one that day tried to correct Linda's use of the word. As a young, insecure teenager who had been bullied and called names about her weight for her entire life, the word *Fat* felt right to her.

She began to measure herself in contentment and laughter rather than in inches and pounds. *Besides*, Linda thought, *there is not a weight limit on beauty.* From that moment on, she decided to accept her size and call it what it was.

The other riders hoisted Linda back onto her horse, placing her on her stomach, with legs and arms dangling down, draped over the saddle like a robber to be delivered to the sheriff, reminiscent of her beloved Western shows. She wondered if Hoss and Little Joe would have done the same thing. "Where is the Lone Ranger and Tonto when you need them?" she yelled out to the others, which resulted in more laughter.

Auntie Vi and Uncle Pete had arrived at Mountain Shadows and were there when the group meandered in. Violet was dressed like a 1940's movie star. She wore a red high-collared dress, black mink stole, and matching red pumps. It was evident that she had just come from the beauty parlour. Her red lipstick was applied perfectly, and her shiny, raven hair was freshly coifed. Sticking out like a sore thumb, Violet relished in the longer-than-usual stares and raised eyebrows from the ranch hands.

Uncle Pete wore a thick wool sweater, even though it was blazing hot outside, and the noonday sun was causing others to strip down to their T-shirts. His black dress pants and penny loafers gave onlookers the impression that he came from money. Auntie Vi and Uncle Pete looked lavish and out of sorts on a dusty dude ranch in the Okanagan.

When spotting Linda, their initial reaction was one of annoyance, as they were taken aback seeing their niece splayed out over her horse. When they noticed that she was in obvious pain,

Violet's first instinct was to give her a sip from her flask, but then thought better of it. She had no idea that Linda would have refused the gesture anyway.

Uncle Pete helped Linda down from the horse and put her in the back seat of his car. Her auntie and uncle had shown up at just the right time, took Linda to the hospital, and after x-rays, found out that she was okay except for a bruised tail bone.

With the season just about ready to wrap up, Linda was bedridden for a few days but enjoyed her fourteenth birthday on August 26th, 1961, with all the other stable hands, the owners, and her auntie and uncle.

It was a celebratory night, so Linda's uncle and aunt were invited to stay for supper. Even when Auntie Vi got drunk and bickered with Uncle Pete, Linda ignored her aunt's behaviour, knowing that if she let it bother her, she would feel emotions she was desperately trying to push down, whispering to herself, *Be happy, be happy, be happy. At all costs, be happy.*

Soon it was back home to North Vancouver to begin Grade 9 at a new school. She was leaving Sutherland High School for North Van High. Four more years until high school graduation and freedom to finally live out her dreams!

Frances with baby Karen

Linda shopping on Granville street in downtown Vancouver

CHAPTER EIGHT

Boyfriends and Weightwatchers

"I come from a family where gravy is a beverage."

–Erma Bombeck

Linda's new motto was, "I would rather be fat and happy than thin and miserable."

In reality, everyone in high school liked Linda, although her self-esteem told her otherwise. Linda noticed that once *she* started calling *herself* names, the bullying and name-calling ceased to exist. She had let the wind out of their sails and beat them at their own game.

Grade 9 evolved into Grade 10, with all Linda's usual horse-oriented activities, and the new school year was off to a pretty good start. Linda had friends and felt she needed to be comical to keep them. She diligently went to school but still disliked academics and would rather be riding.

Besides school, Linda was once again volunteering at Laura Lynn, cleaning stalls, grooming horses, and leading trail rides, all in exchange for boarding her horse, Tosca. She also returned to her job at the veterinary clinic, caring for the animals, cleaning their cages, working at the front desk, and assisting the vet.

During her time off, she enjoyed riding Tosca from the stable in Lynn Valley to her family home near Grand Boulevard, a short distance away. The home was an average 1940's style home, comfortable and practical with all the modern conveniences, including a dishwasher that had been acquired after baby Karen was born, happily ending Linda's dishwashing days at the age of thirteen, which in turn gave her more time riding.

Once home, the neighbours would gather to admire her beautiful horse, who was notably also her best friend. Riding Tosca up and down the back lane, Linda happily gave various neighbourhood kids rides. On occasion, her little sister Karen was brought out to see the dapple grey mare. Even as a baby, she was placed onto Linda's lap. On the saddle, Karen contentedly grasped the saddle horn with her tiny hands while her big sister gripped her snuggly on the old worn leather seat. Sauntering down the back lane high atop the horse, Karen grinned from ear to ear without an ounce of fear.

Tosca behaved like a perfect lady. Linda had done wonders with the once wild and untameable mare. She had effortlessly broken Tosca, resulting in the most sweet-natured beast anyone had ever seen, especially Linda.

That same year, her dad purchased a Kodak movie camera and enjoyed filming Linda and Tosca trotting up and down the lane behind their house at Eighteenth and Moody. As soon as the Kodak film was developed and picked up, many neighbours would be called over to the Bonner's house for Vince's home movie night. The most entertaining part was when Vince played the galloping sequence backwards. The room would roar with laughter, with young and old alike pleading, "Play it again! Play it again!"

North Vancouver was home to Chief Dan George, who lived from July 24, 1899, to September 23, 1981. He was chief of the Tsleil-Waututh Nation, a Coast Salish band whose reserve land was, and is still, located on Burrard Inlet in the southeast area of the District of North Vancouver, British Columbia, Canada.

He was also an actor, musician, poet, and author—his best-known written work is *My Heart Soars*: "The beauty of the trees, the softness of the air, the fragrance of the grass speaks to me. And my heart soars."

As an actor, he was well known for portraying Old Lodge Skins opposite Dustin Hoffman in *Little Big Man* and opposite Clint Eastwood in *The Outlaw Josey Wales*. He was nominated for an Academy Award for Best Supporting Actor for both movies. From 1951 to 1963, he was band chief, but he also worked at several jobs, including longshoreman, construction worker, and school bus driver.

Vince had the pleasure of meeting Chief Dan George on numerous occasions in and around the construction industry. Linda rode horses through several different communities on the North Shore, meeting him as well.

North Vancouver was a horse-friendly community, with all of the forested trails and canyons open to hikers and horses alike, from the beaches to the mountains. One of the favourite horseback riding spots was the old Grouse Mountain Road, which passed by a nudist camp. Many riders secretly hoped they would catch sight of unabashed members in their birthday suits, naked as jaybirds. Unfortunately, or fortunately, their efforts were to no avail. At the nudist camp, any goings-on were kept hidden and left for the rumour mill to spin through possible made-up scenarios and lewd stories, mainly created by teenage boys.

The Van Tan Nudist Club was not well known to North Vancouver residents. They operated off the grid on a seven-acre property halfway up Grouse Mountain and kept a low profile. The Club was founded in 1939 in Vancouver and then later moved to picturesque North Vancouver.

In addition to the many trails around Laura Lynn, Linda and her friends would sometimes venture down to an occasional Powwow on the reserve. Linda enjoyed these events immensely. They also travelled over on the ferry from Lower Lonsdale, across the water to Vancouver, for the PNE parade, to promote the Laura Lynn Stables.

Amidst the carefree days of horseback riding, mini rodeos, Western television shows, and movies at the drive-in theatre in

Burnaby or the Cedar V Theatre in Lynn Valley, an unforeseen tragedy occurred, a horrific, senseless double murder that would instill fear in parents everywhere throughout British Columbia. Especially for Frances, who was already well versed in the local news. She was always abreast of current events, both good and evil.

Linda had made some great pals at Laura Lynn. Two girls, in particular, were twin sisters, Diana and Donna Ring. They were known as the Ring Twins. They boarded their strawberry roan horse at Laura Lynn, which they always rode double and bareback.

Together, Linda, Diana, and Donna would ride throughout the local trails and horse-friendly streets of North Vancouver. While mucking the stalls and grooming the horses at Laura Lynn, there was always laughter and much chatter because all three girls were collectively on the same wavelength. Movies, Western shows, and boys consumed their conversation in addition to their beloved steeds.

Linda and many other teenage girls had a secret crush on the twins' older brother. He was kind and handsome, doting on his sisters. Linda thought that he had the same qualities and appeal as Adam Cartwright, played by Pernell Roberts on *Bonanza*.

In the spring of 1963, the twins moved away with their family to Mable Lake. Linda was saddened and would miss them terribly. The three friends promised to write letters and stay in touch. There was a possibility that Linda could visit, and they all made a pact to share their love of horses forever and ever.

Mable Lake is located in the Southern Interior of British Columbia, Canada. It is a popular community for camping and fishing, a lake fed by the Shuswap River, northeast of Okanagan Lake and west of the Monashee Mountains.

In late 1963 the girls went missing after walking home from school one day. The devastating murders were not immediately discovered. The police dog master in Kamloops, BC, received a call from the Enderby detachment. It had been reported that two teenage daughters had disappeared after school.

An intense search involving the dog master and his RCMP police dog began in a wooded area behind the local school. The dog led the searchers to scattered schoolbooks and clothes. The night search ended tragically when the lifeless bodies of Donna and Diana were found. The scene was horrific.

Soon afterward, a male suspect, identified as Lawrence Herman Haase, walked out of the woods.

The police dog eventually found a working flashlight and a man's bloodstained shirt. Also, the dog guided the officers to a campfire, which was still burning in the woods. In the meantime, the suspect Haase made several statements to the investigating members, confessing to the murders.

After four days, the dog master and his dog found a .22 calibre rifle in an old, rotting log. The evidence allowed charges of murder to be laid against the suspect Haase. It was the dog's extraordinary tracking ability that uncovered the needed evidence at the murder scene. It was the first time in a Canadian court that the evidence provided through a dog master's efforts and his police service dog was accepted one hundred percent. On March 6, 1964, Haase was convicted of capital murder and sentenced to hang.

When the horrendous news came out, in addition to the family and friends of the girls, the entire communities of both Mable Lake and North Vancouver mourned. Frances and Vince were reminded of how fragile life is, and they began to keep an extra rein on Linda and their other three children. However, Linda, being a girl who was very independent, was a cause for concern. She was often gone for entire days and well into the evenings, busy with horses and going to the movie theatre.

Linda was at a loss. She could not understand how bad things could happen to good people. The only murderous activity she was familiar with involved the bad guys, outlaws, and robbers on television and in movies. Until Diana's and Donna's death, guns and killing were candy-coated in Kodachrome and stage makeup— shootouts on the silver screen with no actual bloodshed. Linda would push down her sadness and the many questions she had about the murders until much later.

In August 1964, North America was in the middle of full-blown Beatlemania, and Linda had two tickets to see the Fab Four at the PNE's open-air Empire Stadium. The tickets were four dollars apiece and were up in the nosebleed section, as far away from the stage as possible, a blessing in disguise because after local radio legend Red Robinson, master of ceremonies, introduced the group, they came out and played only two songs before the crowd rushed the stage. The band ran for their life.

Their first song was "Twist and Shout," precisely what the fans started to do to get closer to their rock and roll idols.

Red Robinson was sent back on stage to calm down the crazed fans. When he stated, "We've got to back some people up! There have been two kids crushed already; they'll have to cancel the show," in retaliation, John Lennon said, "Get the f*** off our stage; nobody interrupts the Beatles!"

The Beatles manager, Brian Epstein, looked at John and gave him the thumbs up as if to say, let Robinson do what he has to do.

John then spoke into the microphone to Red Robinson, "Okay, carry on, mate," as his final response.

Linda's cousin, a police officer, was assigned to work on crowd control and snap professional photographs with a costly, high-resolution camera.

After the stampede and the subsequent settling down of the audience, the band continued. Everyone got out alive, and Linda came away with some fabulous photos of The Beatles. She took them to school, only to have her friend Sally break into her locker and steal them.

Sally was a short brunette who perpetually wore striped peddle pushers and thongs on her feet, even in the dead of winter, like a uniform. She was considerably good-looking but always had her nose in everyone else's business. Her thick-lensed, horn-rimmed glasses magnified her big brown eyes, and with her hair pulled back in a tight ponytail, they only served to emphasize the severity of her busy body mentality. To most, Sally was downright meddlesome, but she always professed that she was only trying to help.

Linda and Sally had become friends at the beginning of Grade 8, but their friendship was doomed right from the start, simply because whatever secrets the two friends shared about cute boys or annoying teachers would inevitably be shared with all since Sally had a way of whispering behind Linda's back.

Linda never got her Beatles photos back, and much later, Sally was also the girl who would end up stealing something else from her, something far worse than a few 8 X 10 black and white glossy prints of four sought-after idols. The next theft would eventually break up their friendship forever.

Soon enough, the summer ended, and with that came Linda's seventeenth birthday.

The movie *Sound of Music* had come out a year earlier. Everyone was listening to the Rogers and Hammerstein hit, "Sixteen Going on Seventeen."

According to Linda, even though she had felt like a grown-up most of her life, the magic number seventeen represented adulthood. And the best part was that an older boy named Mike had recently begun to show an interest in her. Not interested in boys in the least, Linda could not help but be flattered by a handsome guy with a cool car, a gregarious personality, and stunning good looks, showing her attention.

Mike Sanderson had the appeal of Elvis Presley but the gift of the gab like Soupy Sales. He was a nonstop talker, mostly about himself. He could do practically anything and matched anyone who begged to differ. He commanded every room he entered because he could be smelled a mile away. Brut by Faberge was an "eau de toilette," and Mike drenched himself in it from head to toe.

In some ways, Mike reminded Linda of her dad, except for his boastful ways, which were tiring and annoying at best—very much unlike her father, who displayed only humble qualities. Still longing to fit in, Linda decided that a boyfriend would seal the deal, and Mike's hard-to-take bragging could be overlooked.

Linda's parents only approved her first date with Mike because it was a group date to the drive-in movie theatre. With other friends present, what could go wrong? They hoped for the best.

The Cascades Drive-In in Burnaby was BC's and Canada's first drive-in theatre. It was started by George and William Steel and Joe and Art Johnson, whose association was named Steel-Johnson Amusements, Ltd.

The concept of showing movies outdoors was first thought of by auto parts salesman Richard Hollingshead. His idea was to give the American car-loving society one more activity they could do in their vehicles. He also had an extremely obese mother who loved the cinema but could not fit comfortably in the movie theatre seats. His idea would also allow his mother to enjoy a movie up on the silver screen. Hollingshead patented his concept in May 1933. The idea was not popular at first until the early 1940s, when in-car speakers were introduced.

Drive-ins started to take off in the '50s. They offered family entertainment because they provided more flexibility than indoor theatres. Families could sit in cars with their babies. They could bring their food and drinks from home, all while enjoying a movie and a night out.

Smoking and drinking alcohol and smuggling non-paying friends in car trunks were untold secrets. Teenagers making out in the back seat was an activity only known to the teens that were participating. Linda and her parents were completely unaware that such things were happening and had become a primary draw to the drive-in for most young people.

Oblivious to the dalliances that could occur, Linda was unprepared. In the past, the drive-in was a special family event—soon, her thoughts and memories of days gone by would be sadly tarnished by a first date that would unexpectedly go wrong.

Linda was excited because she was finally getting to see two movies in one night, a double-feature—first released in 1962, *How the West Was Won* with Gregory Peck and John Wayne, plus *The Man Who Shot Liberty Valance* with James Stewart, John Wayne, and Lee Marvin. Both movies Linda had missed seeing at the box office but was thrilled that top-billed films were always shown a year later at the drive-in.

When getting ready for her date, she was aware of the latest fad, mini skirts, which was every bigger girl's worst nightmare. Some could pull it off, but Linda refused to be uncomfortable, so she opted out of purchasing shorts, bathing suits, or miniskirts. She settled on her favourite knee-length practical grey skirt and navy-blue angora sweater, even though it was itchy.

She was curious who the other couple was who would be accompanying them but was sure they would be fun-loving, Western-loving friends of Mike's since the movies were two of the best Westerns of all time. Certainly in Linda's opinion, anyway.

After pulling up to the house, Mike got out, knocked on the door, and met Linda's parents. The first thing out of his mouth was to tell Frances and Vince how much his car cost, how much money he had in the bank, and about being the first person to own the new Beatles album. They chalked it up to his nerves getting the better of him and wished the couple a lovely evening.

Getting in the car, Linda was initially disappointed that she did not know the other couple in the back seat but quickly forgot about it, as they seemed nice enough, smiling up at her from their embrace in the back seat.

On the drive from North Vancouver to Burnaby, Linda chatted with Mike about her day at Laura Lynn, an upcoming chemistry exam, and how she hated physical education class at school. She then politely asked Mike how his day was, and his response was, "Okay, I guess."

There was a long lineup of cars heading into the Cascades Drive-In, and it was a perfect night weather-wise. The sun was close to setting, and the clear sky would make for a beautiful movie-viewing experience.

After they pulled into their allotted spot, set the window speakers up, purchased popcorn and Cokes from the concession stand, and the Mickey Mouse cartoon was over, Linda anxiously settled into the front seat, close to her side of the door.

Suddenly, she felt the blood drain from her face and instantly run cold. From the kissing sounds coming from the back seat, Linda was brought back to the time when she was twelve, and the babysitter had dressed her up to look like an eighteen-year-old teenager. From the front seat, she did not dare look over her shoulder.

Before thoughts of what exactly was going on behind her could take shape, Mike reached over and put his arm around Linda's shoulder. She, in turn, pushed it off. Mike laughed and leaned in for a kiss. Linda leapt up and out of the car—upsetting her drink and popcorn in the process.

When Linda ran to the washroom, all she could hear were people yelling at her to get out of the way, and with cars honking, she could feel tears stinging her eyes.

When she came out, Mike was waiting for her. In a pleading tone, he stated that everyone makes out at the drive-in and asked why she bothered to go with him if she expected otherwise. He went on to say how much he liked her, and if she liked him back, she would let him snuggle, finishing up with, "If you truly like me, then you need to show me. Otherwise, how'z a guy gonna know?"

Linda could not fathom what "let him snuggle" even meant, and when she stated that she was looking forward to seeing both movies since they came out a year ago, he finally agreed to keep his hands to himself.

Disappointed, gloomy, and pouting for the rest of the night, Mike left her alone. Linda had Mike turn the speakers' volume up as loud as they would go to drown out the couple in the back seat.

Linda chose not to see Mike for quite some time after the movie misadventure. Besides, it was clear that his thin and fashionable mother did not like her. In the meantime, a nice boy named John that Linda was friends with at Laura Lynn had also taken quite a shine to her. He was not as worldly or handsome as Mike, but Linda appreciated John's friendship just the same.

Mike continued to pursue Linda, begging for another date, dropping off flowers at her work and even stopping by her house to chat with her dad.

Deciding between Mike and John, two fellows wanting to be her boyfriend, Linda decided to take her mother up on her offer to join Weight Watchers, merely as a distraction, *but if it worked, then what the heck,* Linda thought.

Weightwatchers was founded in 1963 by a homemaker named Jean Nidetch from Queens, New York. In 1961 she had a plan to teach herself how to eat healthily. She had been overweight most of her life and had tried everything to lose weight—pills, hypnosis, fad diets, and starving herself. All of which only resulted in eventually gaining back all the weight she lost and more.

At the age of thirty-eight, Jean weighed 214 pounds, and a friend mistook her for being pregnant. That comment was the straw that broke the camel's back, and Jean decided to turn to the New York City Board of Health's obesity clinic. Although she lost twenty pounds on the ten-week program, she did not like how the weekly meetings were run.

Jean was following the "Prudent Diet," which taught portion control and prohibited alcohol, sweets, and fatty foods. It included a list and the quantities of food allowed. She took these same principles and started a similar support group. Her meetings included weekly weigh-ins and support. The group as a whole provided empathy, rapport, mutual understanding, support, and sharing of personal stories and ideas. She developed a point system, including prizes for weight-loss milestones. Jean eventually lost seventy-two pounds and kept it off.

Jean's meetings went from six friends in her living room to forty. In May of 1963, she had to rent a public space with over four hundred people in attendance. By 1964 she was selling franchises, and in 1967, the company, Weight Watchers, was international, with one hundred and two franchises in the United States, Canada, Puerto Rico, Great Britain, and Israel. Jean became the company's face and public relations with her slim, well-dressed image, charisma, and flair for motivational speaking.

Frances was considered too thin to attend Weight Watchers but was allowed to go as her daughter's buddy and support person. Thus began a special diet, a compact food weighing scale, and blender drinks, all with Linda's mother's support.

It seemed like a good idea at the time, and in amongst the dieting and weekly weigh-ins, Mike took it upon himself to purchase a diamond ring and propose to Linda.

Linda was ecstatic and young and did not realize at the time that Mike might have ulterior motives. Sure enough, his plan worked, and Linda gave in to his advances and pressure to have sex with him. She was mortified at the whole experience and could not understand why other girls her age were doing it!

What made matters worse was that her first sexual encounter took place in the car that Mike often bragged about. Linda speculated that his automobile was like a bedroom on wheels. All she can remember about her first time was looking down through Mike's 1956 Rambler's floorboards and seeing the gravel road. She wondered how Mike could boast about such a vehicle and not repair the hole in the floor.

When all was said and done, Linda decided that Mike was a sex fiend and concluded that all he wanted from her was sex. The marriage proposal was probably a ploy to get into her pants or skirt or whatever it was she was wearing at the time. She realized this when it was seemingly too late.

People had tried to warn her. In fact, her friend Dennis disliked Mike from the get-go. Dennis was Linda's only guy friend from early on in her childhood, up until Mike arrived on the scene. They were not a couple for two reasons. Dennis drank heavily, and he preferred skinny girls, two things that Linda was not familiar with.

Dennis had confided in her that he used to sip beer from his parents' beer bottles at an early age, not just while they were drinking them but first thing in the morning when he was instructed to clean up all the empties. By the time Dennis started Grade 1, he had thought nothing of being tipsy before the 9:00 a.m. school bell rang. Once he was in high school, he had moved on to harder liquor and carried a mickey around in his back pocket to help him get through the day.

Aside from his apparent dependency on alcohol, Dennis was kind to Linda, and she liked him as a friend only. As only a true-blue friend was inclined to do, Dennis had warned Linda about Mike, saying, "I don't like him, I don't trust him, and you could do way better. There are lots of guys that like chubby girls who are nice, good, upstanding citizens."

Linda appreciated Dennis's concern but was undoubtedly infatuated with her Elvis Presley lookalike boyfriend, even though she despised what went on behind closed car doors. Undoubtedly, Linda would soon see past Mike's phony-baloney persona.

Shortly after the Rambler's back seat incident, Linda was on the Lynn Canyon Trail, riding horses with John, who remained a friend. It was a beautiful spring day, and as they were admiring the new foliage, they got off their horses to give their trusty steeds a drink. Unexpectedly, at that very moment, Tosca lay down and quietly, painlessly died.

Shocked, horrified, and deeply saddened, Linda was dumbfounded as to what to do. There had been no warning signs. Tosca was getting older but managed very well with Linda's loving care and attention.

It was decided that John ride back to Laura Lynn on his horse to get help. Linda called out after him with urgency, "Please call my dad!"

Linda stayed with Tosca and sat down on the ground to rest her head on her beautiful mare's chest. She whispered a few last words and thought back to all their times together. She felt like the human version of Tosca, and both had been mistreated. Linda instinctively always knew what Tosca needed. They were soul mates, decidedly more so than any living person ever could be, Linda surmised.

She remembered the time Tosca warned her about a boy she liked. When Linda introduced a guy by the name of Gary to her best friend and four-legged confidante, Tosca reared up on her hind legs. Linda instinctively knew that Tosca was displaying fright and aggression towards the boy. Linda turned down Gary's movie invitation based on Tosca's behaviour towards him.

A few years later, Gary shot himself and his girlfriend in a seedy motel room. When it happened, as appalling and heinous as it was, Linda could not help but be reminded how Tosca's horse sense made Linda break her date with Gary only a few short years earlier.

Having spent years pushing down her sadness, Linda realized she had forgotten how to cry. The many times she was called a cry baby, a tattletale, or a fat cow came flooding back to her as she nestled into her companion. Mike's advances, Tosca's death, and the murder of her dear friends Diana and Donna—thoughts of the whole lot of them came burning down her face in liquid pain, with guttural sobs expelled directly from her heart. She wept alone in the forest, with what she knew as her closest friend and confidante, a horse whose spirit and listening ears were now gone forever.

Alone on the trail at Lynn Canyon, Linda allowed herself to weep and mourn the loss of her four-legged best friend. She cried about the meanies of the world and the hurt she had endured all these years, sobbing until she had no more tears left. And then she fell silent.

Still, there were other secrets under lock and key. Linda dared not tell anyone or bring herself to think about what she had done with her supposed fiancé, a man she wanted to please but whose expectations she despised. Her first real boyfriend was not a boy or a friend.

It was an all-day event to retrieve Tosca. Vince came with his bulldozer. He had a front-end loader that was perfect for picking up a dead horse. It took him almost all day to get there, and then a horse service came and took Tosca away.

In just a short time, Linda had gone through three of the worst things in her life, and she felt that there could never be anything more traumatic. After all was said and done, Linda's grades began to suffer, and the principal called her mother for a meeting. He suggested Linda quit school and get a job. Even though Linda felt foggy for a time, she realized that she still had Laura Lynn and her dreams of a bright future with animals, particularly horses, in one way or another.

Contemplating a breakup with Mike, Linda's decision was made easy one afternoon when she was out riding with a friend.

After Tosca's death, friends and fellow employees at the stable were always willing to share. So on this day, Linda was borrowing a horse. They just happened to be on an old, abandoned logging road when she spotted Mike's car. When she got closer, it was apparent that he was with another girl, and they were intertwined like only two lovers could be.

Linda silently rode the horse back to the stable. At that exact moment, she took the principal's advice and decided to quit school. It was time. After driving home, she packed up her 1965 Ford Comet, which she had bought and paid for with her own money.

Before saying goodbye to her family, she met up with Dennis for a Coke. Linda told her good friend about spotting Mike in his car with another girl. "They sure were not playing tiddlywinks!" she said. At the news of Mike's unfaithfulness, Dennis was livid.

While they sat there in a booth by the window, who should show his face outside but Mike, staring in at Linda. Mike put his hands in a praying position, and with his best puppy dog impersonation, pleaded and begged for Linda to take him back.

At the silly sight of forlorn-looking Mike, Dennis leapt out of the booth, ran outside, and screamed, "Get the hell out of here! Linda is done with you! And if you don't leave, I will pulverize you!" Mike took off running, and Linda and Dennis laughed until tears filled their eyes.

Before leaving town, she found out that Sally, who stole her Beatles photos, was the girl in Mike's back seat, stealing her boyfriend right under her nose.

Saying goodbye to Dennis and then her parents, Linda was ready for Kelowna, as the life of a cowgirl was calling.

She made one last stop at Laura Lynn for her final farewell. John was there and asked if he could go with her. At the last minute, Linda replied, "Yes, I guess so," thinking that it would be pleasant to have company for the drive.

Linda riding from Laura Lynn to the family home

Ken and Doug more snowman fun with Dad

SEP • 62 •

Dougie, Karen, Daddy and Kenny on a camping trip

Linda during highschool

Watch Lake, Dimps, Doreen and Linda

*Beautiful Tosca, Karen behind a friend sitting in the front
and Linda holding the lead in front of the house*

Linda's first car

Watch Lake, Karen's horse, for the trail ride

Watch Lake, Linda

Linda all dressed up for a date

CHAPTER NINE

Hitting the Trail

"One's destination is never a place, but a new way of seeing things."

-Henry Miller

It was 8:00 in the evening, so halfway to their destination, they decided to grab a bite to eat and get a motel for the night. Over dinner, Linda confided to John about how horrible Mike had been, how she was not ready for a boyfriend and was glad to be rid of him. Saying goodbye to Mike and Sally was the best thing she ever did, and good riddance to both.

The motel room was eight dollars a night, which John and Linda split, and it consisted of a vibrating bed for an additional twenty-five cents, along with a tiny couch. The floral print bedspread, matching blackout curtains, and paintings of circus clowns bolted to the wall gave Linda the giggles.

John insisted that she take the only bed, and he slept on the couch.

When Linda woke up in the morning, John was gone, with a note that read...

Dear Linda,

You are such a nice girl. I realized that you do not want or need a boyfriend, so I decided to hitchhike back to North Vancouver. I hope you have a happy life, and if you are ever back on the North Shore, come by and say hi sometime.

Love, John :)

John signed his name with a smiley face, which had become the trend.

In 1963 a simple yellow smiley face led to tens of thousands of variations and appeared on everything from pillows and posters to perfume and pop art. However, a team of archaeologists led by Nicolo Marchetti found the oldest known smiling face from approximately 1700 BC. After a broken pot had been pieced together, the team noticed that the item had a sizeable smiling face engraved on it.

According to the Smithsonian Institution, the smiley face as we know it in our current society was created by Harvey Ross Ball, an American graphic artist. In 1963, Ball was employed by State Mutual Life Assurance Company in Massachusetts to create a happy face to raise the morale of the employees. Ball created the design in ten minutes and was paid $45.00 for his efforts. His rendition, with a bright yellow background, dark oval eyes, full smile, and creases at the mouth's sides, has become familiar worldwide, with many other graphic artists also taking claim to its invention.

Linda was surprised that John thought he had a chance of being her boyfriend and equally surprised that he left.

That morning, she drove to Mountain Shadows and was hired on the spot. She was given the same position she had when she was fourteen, being responsible for trail rides, grooming the horses, and keeping the stalls clean. This time, however, the sun porch was not available, so Linda would need to find her accommodations elsewhere.

Vince made arrangements for Linda to stay with his father. Grandpa Earl and his wife Esther, along with Grandpa's brother George, had moved from Saskatchewan many years before. Shortly after Vince fled at the age of thirteen, his father lost the farm, and they too packed up lock, stock, and barrel, moving to Kelowna and a three-bedroom home with no plumbing. Since Vince had rekindled a relationship with his dad and visited every summer for the last few years, it was decided that Linda could stay there.

Vince was pleased that his dad, who had struggled with alcohol for his entire childhood, no longer drank, and neither did his Uncle George—a definite selling feature for his eldest daughter, who also did not partake, to be housed there. The only downside was they had no room in the house, so Grandpa Earl and Uncle George set Linda up quite nicely in the space above the barn. She would only need to go into the house to eat her meals.

Linda settled into a happy routine of getting up in the morning, slipping into her work clothes, hopping in her car, and hitting the outhouse, situated at the end of the long driveway, on her way to Mountain Shadows for a long day at the ranch.

Getting to know her grandfather, his wife, and her great uncle George was, for lack of a better word, an interesting adventure.

Grandpa Earl stood no taller than five feet, with curved shoulders. Weighing no more than 110 pounds, he was a spitfire of a man with wild hair that resembled an SOS scouring pad and eyebrows that extended and overtook his deep-set brown eyes. His face always had a look of amusement, but his eyes showed pain and sorrow, a combination that kept strangers at bay and family members afraid to ask.

The Depression-era of the 1920s and '30s was never discussed in Grandpa Earl's house. Still, the traces of trauma in his eyes and hunched shoulders made Linda curious, as she could easily recall her father's many stories of a difficult childhood, which was unlike her own upbringing. She never asked, and Grandpa Earl never told.

Esther was comparatively as tall as Earl but was rounder, with a constant look of perplexity, like she was continually trying to figure things out. Linda had heard that Esther had difficulties communicating, but since she was quick to laugh, Linda thought she wasn't half bad. Esther would giggle at the smallest of things and sometimes when no one said anything at all.

Uncle George, on the other hand, was full of jokes and stories of days gone by. Strangely, his memory of the past and the Depression-era was very different from the stories Linda's father told. Vince's words were of the dry, desolate prairie, lack of money, and abundance of moonshine—painful memories— whereas George's were not, but rather light and jolly, recalling his garden, school dances, and taking the horse and buggy into town on warm, moonlit nights.

Uncle George stood tall and lean in a uniform of worn overalls and a tattered, hand-knitted sweater. He had been a bachelor all his life, and rumour had it that the sweater he never took off was knitted for him by his only true love, who had long since died during their courtship. Linda had heard that childbirth killed her, and the baby she was trying to deliver, George's baby, died too. George never spoke of her again and never dated another woman.

All three of Linda's family members were intrigued and bewildered by her cheerful personality and larger body stature. They often commented on how successful she must be because she certainly was not starving.

This comment made Linda wonder where all her groceries were going. Her parents made her promise to pitch in and help out with dinners. After work at Mountain Shadows, Linda would pick up food to bring back to her grandpa's, such as chicken, pork chops, potatoes, and salad ingredients. But every night, Esther would serve up hotdogs for dinner, night after night.

Linda found out later that Esther was a hoarder, and one could barely get into her bedroom. She had taken to keeping all the food Linda was buying and putting it under her bed, in the closet, and the dresser drawers. Linda dared not say a word, as she did not want to rock the boat, but eventually, she noticed a foul smell starting to emanate from the back bedroom.

Despite Vince's jovial persona, he was also a hidden worrier. When he recalled his unhappy childhood, the bullies, his mother's abandonment, and a father and uncles who got soused every night, he decided that a visit to his father was in order, mainly to check in on Linda and see how she was keeping. Frances enjoyed road trips and was in complete agreement. Besides, it was the middle of summer and time for their usual Okanagan camping and fruit-picking vacation.

Meanwhile, in addition to Vince's worries, she had a few secrets and concerns of her own. Every so often, she did not feel quite right. As far back as she could remember, she would occasionally have a foggy brain and gloomy days. She could not put her finger on what was wrong and kept this side of herself from her loving husband and four children, keeping busy with the daily goings-on that motherhood and being a wife brought.

Notwithstanding, Frances would be gripped with fear on occasion, concerned that she was becoming like her sister and mother, two women that she was not close to or fond of. She desperately did not want to become like either one of them, with temper tantrums, angry outbursts, and days of locking themselves in their rooms. By pushing aside her thoughts and concerns, she carried on.

Leaving first thing in the morning to get an early start to their drive, Vince, Frances, Dougie, Kenny, and little Karen headed up to Kelowna. All was well for now. Seeing Linda in her element brought joy to the whole family. Knowing that she was okay staying at his father's house even if she was out in the barn gave Vince and Frances peace of mind.

Linda had only been back working at Mountain Shadows and sleeping in her grandfather's barn for a little over a month when she got another job proposition. A couple from Scotch Creek had stopped by the ranch one afternoon and could not help but see Linda in action. She was a natural with the horses and had an outstanding, outgoing personality with the guests and other employees. After watching her for a few hours, they approached Linda and asked her if she would be interested in working for them.

They owned a riding stable called The Wagon Wheel in Scotch Creek and offered to pay Linda three hundred dollars a month, and a cute two-bedroom bungalow came with the job. This was an offer she could not refuse, and she said yes, wholeheartedly. Her nights in the barn were getting colder, and the continuous suppers of boiled hotdogs were getting redundantly nauseating, so this would be a wonderful change of circumstances for her.

Scotch Creek is a small community reliant on summer tourism, located on the shores of Shuswap Lake. In 1895, the first white settlers arrived from Minnesota by way of the Canadian Pacific Railway. A flood of migrants followed and picked the land of their choice, thereby becoming early settlers. By 1913, the homesteaders had a legal right to the property that had appealed to them years before. Ferry service began in 1914 between Scotch Creek and Sorento and continued until 1956. As the population increased, the trails were widened, and eventually, a gravel road was built and finally paved in 1960.

In the world of 1966, the average cost of a new house was $14,200.00, the average yearly income per year was $7,000.00, gasoline cost thirty-two cents a gallon, and a new car, approximately $3,000.00. The Vietnam War continued, and on March 26, 1966, up to 200,000 protesters gathered and picketed around the world, demanding that the senseless war come to an end. Heavyweight boxing champion Muhammed Ali, formerly known as Cassius Clay, declared himself a conscientious objector and refused to go to war.

Both the US and USSR fought to see who could get to the moon first. Lester B. Pearson was the fourteenth Prime Minister of Canada, and Lyndon B. Johnson was the United States' thirty-sixth president. Fashion was all about flower power, floral print shirts, and striped bell-bottoms. Shoes, boots, and caps were made from shiny, texturized plastic and vinyl fabric, referred to as "the wet look."

The most popular singing groups included the Beach Boys with "Pet Sounds," The Rolling Stones with "Under My Thumb," and The Beatles with "Revolver," "Yesterday," and "Things We Said Today."

For the time being, Linda was happy working at The Wagon Wheel and settling into her cute cottage, until unexpectedly, one night after work, she heard a knock.

She loved her two-bedroom house, with all the comforts anyone could ever want—running water, indoor plumbing, and a proper queen-size bed. No longer would she be sleeping in a hayloft with the sound of barn mice scurrying throughout the night or existing on a diet of over-boiled hotdogs and stale buns. She had appreciated her grandfather's kindness but considered herself to be a woman of the world, independent, and able to make it on her own, complete with a full-time job and a little western home.

On this warm August night, Linda was relaxing before bed. She happened to have her front door wide open when she heard a loud knock on the door frame. Before she looked up to see who it was, she guessed from the smell of him.

Dressed in blue jeans and a leather jacket, with slicked-back hair drenched in Brute cologne, it was none other than Mike. She stared with mouth agape, and before she could utter a word, Mike said, "Here I am, baby, ready to take you back!"

Linda, in no uncertain terms, kicked him out by pointing at the door and yelling, "Get out now! I never want to see you again!"

The next night after a day at the Wagon Wheel Riding Stable, Linda was just sitting down to dinner at her small kitchen table when another knock came at the door. When she opened it, a little red-headed woman was standing there and did not look happy. Her low-cut, red dress matched her flaming auburn hair and apparent hot temper.

Before introductions were made, the woman burst through the door and said, "Okay, where is he?"

"Where is who?" Linda responded.

Frantic and out of control, the redhead spat out, "Where is Mike, *my* boyfriend! I know he is in here somewhere!"

Linda asked her to calm down and then asked her name. At that point, the aggressive stranger said, "My name is Penny. I am sorry to be barging in like this. Mike told me he was coming up here to get his old girlfriend back, but I still love him."

To which Linda responded, "Yah, you and a million other girls."

She then went on to tell Penny that Mike was a louse, an honest-to-goodness loser and that she would be better off without him. Linda related how she had found him with her best friend in his car's back seat and then told an outraged Penny that Mike was here the day before, but she had refused to take him back.

Linda finished with, "I have never been happier getting rid of that two-timing creep!"

Linda invited Penny to stay for dinner, which she graciously accepted, and never left—well, at least not right away.

The two women, exes of the same cheating boyfriend, became friends, and Penny instantly fell in love with everything Western, especially the cowboys. She got a job as a waitress at a truck stop, and Linda continued with the horses and trail rides at the Wagon Wheel.

Between Mountain Shadows and the Wagon Wheel, Linda had gotten to know many people, specifically cowboys. There were wranglers and ranch hands, herdsmen and drovers, cattlemen and cowpokes (cowboys who rode the range), and cowboys who organized the rodeos and roundups. They all admired Linda.

Soon, however, it was apparent that both girls were being branded as "the wild city girls from Vancouver," primarily because of Penny's wild ways. And the gossip mill began. Unbeknownst to Linda, Penny was sleeping around with every Tom, Dick, and Harry, married or unmarried, cowboy, ranch hand, or long-haul truck driver just passing through. On the other hand, all Linda cared about were the horses, the guests, and the many friends she was making.

Even though the girls were opposites, they both had lots of fun and lots of laughs. There was always whiskey and plenty of beer at the events, rodeos, dances, parades, and parties. Linda found that she loved to dance and was very good at it. She had rhythm, despite failing at ballet and tap dancing lessons as a child, which got her thinking that most people from her past were all wrong about her—the teachers, the bullies, and even the salesgirls at The Bay.

Linda's self-confidence and self-esteem were on the rise. In the Cariboo and the Okanagan, people loved Linda wherever she went. They saw the real her no matter what her size. By default, she also became the designated driver. It was well-known that she did not drink alcohol, and virtually all the men in Linda's circle overly consumed it, so they willingly (sometimes pleadingly) asked Linda to drive them and their pickup trucks home, notably after a night of heavy partying.

Unlike Linda, Penny did drink and would drink any man under the table. Unfortunately, when she did overindulge, her personality changed with every emptied glass, and she became fussy, bossy, and mean-spirited. Not only did Penny begin to show her true colours to Linda, but she also became jealous of Linda's many friendships with the guys—all platonic, but Penny could not stand it.

At the end of the summer, the Wagon Wheel closed down for the season, which meant Linda and Penny had to move out of the house, and both women had to find jobs elsewhere. Linda thought a change would be suitable for Penny, and perhaps she would settle down in a new location.

Linda and Penny got wind of two bank teller jobs at the Bank of Montreal in Clinton, about a two-and-a-half-hour drive away from Scotch Creek.

Linda was familiar with Clinton because of her father's many stories about the Cariboo Gold Rush. First inhabited by the Shuswap First Nations people, by the mid-1800s, the discovery of gold brought the settlers, and Clinton became a busy intersection of trails and wagon roads to Barkerville's goldfields. The location of the settlement made it an ideal resting place for weary travellers and miners en route to the gold. Originally referred to as 47 Mile, the town was renamed Clinton by Queen Victoria in 1863, in honour of Lord Henry Pelham Clinton.

Once "gold fever" subsided, the ranching industry developed, and some of the original ranches such as Maiden creek, Mound Ranch, and Pollard Ranch stood the test of time and remained. By the 1950s, the forestry industry became the mainstay of the economy, and at one time, there were over twenty bush mills and sawmills operating in the area.

When Linda and Penny arrived, they applied and were immediately hired at the bank. In addition to working nine to five, Monday to Friday, Linda started volunteering at neighbouring ranches, while Penny sat idly by, becoming bored. She had grown tired of the dirt and dust and discovered she was not fond of horses, as their odour was unpleasant, and they frightened her.

Linda decided to go home for Christmas to be with her family and also to get more supplies. In the meantime, Penny stayed in Clinton and proceeded to get into trouble.

Arriving home in North Vancouver, Linda was happy to spend time with her little sister and two younger brothers. They watched their favourite shows while Frances prepared all of Linda's favourite meals. In return, Linda helped her mother wrap Christmas presents with her little sister Karen as her aide. Vince did the usual dad stuff of building snowmen, shovelling the sidewalk, and carving the turkey.

On Christmas morning, all the kids were awakened by an excited little Karen, and she was promptly sent back to bed with her Christmas stocking. When the family all woke up, they took turns around the room, each opening one present at a time.

Linda was thrilled with a velvet painting of a horse and a few new blouses for her bank job. The boys received model car kits, Matchbox cars, and Lego. Karen enthusiastically jumped up and down with her latest Mattel Barbie Doll and a Mary Poppins jigsaw puzzle.

Vince had often joked about wanting a five-pound box of money, so Linda took it upon herself to fill a shoebox to the brim with pennies and gift-wrapped it for her dad. The whole family had a great laugh when he opened it.

Linda's dad was comical and kind, but he was a man of few words when sharing his emotions and real feelings. He wanted everything to run smoothly and kept his vow to never show anger or raise his voice. Vince had not been parented due to an absent mother and a drunken father, but somehow, he managed to be a loving father and husband, striving to say all the right things. He sometimes went overboard praising his children. In his eyes, they could do no wrong. He always had a warm-hearted, thoughtful comment to make to his wife and four children. The downsides were his bleeding heart, inward worrying, and often feeling bad for everyone.

On the other hand, Frances had given up on her childhood, as her mother had been strict, moody, and self-centred. Sometimes she was absent, in the sense of not coming out of her room for days on end. The words "I love you" were never uttered. Therefore, Frances struggled with her feelings and emotions, as did Vince, but in a different way.

Linda's parents were from opposite upbringings but similarly had been abandoned and neglected. Together as husband and wife, they parented to the best of their ability, without an instruction manual or guide.

Frances, being an avid reader, took out a book on parenting from the library, written by Doctor Benjamin Spock, his 1946 best seller *Baby and Child Care*. She admired his views and his social and political activism. One of his theories, which was widely criticized, was to treat all children as individuals. He also suggested parents should be more flexible and affectionate. At no time was Frances hugged as a child or shown physical affection. So naturally, she struggled with displaying it to her children and husband. On the other hand, Vince made up for it, showering the kids and Frances in warm embraces whenever he could.

Despite not showing physical affection, Frances found the individuality of Dr. Spock's teaching easy to follow, insisting that Linda have her horses, while Doug and Ken had sports, bicycles, and camping trips.

Frances was thirty-nine, soon to be forty years old, when her last child, Karen, was born. She found herself to have gotten exceedingly tired, so without being asked or told, Vince jumped into the habit of taking Karen to work with him, propping her alongside him on his bulldozer. She was becoming Daddy's little girl, taking over her big sister's spot.

After Christmas and before New Year's Eve, Linda left to go back to Clinton. Her dad pulled her aside and said, "When the right man comes along, never be afraid to say, 'I love you.'"

Linda was unsure how to respond, so she said, "Okay, Dad, I will."

She felt a little sorry for her dad, as many years earlier, when he started his own bulldozing company, he had hoped that Linda would eventually go into business with him. He visualized calling their business "Vince Bonner's Father and Daughter Bulldozing." Eventually, he gave up his dream when Linda's only obsession took over—anything and everything to do with horses.

When Linda returned to Clinton, her car was full of necessities. Work clothes for the bank, extra pots and pans, groceries that her parents stocked her with, and a few of Karen's crayon drawings. With snow on the road, Linda's car crunched into her shared apartment's driveway. Expecting Penny to be nestled on the couch with a book or watching television on their small black and white TV, Linda was instead greeted with a sight straight out of a horror movie.

Dishes were piled high in the sink, all the windows were wide open with the curtains billowing in and out, and much to Linda's dismay, there was a man passed out in her bed. Moving into her darkened bedroom a little closer, Linda gasped at the sight of her closet, which stood utterly empty.

As she stood there trying to wrap her brain around what was happening, the man in the bed, which turned out to be Penny's latest boyfriend, woke up out of a drunken slumber and tried to pull Linda back to bed with him. Filled with shock and annoyance, Linda kicked him out of the apartment. On his way out the door, he exclaimed, "You sure aren't as fun as Penny!"

Turning back around, whispering under her breath *Good riddance* to the now empty room, Linda's eyes adjusted to see every article of her clothing shredded in pieces on her bedroom floor. Looking closer, she could see that someone had cut up all her clothes with a pair of scissors.

Feeling confused by the whole scene she had happened upon, she wondered what on earth had happened. All she wanted to do was settle in after her four-hour drive and reminisce about the wonderful time she had with her family. Instead, Linda straightened up the apartment as best she could, washing her bedding and hanging up her new work clothes. She dumped all her ruined clothing in the trash bin outside, putting away the groceries and her new set of pots and pans.

She checked three or four times that the front door was locked before sinking into a hot soapy bath, not from fear, but rather from annoyance, and anticipating that one of Penny's interlopers could reappear.

Going to bed, she wondered what had happened to Penny. First thing Monday morning, Penny had still not arrived home. Linda went to work, speculating that her roommate would be there and hoping for some explanation.

She got one all right.

The whole week that Linda was back in North Vancouver, Penny had gone off the deep end. She had been dating a married teller from the bank, the local gas station attendant, and the cowboy that Linda had found in her bed. In addition to making errors at the bank, Penny's reputation and character were not stacking up.

Apparently, the married man's wife had confronted Penny, saying that Linda had divulged Penny's secret affair, to which there was no truth whatsoever. Eventually, Penny was run out of town. She just woke up one morning and left, no goodbyes, apologies, or two-week notice. Linda never saw or heard from her again. Thinking back, she realized she should have been more cautious when Penny showed up on her doorstep to clobber Linda for supposedly stealing Mike.

As for the cowboy Linda tossed out of her apartment, Linda ran into him the following week as she watched him slip and slide in his worn cowboy boots down the snow-swept sidewalk. After he fell face first, Linda tried to help him up. Subsequently, they both ended up in a snowbank. They laughed until water sprang from their eyes, and the cowboy apologized for everything. He had started attending AA meetings and turned out to be a pretty good guy once he became sober. He and Linda became friends.

Family Christmas

CHAPTER TEN

Rodeos, Bank Robbers, and Settling Down

"No hour of life is wasted that is spent in a saddle."

-Winston Churchill

In 1968 the top song in North America was "Hey Jude" by the Beatles, and the big movies were *Funny Girl*, *2001: A Space Odyssey*, *The Love Bug*, and *Hang Em High* with Clint Eastwood, Inger Stevens, Ed Begley, and Bruce Dern.

Favourite television shows were *Mayberry R.F.D.*, *Here's Lucy*, *The Doris Day Show*, *Bonanza*, *Gomer Pyle*, and *Rowan & Martin's Laugh-In*. *Time Magazine*'s Men of the Year were Apollo 8 Astronauts William Anders, Frank Borman, and Jim Lovell.

1968 was also the year that Robert F. Kennedy was assassinated. He was a prominent politician and brother to John F. Kennedy, the thirty-fifth president of the United States, who was himself assassinated in 1963. Another significant event was the introduction of the African American character Franklin in the comic strip *Peanuts* by creator Charles Schultz.

1968 was also the same year that Linda fell in love with the Canadian Cariboo rodeo lifestyle. She always speculated this would happen but never imagined how intense and powerful her feelings would be. Once the thunderbolt hit, Linda's life was irrevocably changed.

After Penny's sudden departure from the mess she had made, it did not take long for Linda to find another roommate. Vera was a gorgeous, petite, blonde bombshell who worked at the local hotel. She was ready to move out of her parent's home, which was perfect timing for Linda. Vera was talkative, friendly, likable, and was the same age as Linda. They already had a lot in common.

Linda realized that the new Vera in her life was a lot like her childhood neighbour back in North Vancouver with the same name, pondering the fact that she seemed to be drawn to fun-loving, charismatic people.

Vera never once thought Linda was overweight and treated Linda with respect like any true-blue friend should. Both Linda and Vera loved everything Western, so every night after work, they tuned in to a show or two on Linda's tiny black-and-white television, and every weekend they rode horses, went to dances, and began the rodeo circuit.

Williams Lake, affectionately referred to as Willy's Puddle, is a city in the Central Interior of British Columbia, approximately eighty miles from Clinton. The history of Williams Lake began in 1860 during the Cariboo Gold Rush. It was not until 1929 that Williams Lake became incorporated. Named after Secwepemc Chief William, the city is famous for its Williams Lake Stampede, the second largest professional rodeo in Canada, only after the Calgary Stampede. The rodeo is a truly authentic Wild West experience. Linda felt that every Western movie or television show she had ever seen could not hold a candle to the cowboys, cowgirls, and bucking broncos at Williams Lake.

A rodeo competition consists of two categories, "rough stock" events and "timed" events. Each contest has its own set of rodeo rules and order of events.

The timed events are challenging and have the contestants and audience in a constant state of excitement. Steer wrestling, team roping, tie-down roping, barrel racing, and steer roping, are all categories in which contestants compete against the clock and each other. Linda's favourite event and arguably the most challenging event for any contestant was bareback riding, a real test of balance and strength between human and horse.

Prize money for rodeos was made up of entry fees paid by the contestants. But nothing was more prized than winning a rodeo belt buckle, the rodeo world's most recognized trophy. Larger rodeos give out a slew of awards and prizes, including hand-tooled saddles, horse trailers, and even vehicles.

It was planned weeks before that Linda and Vera would take a carload of friends to an upcoming rodeo in Williams Lake. They did not book any hotel rooms because money was tight, and directly after work on Friday, they were off. They packed white collared shirts, red bandanas, blue jeans, big belts, and silver belt buckles. Freshly polished cowboy boots pulled their ensembles together. Linda was the designated driver because she did not drink, and everyone could party to their heart's content. Naturally, they took Linda's car.

The weekend started with a few preliminary rodeo events, and then it was off to Squaw Hall for a night of dancing. Linda and Vera were excellent dancers and rarely sat down for the entire evening.

Gone were the days of being the biggest girl in ballet class or tripping over her tap shoes. Linda could move rhythmically on the dance floor unabashed and never tiring. From the polka, the two-step, and the triple step, to the silly Chicken Dance, it was all about good clean, fun.

Linda never tried her usual dance numbers from back home on the coast, such as the swim, the mashed potato, the twist, the shake, the hitch hike, and the pony, because as she was told many times over, those were sissy dances that only city slickers partook in.

The women came in all shapes and sizes. There was no competition or concern with body weight. Everyone danced, and everyone gave it their all! They dressed to the nines, looking and feeling attractive.

The only noticeable difference was the glamorous groupies, given the nickname "Buckle Bunnies." Linda and her friends did not profess or even want to be in the same category as these magazine-pretty women.

Buckle Bunnies typically wore short-shorts, mini-skirts, low-cut tops (always flannel and plaid), painted-on jeans, and cowboy boots that resembled high heel shoes. These cowgirl wannabes often told elaborate stories to get countrymen interested in them. Their most common lie was that they were true country girls with horses and ranches. As the rumour mill indicated, they were looking for buckle-winning cowboys to sleep with, skilled men who always won big at the rodeos.

Even though these women carried sordid reputations, Linda and Vera liked to think that perhaps some of the Buckle Bunnies had good intentions.

When the last call was announced, Linda and her gang decided to head over to the main street's after-hours café. Driving from the hall to the restaurant, they noticed the streets were filled with partiers and hooting and hollering cowboys, all boisterous and seemingly drunk. The hoopla gave off the same feel as a New Year's Eve party, minus the kissing under the mistletoe at midnight.

Once at the café, Jack, a good friend of Linda and Vera, was so drunk that he passed out on the table with his face firmly planted in his french fries, ketchup and all. The girls knew they had to get him out of there, but even with Linda under one arm and Vera under the other, they could not budge him. Jack was skinny, at least six feet tall, but was solid muscle, so it was no easy feat. Since he was in a drunken stupor, his body felt like dead weight.

Linda and Vera looked out onto the street and spotted some cowboys idly smoking nearby, so Linda approached the men. She asked them if they wouldn't mind lending a hand to help her hoist Jack up out of the booth and drag him to the car. They both enthusiastically said "yes!"

Linda noticed one of the men was of somewhat smaller stature, but thankfully, with the help of these two strangers from the street, they all managed to load Jack into Linda's car.

Once Jack was safely tucked into the back seat, surprisingly, the smaller man jumped into the car with Linda and her friends and asked for a ride. As if seeing him for the first time, Linda noticed he was dressed to the nines. With silver spurs on his childlike cowboy boots and sequins on his turquoise shirt, he proudly wore a matching turquoise cowboy hat that glimmered in the moonlight, like a star-studded buckaroo from an animated children's book. He certainly was a dapper dan, Linda thought.

She drove the loaded-down car to the outskirts of town only to pull over for the night. The smaller man, whose name was Hank—an authentic Western name, to say the least—chose to stay with his new gang of friends, refusing to leave. Readily accepted into the mix, they all curled up wherever they could find an inch of space and slept in the car, as all the hotels were booked, and there was no other alternative.

In the morning, the cramped partiers awoke to find Jack draped over the top of the front seat. Both his wallet and their "new friend" were gone.

They collectively decided that both of the guys had stolen Jack's wallet when they helped him into the car. When Jack left Clinton, he had over one thousand dollars in his wallet. Now he was broke, much to his dismay. Linda kindly lent him a couple of bucks to get him through.

They spent the rest of the weekend at the rodeo, cheering on the cowboys, enjoying the halftime show, watching the little kids ride the baby calves, and chowing down on butter-drenched corn on the cob, barbequed burgers, snow cones, and hot-off-the-griddle bannock, served up by the local First Nations.

Bannock is a quick flatbread, similar to cornbread or a scone. It can be made with various available resources. The original recipe consisted of flour made from maize, roots, tree sap, and leavening agents. Combined with water or milk and other possible flavouring agents, it is fried in rendered fat, vegetable oil, or shortening, baked in an oven or cooked on a stick. It is a common treat in many North American groups of Indigenous people.

Arriving back to Clinton late Sunday night with a carload of bedraggled and hungover friends, Linda reproduced the fresh memory of what a great time she had.

First and foremost, she was proud that she did not need to sleep around as some other men and women did. She was pleased that her male friends thought of her as a friend, and she did not mind in the least being the designated driver. Linda marvelled to herself how kind everyone was. She decided that bullying and name-calling, especially about her weight, was a non-issue here, at least for the time being, ultimately deciding right then and there, that the Cariboo was truly where she belonged and where she wanted to be from here on in.

Linda reflected that as far back as she could remember, since she was old enough to know about couples, marriage, and wedded bliss, the last thing she wanted was a husband, children, and a white picket fence. Moving forward, she would focus on friends and having fun.

First thing Monday morning, a couple came into the bank directly up to Linda's counter. They explained how they were having a picnic the day before, on Sunday afternoon in Williams Lake. While sitting under a weeping willow tree, a slight breeze came along, and a wallet dropped out of the tree they were sitting beneath, hitting the husband on the head and bouncing off onto their picnic blanket. They could not figure out how the wallet got in the tree but assumed that someone might be missing it. Handing the wallet over to Linda, she was astounded to see that it was Jack's wallet, minus the money, but with all of his identification intact.

After the Williams Lake Rodeo, Linda and her friends were able to find a different rodeo every weekend. No matter how big or small, they made a point of travelling around the rodeo circuit. From Ashcroft in southern BC, to up north of Quesnel and west into the Chilcotin wilderness, Linda and Vera never missed a rodeo. They drove to 100 Mile House, Ashcroft, Bella Coola, Williams Lake, Redstone, and Quesnel—with each rodeo reflecting the spirit of that community and offering its unique twist on the traditional rodeo format.

After a weekend of dancing, the exhibition, and roundup festivities, it was then back to Clinton, working at the bank, and spending all of their spare time horseback riding. During Clinton's own celebration of Western Heritage week, including an old-time ball on the last night, even the bank was decked out entirely in a Western theme.

They could rest assured that the fun did not end when the sun went down, from the kick-off in April to the wrap-up in September, with the year-end BC Rodeo Association finals in Williams Lake.

All good things must come to an end, and Linda's dad missed her terribly. On a Sunday afternoon in late fall, Linda's telephone rang. It was her parents. When she heard her dad's voice, she was gripped with fear that something had happened. A year earlier, her dad had suffered a heart attack, which he survived, staying in the hospital afterwards to recuperate. As it turned out, he had been working much too hard and worrying even more about everyone and everything. Part of his recovery was to slow down, so he had scaled things back at work, started eating healthier, walking daily, and working less.

Frances and Vince explained to Linda that they had decided to invest in some property. For $16,000, they purchased fifty acres of land in Mission, British Columbia, and they wanted Linda to come home. It had been Vince's dream to own property, to build a log home, a barn, have a massive garden, a few trout ponds that would double as a swimming hole, and horses for his eldest daughter.

The land was completely covered with trees, beautiful cedar trees, and Vince could hardly wait to start bulldozing, clearing, and building. Using his logging skills, he would selectively cut down trees from the property for a log house and barn.

Vince hoped that Doug and Ken would help develop the land, build the house, and create Western theme riding trails—a perfect scenario for his horse-driven daughter to manage a stable, in addition to providing a weekend getaway for his whole family.

Frances was not particularly thrilled with the idea, but she loved Vince and wanted his dream to come to fruition. She felt that they had acquired a comfortable, predictable life in North Vancouver, with a five-bedroom home, lots of friends, a bridge club, curling, and a few trips abroad under their belt. However, Vince was not a world traveller type and was a country boy at heart. Even though a property out in the boondocks felt like they would be digressing, Frances thought the acreage would be an excellent hobby for Vince and provide a father-son activity, developing building skills for the men and togetherness for their children.

Linda's answer was clear and obvious. She would quit the bank in Clinton and move home to help her father.

Somewhat reluctant to leave but faced with an offer she felt she could not refuse, she gave her parents a whole-hearted yes, and within two weeks, she was back in her childhood home in a neighbourhood that had not changed.

Between her heart, gut, and brain, Linda was conflicted, but family came first, above and beyond her mind churning with anxiety.

Mr. Gurney was the bank manager at the Canadian Imperial Bank of Commerce at the corner of First and Lonsdale in North Vancouver. He had the pallor and pot belly of a businessman—a stout, balding man with a mustache and a neck that spilled out over his collar—with an outdated, brown three-piece suit and wing-tipped shoes. Mr. Gurney reminded most people who knew him of the characters, Mr. Drysdale, from the hit show *The Beverly Hillbillies* or Mr. Mooney from *Here's Lucy*. Seemingly the only difference was that Mr. Gurney was not a bank manager in a television show, but one in real life, and he had a loaded gun in his desk drawer.

After arriving home just before Christmas, Linda got a job at the Sears mail-order store, but she was laid off when the holidays wrapped up. Getting a job was never a problem for Linda, and within two days, she was working again.

With her previous bank experience in Clinton and her habit of never sitting around for long, Linda was immediately hired at the Bank of Commerce at First and Lonsdale in North Vancouver. My Gurney took quite a shine to Linda, but with him being at least forty years her senior, she was not interested in his advances. Regardless of giving her boss the cold shoulder, it was plain to see that her charismatic personality and banking knowledge impressed everyone around her, which made her a shoo-in for the job. She instantly became Mr. Gurney's right-hand woman.

Even though four years earlier in Grade 12, the principal of Sutherland High School told Linda's mother that she would be better off quitting school, unbeknownst to anyone, Linda excelled with numbers. Her memory was marvellous and considerably unbelievable.

Every second Friday, payday to most, Linda's line at the bank was longer than any other teller's. The main reason for this was that she never forgot a face, and she had memorized all the customer's bank account numbers. Therefore, people rarely needed to bring in their identification and did not bother to remember their account numbers. Linda did it for them.

On one Friday, Mr. Gurney had Linda accompany him to the bank's head office branch across town on Hastings Street— not a usual practice, but the bank was low on accessible funds. Therefore, more money was needed, as it was payday.

With no armoured vehicle or bulletproof-vested guards escorting them, off they went, just an ageing bank manager with his favourite right-hand gal at his side. When Linda expressed her concern with transporting so much money back to the branch, with a smile and a wink, Mr. Gurney reassured Linda not to worry because he had brought his gun.

Growing up, Linda was told that her mother almost delivered her in a bank as it was being robbed. It was a fun family story, and Vince often shared it to bring a smile to Frances's face, in addition to recalling days of old. At the time, it was a close call and possible tragedy, but now they only saw it as a humorous story.

Shortly after being hired, Linda was promoted to head teller and had become a casual acquaintance with a fellow employee, a woman by the name of Myrna, whose husband was an RCMP officer.

Myrna was older than Linda, and they did not have much in common at all. Nevertheless, Linda liked everyone, and Myrna was no exception. She wore her hair backcombed and dressed somewhat old-fashioned, unlike the other tellers. Everyone else wore modern pantsuits—bell-bottom pants in stretch polyester or seersucker. Myrna opted out of trends, went the practical route, and was always kind and easy to chat with.

Linda, on the other hand, opted out of trendy fitted pantsuits but had a nice selection of stretch polyester pants, vests, and blouses purchased at the local K-Mart in the plus-size department. She often wore black and chocolate brown shades, as darker colours were said to make one look thinner.

On Wednesday evenings, Linda went home, had an early dinner, and then it was a fun-filled evening playing bingo, which had become a popular pastime for Linda. As legend has it, the game of bingo first originated in Italy in the 1500s. From there, it moved to France in the 1700s. In nineteenth century Germany, it was used as a teaching tool for children to learn their timetables. The game travelled to North America in the 1920s, where its name evolved to beano. Players used to shout the word when they found all numbers in a row. The end of the game came when a player filled an entire line.

Hugh J. Ward popularized the European game at carnivals and copyrighted and published a rule book in 1933.

An American toymaker named Edwin Lowe adapted the game using a rubber numbering stamp, cardboard, and dried beans. He gathered his friends, and they all began playing. It is said that one player got so excited and enthusiastic that when he won, he hollered "bingo" instead of "beano." The name stuck. By the 1940s, people were playing bingo everywhere.

Late one Friday afternoon at the bank, a frightening event occurred. Myrna was handed a note by a handsome young man who had been waiting patiently in her line. The message said, "Act normal and give me all your money. This is a stick-up." Reminiscent of a late-night Western, Myrna calmly and quickly followed the would-be robber's requests. Always in support of her husband's career as an RCMP officer, Myrna was careful not to cause a fuss.

The theft was pulled off without a hitch until Myrna was able to identify the man due to her keen sense of detail. After she described him to the police, he was caught only a few blocks from the bank. He was in no rush to get away and was seen walking up Lonsdale wearing a strangely bulging jacket. With his James Dean-like appearance, he was easy to spot, and the arrest was made before the weekend was to commence.

It turned out the robber was a friend of Linda's from high school. From all the Western and detective shows Linda had watched over the years, she worried that it would come down to guilty by association. Fortunately, it did not.

After the stick-up, and the robber was caught and identified, all the bank employees left work for the weekend, showing up first thing Monday morning, business as usual. Other than Myrna sharing the excitement around the water cooler, the robbery was never spoken of again. Traumatized employees quickly learned to suck it up, push it down, and carry on.

In addition to her weekly games of bingo at the Catholic Church on Wednesday nights, Linda also roped her mother into joining her, and they often sat with their next-door neighbour Anna Hocevar and her friend Fay Emberly. Living next door to the Bonners, Anna and Mike's four children, Michael, Stephen, Mario, and Marlene, became great friends with Linda, Doug, Ken, and Karen. But on Wednesday nights, it was ladies of the households who made a quick supper for their families and went out to play bingo together.

It turned out that Frances enjoyed herself immensely and realized that she adored bingo, hook, line, and sinker. More importantly, she discovered that she and Linda now had something in common, an activity they could call their own, besides Weight Watchers.

Everyone loved Anna. She was an energetic and petite Italian woman who had a knack not only for playing bingo but also for entering contests on the radio and winning. From alarm clocks to transistor radios, toasters to cash, trips, and free meals at restaurants, she would be the winner. On one memorable occasion, a radio game instructed people to go to a particular street corner in North Vancouver. Anna got there first, won the prize, and then looped around a second time. The radio announcer said, "I thought you were here a few minutes ago and already won?" Without skipping a beat, Anna responded with, "Oh no, that was my twin sister!" Anna was a witty, quick thinker and as lucky as they came.

Another skill that Anna excelled in was cooking. Her spaghetti sauce was famous with other families in the neighbourhood and could have easily won a few contests all on its own. In fact, it did! The favoured Italian dish was featured in *Canada's Largest Chicken Contest*. Only thirty-two recipes made the cut.

Linda was living back at home and missing the Cariboo, the rodeos, and the cowboys. What else was missing was her carefree thoughts about her weight. Even though she was back at Weight Watchers with her mother, her body weight fluctuated like the rising tides and the ever-changing weather. It amazed her how extra weight on the scale could dictate how she led her life and the social discomfort that crept in almost without her knowledge.

The long and the short of it was that in the city, Linda felt judged. In the country, she felt accepted. Whenever strangers, friends, and family mocked or belittled her, Linda made a joke as a go-to secret weapon, using humour as a shield to protect herself. They were unaware of what was underneath—as the saying goes, "The pillow in your bed sees the most honest tears."

With each lewd comment from a passing vehicle or thoughtless put-down from a salesperson, Linda's skin grew thicker. She was becoming less upset or insulted and managed to take criticism well.

Ironically, Linda was humble and kind. She knew how to treat people well. She knew what it felt like to be mistreated and never judged a person for how they looked or how they did things. Instead, she focused on work, bingo, and weekends at the Arlington Hotel, dancing up a storm.

The Arlington Hotel is a three-storey, late Victorian, Italian-style commercial structure on West Cordova near Vancouver's historic Gastown area. Built in 1908–1910, it was considered to be the most modern office building in the country for its time. It was described at the time as an "object of pride to every citizen."

Originally, the Arlington served as commercial space on the main floor with lodging and residential space on the above floors. There was an adjacent billiard parlour that provided recreation for lodgers. After years of neglect and deterioration, it was renovated and brought back to life in the mid-1960s, with dancing, live music, dining, and billiards.

The Arlington had become a favourite go-to place for Linda and her friends, and it became a routine every Saturday night for drinks and dancing, with Linda once again driving a carload of people in her Rambler as the designated driver.

No one could hold a candle to Linda's energy and dance moves. With lights low and the music's pulsing beat, all of her dance partners were surprised that a bigger girl could move with grace, finesse, and rhythm.

Before last call one Saturday night, a second-guesser sauntered over to Linda and said, "I would consider dancing with you if you were thinner." Without missing a beat, Linda responded with, "And I might consider dancing with you if you had more hair." Her table of friends erupted with laughter while the nay-sayer crept off in the other direction.

Meanwhile, Vince, Doug, and Ken had been travelling out to the property every weekend to clear the land, cut down trees, and put them through a portable sawmill. The plan was to stay in the family's camper while building a small cabin. The little bungalow would give them a comfortable, warm place to stay while they began and finished the building projects.

At some point, Vince's brother Hank suggested they use a bigger, more efficient mill that he had stored upcountry on his farm. Vince and the boys borrowed a friend's single axle dump truck to retrieve it. They painstakingly took it apart, loaded it piece by piece onto the dump truck and brought it to the property in Mission. Once there, they put it back together like a jigsaw puzzle.

Vince had done so many odd jobs and favours for people over the years, it became a payback time when people learned of his passion project. Neighbours, friends, and even acquaintances rallied around Vince and the boys to pitch in and offer their physical labour and expertise. They became morale boosters and a support system.

Frances and Vince marvelled at Doug's intelligence. When he was a little boy, he never wanted help putting together his models or Lego. He was an independent, systematic thinker and felt he worked better alone. Seeing this quality in his son, Vince suggested that Doug try to design the log home. Combined with Vince's skill, thoughts, and ideas, Doug accepted the challenge.

In his late teens, Doug relished the endeavour. He drew a 20' X 30' rectangle with a foundation on poured concrete piers 10' apart. The plan included a central living room, open kitchen, bathroom, and two bedrooms downstairs, with an ample open space upstairs, and two substantial front porches, one upstairs and one downstairs.

The preparation for the building took a few years of felling trees and cutting lumber. When the construction began, so did carloads of neighbours wanting to help. A few tradesmen, friends of Frances and Vince, came out to help with the electrical and forgot their voltage meter to test the lines. Young Doug, still a high school student, suggested a hack with an old battery radio that would show suitable circuits. To everyone's amazement, it worked beautifully.

Then, unexpectedly came another tragedy, an unforeseen accident that Linda's brother Ken witnessed and would never forget. Ken had worked alongside Vince since he quit school in Grade 9. Vince's bulldozing business had grown over the years. At one point, he had four bulldozers, a few employees, and his son Ken.

After clearing some land on a hot summer afternoon, they had pushed together some stumps to make a brush pile with the bulldozer. Ken had been given the job of sharpening the chainsaw while Vince threw paint thinner on the diesel-soaked pile. Unexpectantly, it blew back on him on ignition. Even though he was far enough away, he had trouble lighting the matches, and by the time he threw the flaming stick, the fumes had risen on the hot summer day and had ignited towards him.

Sitting on the back of the pickup truck, with the tailgate down, Ken was lost in his thoughts when he was abruptly shaken to alertness by a loud explosion. Looking up as if in slow motion, he saw his father flying through the air with his arms, chest, back, and hair on fire. Vince was franticly patting out the fire when an employee grabbed an old blanket to smother the flames. Vince downed a bottle of rum to ease the pain and then went into shock.

The employee drove Vince to Mission Memorial Hospital with Ken and his buddy following behind in Vince's truck. Neither of the boys had a driver's license or knew how to drive, but they sure learned quickly that day.

Once Vince's burns were treated, Ken sat by his side. Gripping Ken's hand, Vince leaned in towards Ken and confided in him that he was in the worst pain of his life. Ken held back the tears and tried to be strong for his father. The recovery process was lengthy and excruciating.

Simultaneously, Linda was getting ready to move into the completed log home and was excited at the thought of offering trail rides on the trails Vince had developed. She had applied at the Canadian Imperial Bank of Commerce in Mission. Aside from the anticipation for an upcoming bright future, something she had always dreamed about, Linda still had a nagging desire to be in the Cariboo. But this would remain her little secret because she never wanted to sound ungrateful for all that her father and brothers had done.

Vince, Ken, Doug, and many volunteers also built the barn entirely out of logs, adding to it a shingled roof. Complete with horse stalls, a tack room, and stairs to the loft where the bales of hay were kept, what made the barn unique and functional were the big sliding barn doors in the back, constructed so a pickup truck could back in to unload.

Having grown up impoverished on the prairies, Vince was skilled at making the best of every situation. He also knew the importance of water.

Finding natural springs on the fifty acres by using a well witcher, he dug up three human-made ponds. Next to the small cabin was a swimming hole with a diving board and raft. Another pond further up on the property had a rope swing. The third was next to the barn, which supplied water for the horses.

Witching wells/dowsing is an old-fashioned method and type of divination employed in the attempt to locate groundwater, buried metals, gemstones, oil, gravesites, and currents of the earth's radiation without the use of scientific apparatus.

Using a Y-shaped twig—a witching stick (Vince knew a guy)—you walk around the area where you think water might be. To some, this is a natural phenomenon, kind of like an Ouija board in the sense that the person using it inadvertently moves it because there is a force. By squeezing the two ends, there is a tension that pulls the stick towards the water source.

Vince also placed rain barrels next to the barn, the log home, and the smaller cabin. In the 18–1900's, wooden barrels would be used as shipping containers for dry goods. When the goods were unpacked, the barrels could no longer be used, so they were placed under the eaves to collect the rain. During Vince's upbringing, every farmhouse had a rain barrel. Throughout the hot, dusty days of summer, because the rainwater was closer to the house than the well, the water was heated to use for washing hair, clothes, and for baths. The barrels also acted as water containers for the lawn and garden. Vince's primary purpose for having rain barrels was in case of fire—available water just in case.

Shortly after Linda got into the swing of things, out of the blue, there would be another fire, and it would not be a body that would burn, but in Vince's eyes, it was equally as tragic.

Coldwell kids getting a horse ride

*Martha, cousin Marjorie, Grandpa Earl (Vince's
father) and Karen in Kelowna*

Linda at the Haney Fairgrounds in Maple Ridge

A new Cat for Vince

CHAPTER ELEVEN

A Proposal

"Believe me, the reward is not so great without the struggle."

–Wilma Rudolph

While Linda was waiting in the wings for the property to be ready, in addition to her work at the bank, she got a job volunteering with a fellow who owned American Quarter Horses. They were show horses, and he needed young women to show them at various events throughout the Lower Mainland, a few of which were the PNE, the Cloverdale Rodeo, and the Maple Ridge Fair. It would be a paid position, but first, Linda needed to be trained.

Ed was in his sixties, not considerably handsome, but pleasant and seemingly kind, and a horse lover through and through. He always wore big red suspenders over a bulky wool plaid shirt tucked into his GWG blue jeans. His thick, calloused hands were an indication he was a hard worker, and his overextended belly showed his love for greasy burgers.

Shortly after Linda started volunteering in preparation for an eventual job, Ed asked if she could manage his estate while he went on a Texas horse-buying trip. She gladly accepted the offer and spent two months working at the bank in North Vancouver and then driving forty minutes to Maple Ridge every day to maintain the horses, sleeping overnight and commuting back to North Vancouver every morning.

Linda single-handedly cleaned the stalls, groomed, fed, and exercised Ed's prized horses, knowing that it would all pay off eventually, and she would be given the dream job of a lifetime.

His seventeen-foot trailer was a bachelor's pad, complete with overflowing dirty ashtrays, empty liquor bottles lining the countertops, and a stench permeating the entire dwelling that could easily offend even a pig farmer. Linda cleaned up as best she could in addition to all of her other duties.

When Ed returned, and Linda was to begin the training he had promised her, she was told that she was too large to be a horse showgirl and just not pretty enough. He stated that he had found a more petite lady who would be perfect for the job. Besides, he added, the new gal had naturally blonde hair, and men love that.

Linda was hurt and angry, feeling used. Two months of her time and expertise were given to a hotshot who she figured had no intention of hiring her in the first place.

Concurrently, Linda's dad was recovering from his accident, and Linda was moving from her family home in North Vancouver to the property on Carr Street in Stave Falls, Mission. She quickly got over the humiliation of not being hired by a total cad! There were other opportunities on the horizon, with bigger and better things to come, she speculated.

Phil Russell could have been a body double for actor Paul Newman. Adored by all the ladies, he had become Vince's right-hand man for a time. He lived across the street in North Vancouver and never hesitated to drive out to Stave Falls to work on the acreage.

Another man in Vince Bonner's life was Burt Wiens, a kind-hearted, devoted foreman who Vince and Frances thought of as family. He, too, was handsome, a few years younger than Vince, with dark hair and an outdoorsy complexion. Burt had a wife and four children, two boys and two girls. Over the years, the two families had gotten together for meals and lots of laughs.

Phil, Burt, and Vince were all blue-collar workers who enjoyed engaging in hard manual labour, primarily construction, in the field of bulldozing and excavation. Vince's background in logging was an asset to his business and land clearing details. Burt, on the other hand, was a true jack-of-all-trades. Handsome, with a brush cut and an outdoorsy complexion, he was fit and muscular.

When the rainy season set in and most of the earth became muddy, sludgy sinkholes, Vince still kept Burt employed, as he had a family to feed. Seasonal work in rainy Vancouver was unpredictable. When there was no bulldozing, Burt could often be seen around the Bonner's North Vancouver house, doing odd jobs or out at the property to pitch in wherever he could.

Vince paid the men who worked for him before he took a wage and depended on Frances's bookkeeping skills to pay their bills and keep their heads above water.

Rolley Lake Riding Stable was the name that Vince and Linda decided to call their new place. It was named after a lake and campsite in the area called Rolley Lake, which happened to be ideally situated in conjunction with the manicured trails Vince and Burt had groomed from old logging roads.

Once the riding stable was completed, they had created and decorated an Old Western-themed graveyard called Boot Hill. It consisted of headstones and graves for infamous characters of wild-west history, such as Jesse James and Wyatt Earp, who were notorious bank and stagecoach robbers from those days. Another trail called Hang Man's Trail consisted of a replica of an actual cowboy hanging from a tree with a noose around his neck. It was all in fun, but the tricky part was getting the horses to pass by, as they were spooked every time, which caused anticipation, laughter, and a sense of fun from all the riders.

Advertisements for the riding stable were posted in the *Mission Gazette* and *Maple Ridge Times* newspapers, offering trail rides, riding lessons, and boarding for horses.

Weekends had become busy, with Linda leading trail rides and teaching riding lessons in the professional-sized riding ring.

Vince had cleverly saved the sawdust from the sawmill to dump in the corral. Everyone from miles around was intrigued and interested in the Rolley Lake Riding Stables.

Linda had purchased horses from the Matsqui Horse Auction and was thrilled with her beloved white gelding named Jack. She had convinced her parents that her little sister should also have a horse, which she named Cricket. Two other horses that were added to the mix were Big Dolly and Little Dolly.

Every morning after cleaning the stalls and feeding the horses, Linda left her new home to work at the Mission branch of the Canadian Imperial Bank of Commerce. She had made an easy transfer from the North Vancouver location to the Mission branch with raving reviews from Mr. Gurney, who was so distraught to see his favourite employee and protégé go that he put in for retirement the next day.

Linda would have preferred to work solely with the horses and riding stable customers, but in its newness, the stable was not yet off the ground, and financially she had to make do for just a little longer as an employee at the bank.

Aside from making new friends at the bank and receiving immediate praise for her dynamic personality and banking skills, Linda found herself smack dab in the middle of an embezzling scheme gone wrong. It was not that Linda had anything to do with it, but it was hard not to feel involved, as it unfolded before every employee's eyes. Besides, Linda had become friends with the woman in question.

Janet was the head teller and was well-liked by all the staff and customers. Linda particularly liked her, as she had been very kind to Linda, welcoming and friendly. She was in her late twenties, with bright, compelling green eyes. Her brunette shoulder-length hair was cut in a shag, with feathered bangs. She dated an RCMP officer and lived alone in a modern townhouse—always quite the envy of the other tellers.

Unbeknownst to everyone at the bank, Janet transferred funds from old dormant accounts that had not been used in years. If the customer would one day show up, Janet would transfer funds back into their account from other accounts. She was also skimming off the top and pocketing what she could.

Meanwhile, her outlandish spending was going unnoticed—Caribbean trips, beauty treatments, and an extensive wardrobe. It was not until after the investigation took place that co-workers realized they had never seen Janet wear an outfit more than once, and she was never without a suntan.

During Linda's first few weeks at the bank, the whole scam came crashing down. The bank was closed for auditing, and a bookkeeping system was discovered that provided evidence that Janet was the one to blame. A trail led the police and investigators straight to Janet's townhouse.

There was an eventual arrest and a court hearing, after which poor, likable Janet went to jail. It was almost as entertaining as one of Linda's shows, but more upsetting because Linda was honest and could not imagine the gall and confidence it would take to be a thief. Episodes of Perry Mason could not hold a candle to the sting that went down, resulting in Janet's arrest.

Laura Lynn and Mountain Shadows was Linda's roadmap for working and managing the Rolley Lake Stables, and her life-long passion for horses and anything Western acted as her comforting guide. Vince and Linda both knew the stables would soon be a success—until a grey November evening in 1969, when an unexpected, tragic occurrence took place.

The date was November 11th, Remembrance Day. Historically this date is observed across Canada and many Commonwealth countries to remember those who died in military service and honour those who served in wartime. Also, November 11th represents the Armistice agreement of 1918 that ended the First World War.

For the Bonner family, November 11th would become the day that dreams and hard work would be reduced to ashes and rubble, resulting in tears of pain, heartbreak, and earth-shattering anguish for Vince.

When not working at the bank, Linda worked at the stable. She was dedicated and loved every minute of it. One evening before retiring to bed, she had brought two of the saddles into the house from the barn's tack room and planned to clean and polish them after her duties at the barn.

She was tired from a full day at the bank but never too tired for the horses. Various tasks required to maintain the stables had turned into hobbies for Linda, as one would enjoy doing a crossword puzzle or knitting a scarf. Linda always had a long list of chores that she looked forward to and delighted in.

On this particular night, she was feeding the horses with the neighbour's golden retriever/yellow lab cross close by her side. Vince had become friends with the family who lived on the property next door, a lovely older couple whose children were all grown. The gentleman was a retired carpenter, and his wife was a homemaker, with the best homemade soup known to all.

Over the last few years, while Vince was working the property, he would look up to see the couple's dog with a note in its mouth every other day or so. The message read, *"If you have the time, the soup is on, and freshly baked bread just came out of the oven. Come on over for a bite to eat."*

Vince would write back, *"Be right over!"* and place his response in the dog's mouth and off he would go.

At the time, Karen would have been nine years old and would often go with their dad on the weekends to the property, which the family had nicknamed "the farm." While there, the golden retriever/lab, named Ateu, would remain at Karen's side for the entire duration of the weekend. He had a habit of gently holding onto the end of her sleeve while they roamed around the property together. Karen trailed after her father, and Ateu followed after her. The three of them had adventures together.

On the night in question, Linda was alone on the property. With her transistor radio on in the barn, Linda became startled by the horses' sudden change in behaviour. They had begun snorting and clamouring from side to side in their appointed stalls—one horse, out of character, reared right up on its hind legs.

Suddenly, Linda and Ateu jumped at the sound of what the horses were reacting to, a crackling sound and then an explosion coming from the cabin's direction. Instinctively, the animals knew there was danger.

Dropping everything and running towards the house with the dog at her heels, Linda saw flames shooting from the roof. Darting inside, she grabbed the phone with its long extension cord and ran back outside, phoning the fire department in Mission and Maple Ridge. Confused at what was happening, she still managed to think fast on her feet and do what she could.

Then she called her dad, knowing that what she needed, as the flames engulfed the log home, was her father.

Answering the phone late in the evening, with his usual, "Hello, Vince Bonner Bulldozing, what can I do you for?" Vince instantly was on guard as he heard the panic screams coming from the other end of the telephone.

"The house is on fire, the house is on fire, help, help, help. I don't know what to do!"

Vince could not calm his daughter and felt helpless and at a loss. He immediately knew there was nothing he could do except jump in his truck and drive the one hour from their North Vancouver family home to the Mission farm. He arrived at the same time as both of the volunteer fire departments.

Meanwhile, after hanging up with her dad, Linda ran back into the burning house and dragged the two expensive saddles outside. She called for the dog, and he came out of the barn, pulling and tugging one of the horses by the reigns, trying to do his part.

Standing outside, Linda and Ateu walked in circles, watching and waiting for someone to arrive. The heat was radiant, intense, casting its yellow glow into the night, like something out of a horror movie, frightening and unexplainable. The dog never left Linda's side.

By the time Vince arrived, it was too late.

The air smelled like a campfire, except that there were no marshmallows and camp songs to go with it. This was far worse than any bonfire or tree clearing that Vince had burned on the lot before building. Instead, twisted plastic, charred logs, and burned-up dreams stood before father and daughter, lifeless.

All that remained was a charred and smouldering outer shell. The roof was gone, and with it, hours and hours of laborious love and hard work. Of what remained, nothing was salvageable, other than what Linda and Ateu had managed to pull out before the heat and flames took over.

The only thing to be thankful for was that no one was injured, and the fire did not spread to the old-growth forest or the barn full of terrified animals.

The late arrival of the fire department was due to a mix-up. There was another Carr Street in Maple Ridge, and the fire department went there first, not finding any fire at all. Those fifty acres of land, cabins, and barn were located at 12468 Carr Street in Mission, although the property was closer to Maple Ridge and was in the Maple Ridge phone exchange. Two streets were named the same but were in two separate communities.

Investigators were not sure how or where the fire started. One fireman speculated the television, another the wiring, and a few suggested arson. They wondered how it went up so fast. Even though there had recently been suspicious goings-on in the neighbourhood, no one could come up with a reasonable explanation.

Earlier that year, there had been a murder on the same street. A ninety-year-old couple, whom everyone adored, lived a few doors down from the property. While the husband was at church one Sunday, his wife had chosen to stay home and was bludgeoned to death. Her measly pension cheque was missing. The husband was blamed first, as he was found with blood on his hands. Then it was speculated the handyman had something to do with it. After fingerprints were found on a rock outside, together with a confession, the handyman was charged and convicted of the murder.

The entire neighbourhood in the sleepy little hollow of Stave Falls began locking their doors and looking over their shoulders.

Another questionable person was a man Linda had started dating, by the name of Johnny. He was a drywaller from Ontario, a rough-around-the-edges type who was not into horses at all. He had taken a liking to Linda, but she quickly broke up when she caught him in the barn making out with one of her customers. He stormed off, disgruntled. Sometime after the incident, a friend showed Linda a newspaper with a write-up about Johnny and how he had been sent to prison for setting a fire at a horse-riding stable in Ontario.

There were also a few people who would offer to clean stalls and do odd jobs in exchange for riding the horses. Linda had remembered doing the same thing herself at Laura Lynn. Still, she knew and understood why she was not always allowed to take free rides, as the paying customers come first—sometimes leaving the volunteers disgruntled. Now she wondered if she had rubbed someone the wrong way by saying "no" to a few of her volunteers. *Had they retaliated by setting the gorgeous log home ablaze?* Linda wondered.

When all was said and done, the drive home to North Vancouver passed in a blur for Vince. He felt empty and devasted.

Once inside the door, Vince crumpled into Frances's arms and wept the tears he had been holding back. He cried for the loss, sobbed for his daughter's dreams and his sons' hard work. He grieved for the joint efforts of family, friends, and employees that had all gone up in smoke in less than an hour.

Linda had to work the next day, and she had not slept all night. Again, she wondered why bad things happened to good people. With a strong work ethic and much practice in shoving down her feelings, as in, "the show must go on," Linda wasted no time carrying on.

The kind couple from next door suggested that Vince pull their available seventeen-foot trailer over to the property with his bulldozer so that Linda would have a place to live in since she now had nowhere to stay. Co-workers from the bank donated everything Linda would need—pots and pans, bedding and food. Linda felt blessed in the midst of the horror of it all.

She had no idea that things were about to go from horrendous and devastating to excruciating and vile.

Linda felt as though she was living in a haze. The guilt was unbearable, and she went through the motions of work and caring for the horses like a zombie. Unfeeling, unemotional, and uncaring—not at all like her usual cheerful self. She could not escape the visions of the many people who had put so much time and effort into the log home, only for it all to be reduced to ashes and soot in what seemed like seconds.

She kept her thoughts and feelings to herself, never realizing that sharing her pain would help her cope.

A few nights after the fire, Linda was set up in the neighbour's trailer and back at work, almost as if nothing had happened. She was alone. After work, when she was at the barn going through her usual ritual of feeding and grooming the horses, she heard a car drive up and two doors quietly close—followed by some rustling, stumbling, and slurred, incoherent whispering.

Linda knew instinctively that she was in trouble. She was not expecting anyone, and if it were friends, they would have called out to her. She froze. With very little light in the barn, her eyes had adjusted, more so than the strangers who were quickly approaching. Dark, faceless bodies were moving towards her.

Her brain was racing, but no sense could be made out of her thoughts. She went to speak, to try and talk her way out of whatever was about to happen, but her voice was strangled in her throat, and her breath caught. The last thing she remembered was the soft, gentle eyes of her horses, whose languid gaze saw the whole thing.

She forced a deep guttural scream, but the adjoining properties were not within earshot. No one would hear her protests and wailing. This she knew, but violence never has deaf ears.

As the two brutal strangers were finished with her, they spoke. Their alcohol-induced words burned like vinegar pouring into her already deep wounds, threatening that if she tried going to the police, they would say that she was easy because of her fatness, that she enticed them into sex because she could never get a man any other way. Besides, they had friends who would back up their story. The police would undoubtedly believe them, as who would regard someone as fat and disgusting as her?

Their contention and malice covered her like a barrage of foul-smelling garbage. The stench sank deep into her skin. She felt shameful and dirty and knew that a million bars of soap and scrub brushes would never remove the reek.

After the men left, she apologized profusely to the shadowy silhouettes of her compassionate, well-mannered friends in the barn. As on-lookers, they were as helpless as she was, the horses she loved and lived for, who loved her unconditionally in return.

In the small trailer, there was only a sink. Linda did her best to clean up, but she had another sleepless night before going to work.

Two weeks later, when the morning sickness bombarded her, she telephoned her mother and sobbed into the receiver, telling her about the attack and how sick she felt. Frances stood by her eldest daughter—her firstborn, the once sweet, precocious, comical daughter, who dreamed big and was kind to all.

Linda chose to confide in Dennis as well, and his only reaction was to find the creeps and beat them up and then offer to marry her, to raise the baby together. As sweet as his suggestion was, he was a heavy drinker, and his proposal seemed worse than shamefully raising the baby alone.

An appointment was made at Lions Gate Hospital in North Vancouver. Linda was interviewed in front of a doctor's board to see if she was eligible for an abortion. Her mother went with her, held her hand and stoically represented her daughter at the upsetting meeting, as the all-male panel of doctors grilled Linda and assessed her.

Before leaving for the procedure, the last thing Frances said was, "Please do not breathe a word of this to your father." Not only would he seek out the culprits, but he would surely kill them. Add that to the stress of the fire, and this would end up destroying him.

Linda bottled up her emotions yet again.

Dennis drove Linda to her scheduled abortion, and on the steps of the hospital, Dennis proposed again. In a state of numbness, Linda knew she was being given a choice, a way out of committing the unthinkable. She turned Dennis down by shaking her bowed head, feeling the hot tears stream down her face, unable to utter a word. She had no thoughts of regret or what the procedure entailed and no one to offer up any details or an alternative plan. Aside from Dennis, she was entirely alone.

Next up was another gathering of family, volunteers, and Phil and Bert, to sandblast the charred logs and rebuild the home. Since the building of the first log home, Phil had become a dentist and left his wife for a dental assistant. Having moved to Abbotsford, he still gave up his weekends to help out.

With the work crews coming and going, Linda continued at the bank and continued to run the stables, living out of the donated trailer.

The older couple next door eventually moved away and rented their house and property to two men from Vancouver. The whole Bonner family would miss them, especially their brilliant dog and loving companion, Ateu.

However, by 1971 the work had mounted at the bank, and the stable was struggling. The bottom line for Linda was that she missed the Cariboo. Her weight was at an all-time high, and with that came continuous comments from strangers and acquaintances. The worst was when people hollered out of their car window when she walked down the street. She always tried to park as close as possible to where she needed to be for this reason, not because she was lazy, but rather to avoid being seen and having to endure lewd and hurtful remarks.

At the bank, she was behind a counter, and customers always commented on what a pretty face she had or how friendly and knowledgeable she was. On the dance floor, with the lights down low, she revelled in her dancing skills, and there she knew she was okay and even admired for technique.

Besides knowing that many people liked her, Linda often wondered what gave strangers, invaders of her space, the right to say such prejudicial things, especially when they did not even know her. It seemed she was living in a society not even willing to give her a chance.

For years, her mother had questioned her weight, often asking Linda if something had gone on that she was not telling anyone. "Was there an incident? Did someone molest you or hurt you?" Frances would plead. Her response to her mother was always a curt, "No, Mom, nothing happened."

Neither mother nor daughter ever spoke of the years of name-calling, the horrific murder of her friends, untrustworthy and damaging caregivers, a creepy first boyfriend who had rushed her into something she did not want to do, and especially not the two men at the barn and the resulting abortion. It was blocked and buried deep within both of them. As much as her mother's questioning bothered her, Linda would think long and hard and could never pinpoint one or another incident that would cause her to overeat. She sometimes wondered if she had a slow metabolism or if something was wrong with her thyroid. After all, she did not smoke, drink alcohol, coffee, or tea. She was friendly, kind, comical, and fun to be around. So what if she had a healthy appetite?

As the years went on, she made a habit of thinking only of the result of her overindulgences with food, the extra weight that she carried, never connecting the horrendous events and trauma she had endured in her life as the reason for why she did overeat, never realizing that trauma could cause her to look to food for her comfort. Instead, in a state of numbness, it felt better to push everything down rather than face the pain and develop a healthy way of coping with it.

Linda came to the conclusion that the only place she ever felt truly accepted and safe was up north in the Cariboo, where she was free to be herself, regardless of what her weight happened to be.

She had grown weary after two years of living on the property. The fire, rebuilding, and lack of revenue all combined took a toll on all of them, her father, her mother, and herself. In addition, her guilt had become all-encompassing. With her parents' blessing and a heavy heart, Linda gave away Big Dolly and Little Dolly to good homes, quit her job at the bank, and packed up her truck to head back to Kamloops. Rather than leaving the newly refurbished homestead vacant, her mom, dad, and sister Karen were set to rent out their North Vancouver home and move out to the farm after Linda left.

She hoped the drive would bring a semblance of peace. At the thought of moving back, Linda felt a glimmer of hope and was excited to be reconnecting with what she liked to refer to as the Wild West—old friends, rodeos, cowboys, and no judgement. There she was referred to as Lynn, and she felt accepted. The name Lynn was like a new identity that Linda felt she needed.

Driving towards Chilliwack and on through to Hope, the Fraser Canyon, Merritt, and finally, Kamloops, the weight lifted from her shoulders, and seemingly her waistline, as Linda clocked the miles.

Almost instantly, Linda applied for and got another banking job at the Canadian Imperial Bank of Commerce on Third and Victoria in Kamloops.

A lot had happened since she had left the rural life three years prior, and Linda was happy to be in the saddle again. Being in the midst of the dusty, desert-like hills and distant mountains brought peace of mind to her usually clouded thoughts.

Even Domtar Pulp Mill's aroma was overlooked because it provided hundreds of jobs, despite the citizens' complaints about the smell. Linda smiled at the thought and scent of it. She revelled in her work ethic that had been passed down from her father. Just the thought of her dad gave her strength, even though there were many secrets he would never know.

It would soon be 1972, and Canadians were anticipating the Summit Series when Canada brought together their best hockey players to play against the Soviet Stars in an eight-game exhibition series. In the final game of the series, Canada did not just win in the last few seconds, they won after trailing behind and enduring controversy throughout. It was one of the most-watched games in Canada and perhaps worldwide.

Linda's entire family were hockey fans, even her mother. They had season tickets to all the Vancouver Canucks games at the Vancouver Coliseum, while Linda lived out her cowboy-flavoured Western lifestyle.

1972 brought hippies picketing the Vietnam war, and young people everywhere were chanting "Sex, Drugs, and Rock & Roll." Wrangler jeans were $12, and a Kodak Pocket Camera cost $28.00. In Vancouver, the average home was $30,000-$40,000, and renters paid approximately $165.00 a month. The gasoline cost was fifty-five cents a gallon, and movie tickets were $1.50–$3.00.

Popular Western movies were box office hits such as *Joe Kidd* with John Saxon, Clint Eastwood, Stella Garcia and Robert Duvall; *Bad Company* with Barry Brown, Jeff Bridges, David Huddleston and John Savage; *The Cowboys* with John Wayne, Bruce Dern, A. Martinez and Robert Carradine; and *The Life and Times of Judge Roy Bean* with Paul Newman, John Huston, Ava Gardner and Jacqueline Bisset.

Even though 1972 brought America's Watergate scandal, it was also the year that Billie Jean King overtook Evonne Goolagong at Wimbledon. Women dominated the Grammy Awards, and Gloria Steinem's *Ms. Magazine* made its debut. Women all across North America were finally starting to be heard. Author Betty Friedan's book *The Feminine Mystique,* a nonfiction book in which she contested the post-World War ll belief that it was a woman's destiny to marry and bear children, was flying off the shelves. Many women agreed that homemaking in the suburbs sapped them of their individualism and left them unsatisfied.

Not one to protest or speak outwardly about the women's liberation movement, Frances was nevertheless on board with what women were saying and speaking out against, often recalling her dreams of becoming so much more than a housewife and mother. Therefore, she was open to whatever her two daughters decided to do with their lives.

Linda was twenty-five years old, the same age her mother had been when she married her father. Unlike her mother, Linda was not interested in becoming "the little woman," or another unsettling term, "barefoot and pregnant."

Linda knew she did not have a domestic bone in her body, and even though she liked children, she also did not want any. However, shortly after arriving in Kamloops, Linda met the man who just might change all that and eventually become "the one."

Resuming her old friendships and making a few new ones, Linda was introduced to the Hefley Creek country dances, the Blue Room at the Plaza Hotel, and a cowboy named George Alcide Proulx. He preferred to be called by his middle name, Alcide.

Alcide was a tall and considerably handsome hillbilly type and was admired by many unattached women. Even a few married gals had their eye on him—a dairy farmer, cowboy, and man who could work the land, from excavating to riding the range to milking the cows.

It all started at the Hefley Creek Hall on a Saturday night in the spring of 1971. Heffley Creek is located along the Southern Yellowhead Highway, separated from Kamloops by the Thompson River. It was a farming community since the 1860s. The namesake Adam Heffley entered BC as a miner during the Goldrush of 1858. He was one of the handlers for the famous camels that were unsuccessfully used as pack animals on the Cariboo Road. Heffley raised horses on his ranch and took pride in racing horses with Chief Louis of the Kamloops Indian Band. Heffley died of a heart attack in 1871, and his property was sold at auction.

Heffley Creek Hall was made famous for its Saturday night Stomp, a Western BC term for dance. Men wore authentic Western dress-up clothes, string ties, silver belt buckles, freshly laundered Wrangler jeans, polished boots, and crisp, wide-brimmed cowboy hats at the Stomp. On a sleek and slippery hardwood floor, the men often outshone the women as couples rallied to polka, waltz, and shimmy on down to the local country and rock and roll bands.

After settling into her new apartment, Linda easily resumed the routine, at the end of a long work week, to attend the Stomp most Saturday nights in Heffley with a few of her friends from the bank.

The dances were always dry events; all ages were welcome with never any liquor in sight. However, people often made trips out to their cars to satisfy their needs if they required something more potent than a pop.

When the liquor began flowing outside for her friends, Linda settled into her diet Pepsi inside as the band struck up their rendition of "A Hard Days' Night." After the first sip of her diet soda, she was tapped on the shoulder by a well-dressed, potbellied stranger. He introduced himself as George but said his real friends call him Alcide. He reached for her hand, and Linda accepted and cheerfully introduced herself.

Linda felt pretty and a tad smaller than usual, with her five-foot-seven-inch frame next to Alcide. It was apparent that he loved to dance and proved to be an excellent dance partner. As the night came to a close, Alcide invited Linda over to the family ranch for a good old-fashioned country supper the following evening. Linda eagerly accepted and drove her truck out to the ranch the following afternoon.

At meeting Alcide's family, Linda was well received and got along with everyone. Even though all the family women busied themselves in the kitchen, Alcide invited Linda to the barns to meet the horses. One horse that Linda took a liking to was Chief, which belonged to Alcide's sister Dolores. She was also a bigger girl, so her horse was outfitted to carry her weight with no effort. Linda noticed that the entire family was of larger body stature. This comforted and reassured her.

After a farm tour, they went back to the house for a wonderful dinner of roast beef, mashed potatoes, corn, beans, gravy, and biscuits, with hot apple pie and homemade ice cream for dessert. Everything they ate pretty much came from the farm and disappeared in minutes, as most meals do on the farm. Besides, Alcide and his siblings were hungry from a hard day of farming, and Linda admired their appetites. In the meantime, Alcide delighted in Linda's ability to talk ranching, farming, and finances.

It was not long before Linda was heading out to the dairy farm every Sunday, after a night of dancing. Alcide was kind and charming. Linda found his best quality was that of a hard worker, in addition to being a jack-of-all-trades, which warmly reminded her of her dad.

Occasionally, Alcide would stop into the bank and take Linda out for lunch. A few months into their relationship, it was on one of these lunches that Linda started noticing something was amiss.

Linda considered herself to be a pacifist. Even though she was raised on Western shows and was not ignorant of the world's ways, she did not like war, violence, or fighting of any kind. In contrast, Alcide had an obsession with guns. What was odd was the pistol he carried in his lunch kit. He also had a habit of opening and closing his lunch kit numerous times a day, in an admiring sort of way. His actions were unsettling to Linda, but she chose not to mention it.

Setting her thoughts and feelings on the back burner for a time, Linda was excited to have been invited to the ranch in Barriere to help move the cattle to the summer range, which was in reference to the grazing land. At the end of the summer, the livestock would be moved back home to the ranch, barns, and food source referred to as the winter range.

After getting all geared up, Linda was to ride Chief and head out for an all-day expedition. The air was light and sweet-smelling, the fields were parsley-green, and the entire scene was spirit-lifting.

About an hour into the ride, Linda was instructed to hang a right and go up a slight incline. She did what she was told and powered up the slope. Instantly, without a moment's notice, the bank gave out, causing Linda and Chief to topple over. There was nothing rider or horse could do to save themselves, and within seconds Chief had landed on Linda's back.

Unable to move, once again reminiscent of hurting her back at Mountain Shadows, Linda was transported to the ranch and driven forty miles to the hospital. After X-rays, she found out that she had a cracked tail bone and would have to stay in the hospital. The prognosis was good, but she was told that horseback riding would be off-limits and not a part of her life for at least three months.

Linda was scheduled to spend a week in the hospital and then begin her therapy and road to recovery. During one of Alcide's visits to the hospital, he bent down on one knee and proposed marriage with the most massive diamond ring Linda had ever seen. She quickly accepted Alcide's proposal.

Sumas Dancer

Linda with cowboy bob at the Cloverdale rodeo

Frances and Vince on a cruise-ship dancing

Dolly and Linda

Vince happy working

The log home Vince, family and friends built

CHAPTER TWELVE

Avon Calling

*"I cannot compromise my respect for your love. You
can keep your love; I will keep my respect."*

-Amit Kalantri

Back home on Carr Street, Frances, Vince, and twelve-year-old
Karen were settling into life on the hobby farm that Vince had
been creating and developing for years. The riding stable was gone,
but the horses, barn, and corral remained.

While recognizing that this move was everything Vince loved,
Frances wished she could be anywhere else. She had been reluctant
to move, but her husband and youngest daughter were eager and
happy to re-locate to the fifty acres of land and the rustic set-up.
So they did.

It became evident that Frances had begun to feel very depressed,
withdrawn, and unable to change gears to live in the country. On
the other hand, Karen was making friends, taking the school
bus to her new school, and riding her horse Cricket on the still
manicured trails. Vince was semi-retired and enjoyed working in
the garden, tending to the animals, and keeping up the ponds he
had stocked with rainbow trout.

Ken and Doug were both working and hoping to eventually build their own homes on the property with Vince's assistance. Both brothers were dating and happy. Ken was doing bulldozing jobs for Vince and was engaged to be married, while Doug worked at a local newspaper.

Frequent visitors were Bernie and Peter, the couple who lived and rented the house next door. Frances and Vince found Bernie to be delightful but were not too fond of his partner, whom they felt was cantankerous and unkind.

Regardless, Vince treated both men well and could often be seen taking baskets of vegetables down Carr Street's length, delivering his bounty of green beans, potatoes, and cabbages to various neighbours. At the same time, Frances had taken to having coffee dates with Bernie, not because she invited him, but because he made a point of dropping by.

Of course, Frances and Vince knew about homosexuality, but the topic had never come up, so it was not readily discussed. Frances found herself enamoured with Bernie's femininity. Somehow it gave her the giggles, but never in public, as she was mortified to offend anyone.

On one occasion, Bernie knocked at the door, frantic because he had run out of Peter's deodorant, and he would be home soon. He was in such a tizzy that he had Frances in a flurry as well. She ran around the house looking for something suitable and gave him Vince's Mennen cologne to hopefully tide him over until shopping day. Living in a rural community twenty minutes from shops and services meant that a trip into town only occurred once or twice a week. A multitasking list would be composed, and one never went for just one item.

Another time, Frances heard a loud pounding on the front door, only to find Bernie in a flap over Karen's horse Cricket, who had just kicked Stanley in the mouth. He was desperate for a band-aid and wondered if Frances could lend him one. It was not until much later that Frances found out that Stanley was the French poodle. The whole time she thought Bernie was talking about one of his house guests. The entire episode turned into a comical misunderstanding and pleased Frances to retell the tale of mistaken identity.

Bernie and Frances ended up swapping recipes, favourite laundry detergent, and grocery flyers from the newspaper. They shared their thoughts on Victor Newman and various other characters from their mutually well-loved soap opera, *The Young and the Restless*.

For a time, Frances came in and out of her down days. Unknowingly, Bernie was instrumental in bringing her up and out of her darkness and gloom whenever he came around.

Linda, Doug, and Ken were unaware of their mother's state of mind. Karen was the only child left who was living under the same roof, but being thirteen, she carried on with school and being a somewhat self-centred teenager.

Vince, however, was at a loss and unsure of what to do or say to his wife when she became withdrawn and uncommunicative. He knew that over the years, she had changed. Her blue eyes had lost their twinkle, and she failed to laugh at his jokes as freely as she used to. She had grown silent. Even though he was a hard worker, a thoughtful husband, and a loving and caring father, Vince had grown up in a time when a conversation about one's struggles was unheard of, and concealment about sadness and heartbreak was commonplace.

Out of the blue, one grey November morning, Frances suggested a trip, somewhere hot and sunny. She privately thought that it might clear up the cobwebs in her mind and get her out of the doldrums and off the property she was gradually coming to despise. Vince agreed, and Karen was delighted.

Years earlier, in the late 1960s, Frances and Vince had won a trip to Mexico. They were in a bridge tournament and had won a glass decanter for winning the card game, and surprisingly enough, they also won the door prize, an all-inclusive trip to Acapulco. It was there that Frances's moods lifted. She felt like a twenty-year-old again, hopeful, light, and happy. It was then she speculated that bright sunny days often made her feel better.

In 1973 Vince was fifty-eight, Frances was fifty-three, and Karen was 13 and in Grade 9. With the three older children, now young adults, off working and making their way, they felt Karen was somewhat like an only child, so they thought, *Why not spend some of our hard-earned money on travel?*

Together Karen and her mom would lay the travel brochures out on the kitchen table, and like a puzzle, they worked at piecing together just the right destination, admiringly looking at hotels and vistas with their tiled Spanish floors, swim-up tropical bars and endless sandy beaches. It was decided that Mazatlán, Mexico, for two weeks over spring break would be their destination.

Reminiscent of horseback riding and dude ranches with Linda, Vince's kind of parenting took on body surfing, cliff diving, and Mexican fiestas with Karen. Frances relished the hot sun and enjoyed watching Vince entertain their daughter. It was on this trip with her nose in a book that she felt her old self re-emerge, and she couldn't be happier. This experience began the mental health travelling bug. Once or twice a year, off they would go to Mexico, Hawaii, or California. Sometimes Karen would bring a friend. And on every trip, Vince was a contributing factor to the fun.

Although Vince thoroughly enjoyed the getaway, he was a perpetual, secret worrier and did not enjoy leaving the farm. He often feared the possibility of another fire. He fretted about his farm animals, which had grown into a menagerie of various critters such as pigs, chickens, and a slew of mismatched pets—cats, dogs, a burly old sheep, and Burt the bull. Ever since he had taken early retirement, Vince put his energy into his extensive garden and hobby farm.

However, shoving down his misgivings about leaving, he put on a brave, caring face and traded his deep-rooted worry for the joy on his wife's face and spending time with his youngest daughter. He concluded that for two weeks a year, he could cope just fine.

Occasionally, Linda called home to check in but was waiting for just the right time to introduce Alcide to her family. After the news of her engagement was common knowledge, the gossip mill began, as tends to happen in small towns. A few of Linda's friends, who had known Alcide longer, thought it essential to fill Linda in on a few things her fiancé might be keeping from her.

Linda learned that Alcide had an ex-wife and two children. Having such an involved and remarkable father, Linda instinctively knew what a father's duties were. She was raised by a dad who desired to be with his children. Many memories flooded her mind of Ken and Doug's camping and fishing trips, little league and soccer games with their dad, and Karen as a little girl, being inseparable from their father, sitting beside him on the bulldozer while he was working, and now she was taking trips with their parents.

Linda always had a great father-daughter relationship of her own. All of her years, her dad had gone out of his way to take her horseback riding and find her stables and ranches where she could volunteer and learn.

She wondered why Alcide never spent time with, or spoke of, his two children. When she casually asked him about his kids, and their mother, Alcide's explicit language could have rusted the family's milking buckets. He had nothing nice to say and finally stormed out to his pickup truck and lunch kit, where he kept his gun. Linda liked most things, but she did not like drinking, guns, or foul language.

It was abundantly apparent that he was not fond of his ex-wife and failed to pay child support or work on a relationship with his children. Upon learning this new information, Linda started to wonder if she was with the right man.

Linda's new roommate Betty was a fellow employee at the bank and into cowboys, horses, and anything Western. Linda was still unable to ride because of her horseback riding accident with Chief, so Betty and Linda spent time together after work watching shows and talking about her dilemma with Alcide.

Standing five feet two inches tall, Betty may have been short, but she made up for it in width. She had a mop-top of curly blonde hair and a cute turned-up nose covered in freckles. Her nickname was Betty Crocker because she loved to bake muffins, pies, cookies, and cakes—an actual Suzy Homemaker type through and through. Betty was also an Avon representative.

Avon was initially called the California Perfume Company, founded in 1892 by David H McConnell, originally a door-to-door salesman who sold books. He partnered up with Alexander Henderson, and by 1932 they specialized in perfumes, toilet waters, powder, rouge, and lipsticks.

The name was eventually changed to Avon in 1939, with a slogan of a ringing doorbell followed by a sing-song voice exclaiming, "Avon calling!" Eventually it became the most prominent multi-level marketing company in beauty, household, and personal care worldwide. Avon ladies were some of the first conglomerations of American and Canadian women to be financially independent with a respectable profession.

Betty was perfect for the job. She loved people and made being an Avon representative look easy. Betty was a natural at going door-to-door, placing orders, and believing that her products were unique and of the highest quality. She wore Sweet Honesty perfume and always sold out of Skin So Soft Bath Oil because not only did it soften one's skin, but it also acted as a mosquito repellant. There were many cowboys on her list who smelled tremendous and were bug-free.

One late night while snacking on a freshly baked chocolate chip walnut cookie, Betty came up with a scheme, a way Linda could find out a little more about Alcide and whether or not he was the man she should spend the rest of her life with. Betty knew that Alcide's ex-wife occasionally purchased Avon products, so she suggested that Linda take some Avon catalogues and go directly to the source.

Linda felt a rush of adrenaline at the thought of investigating and getting to the heart of the matter. She hoped that she might receive valuable information while making a connection with another woman Alcide had once loved, all while offering up some common-place Avon products.

Even though she had already accepted Alcide's proposal, she knew something was not quite right with him. She felt it her duty before going any further with the relationship to embrace Betty's plan.

"Ding-dong, Avon calling!" Linda announced outside the door of Gloria's tiny bungalow. Alcide's ex-wife let Linda inside her meagre, run-down living space and was happy to take the Avon catalogue that Linda offered. She put the tea kettle on, and even though Linda did not drink tea, she gladly accepted.

Linda was able to make idle chit-chat, talking about the weather, her job at the bank, eventually asking Gloria what she did for a living.

She opened up immediately and said, "I am a single mom with two beautiful boys and barely getting by because my cheap ex-husband is a good-for-nothing louse."

Before Linda could respond, Gloria went on to say, "Maybe you have seen him around town. He is kind of a big-shot around here, thinks he's the cat's meow!"

Linda had been raised with honesty being the best policy, so she had to come clean, not about being a fake Avon Lady, but more so what her connection was with Alcide. She said, "Gloria, Alcide has asked me to marry him, and I feel there is something not quite right about him. Could you please tell me a little bit about him, if you don't mind?"

After a long pause, Gloria's words were direct and straightforward. She said, "Don't do it." Just then, the kettle started to blow its whistle, and Linda almost jumped out of her skin. While pouring the tea, Gloria explained that Alcide had anger issues and an obsession with guns. He could be wonderful at times and then suddenly slip into a cantankerous and nasty mood.

Linda instantly thought of his lunch kit behind his truck's seat, the one that kept his pistol. Just thinking of the potentially dangerous contents gave Linda a reason to cringe. She realized right then and there that his behaviour was indeed sometimes like a boiling pot about to lose its lid.

Linda broke it off with Alcide without explaining why. She was once again single, and she did not mind it in the least.

Many years later, Linda found out that Alcide had murdered his next-door neighbour, which made her feel light-headed that she almost walked down the aisle with a killer. When all was said and done, it was discovered that the murder was in self-defence, and no charges had been laid. At this point, Linda could not see into the future, and all she could see in the present time was how Alcide's ex-wife lived in poverty and how he ostensibly neglected his children. Everything she learned from her fake Avon visit was a wake-up call and her saving grace.

Gut instinct is an immediate understanding of something that does not require thinking over. You just know. Linda learned that trusting her intuition was the ultimate act of trusting herself. After breaking up with Alcide, she wondered if she should quit her job at the bank, say goodbye to her friends, and go home. On instinct, she chose to stay a little longer in Kamloops, the place she loved to live.

Linda had always been in awe of the mountains and the effect that the sun's glow had on them, creating soft, green-and-gold hues. It was an easy decision for her and Betty to attend an upcoming rodeo in Clinton, scheduled for the fast-approaching weekend. The setting there in the mountains was very inviting.

The sights and sounds, mixed with the dusty aroma of sweaty riders, wranglers, and ropers, had not changed. Linda was thrilled to be single and unattached, footloose and fancy-free, surrounded by leather saddles and dry, golden straw, a scent that could easily be bottled and quickly sold to the highest bidder, in her opinion. They planned to watch the rodeo, eat some great food, dance with a few cowboys, and have some good, clean fun.

While Linda and Betty sat in the stands, enjoying the barrel races, a handsome cowboy caught Linda's attention, a man she could not take her eyes off. He was a calf roper. This timed event required the rider to catch the calf by throwing a loop of rope from a lariat around its neck, dismount from the horse, run to the calf, and restrain it by tying three legs together in as short a time as possible.

Barrel racing has long been a favourite event in the rodeo world and one of the fastest. While cowboys are holding down bucking and spinning bulls, cowgirls on horses are charging through the gate in a race against the clock. The faster the rider completes circling three barrels in a cloverleaf formation, the higher up on the leaderboard horse and rider will be.

The race begins with the rider entering the arena at a full-on gallop and running towards the first barrel. The rider then steers her horse toward barrel two, circles it, and charges toward barrel three. After rounding barrel three, the rider pushes her horse toward the finish line at top speed. The goal is to negotiate the cloverleaf pattern in the fastest time without knocking over any barrels.

The pent-up energy and excitement of bronco busting, calf roping, and barrel racing had the crowds in the stands cheering and on the edge of their seats.

While the audience was hooting and hollering, David Coldwell looked up to the bleachers and instantly caught Linda's eye. As he became infatuated with her, she was doing the same with him.

Jumping over the corral fencing, he made his way up to where Linda was sitting. He introduced himself, and they spent the rest of the afternoon watching the rodeo and getting to know each other. David offered to buy Linda and Betty dinner, but Betty chose to decline. She could see the apparent sparks flying and thought it best for them to be alone. "Besides," she whispered to Linda, "I am so glad you are already over and done with Alcide. This guy seems to be a considerable improvement."

After dinner, despite just meeting, Linda and David held hands as they made their way around the horse trailers and festivities. Heading towards the dance hall, who should they happen to run into but Alcide, and he was not looking pleased. Before any greetings, Alcide laid into Linda. He was hollering at her that she needed to take him back and demanding she go with him that instant.

Sensing Alcide's hostility, David put his arm around Linda's shoulder and said, "This lovely lady is with me, so I reckon you oughta back off buster, or else!"

David's words made Linda's heart melt, and apparently caused Alcide to re-think his ultimatum to Linda.

If one were to describe David, the definition would be a man's man. At least, that is how Linda saw him. Linda quickly learned that it was known to all that nobody messed with David Coldwell. He stood straight-backed and confident, but deep down inside, he was shy and a real gentleman.

David's friends would lovingly tease him about being a Hoss Cartwright look-alike but a much younger version. Everyone knew that he was a very kind soul and a gifted horseman, educated in farm and country life, just like the television character from the popular hit television show that Linda tuned in regularly to watch. She also noticed and loved how the Coldwell name was similar to Cartwright, her treasured family from *Bonanza*. Linda had fallen in love, and not just with David.

After meeting his whole family, she began visiting the Coldwell ranch in Jesmond every weekend after that. Jesmond is a ranching community in the South Cariboo region of the Interior of British Columbia. It is located west of Clinton on the road from Kelly Lake.

The family's ancestor was Harry Coldwell, who was born in England in 1882 and moved to Vancouver in the spring of 1913. After two seasons, he moved to Ashcroft to hopefully get away from the damp, rainy climate. Harry appreciated the dryer weather and spent a few years building houses at Gang Ranch and Dog Creek. In 1914, Harry bought a place called Mountain House and in 1919, he changed the name from Mountain House to Jesmond, after the English town he was born in. By 1921, Jesmond had a store, gas station, and post office. After Harry died in 1970, his son Pete took over and then passed it down to his son Raymond in the 1980s.

The Coldwell Ranch has been inducted into the BC Cowboy Hall of Fame as a Century Ranch, and Charlie Coldwell, who now runs it, has continued the family tradition of guiding, trapping, and ranching. He was recognized as a Working Cowboy by the Hall of Fame as well.

Linda fit right in, and the whole family admired her. She rode the range with the fellas, worked in the barns, and even helped to mend fences.

David and Linda were always together. She surreptitiously marvelled at how much David was like the popular movie actor Dan Blocker, who played the character Hoss Cartwright on *Bonanza*. She understood why others thought so too. Linda's heart sped up every time David entered the room, and his affection and big bear hugs were unlike any love, respect, or admiration she had ever experienced.

As soon as the bank closed on Friday afternoons, Linda took off to Jesmond, the Coldwell Ranch, the horses, and David. The weekend was filled with laughter around the supper table, card games, and hours of tending to the animals. They got out for a ride whenever the chores were done.

Every Sunday night after a big family dinner, Linda's heart ached on the drive back to Kamloops until they could all be together again the following weekend. During the week, David would often write her endearing letters and short notes that were simple and informative and always very sweet.

The Coldwell Ranch was also a popular destination for wild game hunters from all over the world, which was a very lucrative enterprise.

Linda was interested to learn that wild game is classified into three categories: small birds, like thrush and quail; game proper, a category subdivided into winged birds like goose, duck, grouse and partridge, and includes ground game like squirrel or rabbit; and big game, which is mostly venison, deer, elk, moose, caribou, bear, and wild boar. Back in the '50s, '60s, '70s, and '80s, game trophy hunting was also a prominently accepted activity and still is in many parts of the world.

Walking into the Coldwell's living room, one felt they were being watched by the many disembodied animal heads mounted on every wall space. Cougars, leopards, deer, and bears adorned the house in all of their massive glory; stuffed heads, furry faces, glistening eyes, and sharp, jagged teeth, forever frozen in time. If thoughts could still circulate their brains, they would have high-tailed it back outside into the uninhabited, uncultivated region of vastness. Instead, they were proudly placed as trophies by the handiwork of a taxidermist.

Linda did not partake in hunting, but she certainly enjoyed a moose stew or wild deer meat roasts every Sunday night before she went back to Kamloops.

Ranch life consumed Linda, and she had begun to hit it off with David's mother, Mrs. Joyce Coldwell, also the local teacher at Big Bar School. She had a romantic, old-fashioned marriage, and Linda appreciated her, as well as her husband. Joyce and Linda had developed a unique bond. They both struggled with their weight. Or rather, longed to be a different size.

They shared recipes, dieting tips, and their love of the wild game the ranchers hunted and killed for food and sport. Linda and Joyce were both off and on with the healthy Weight Watchers diet plan, but they both wanted a quick fix, so they were frequently in discussion and tried many fad diets, just like millions of others.

Back in 1959, one of the first fad diets to hit North America was Metrecal. It was advertised as "Satisfying Food for Weight Control," which consisted of a chalky, protein-rich powder, a drink that was to be consumed four times per day. The product line expanded to include clam chowder and cookies.

SEGO was a meal-replacement shake that hit the market in 1961, along with dozens of other diet drinks that filled the shelves in the early part of the decade. Next up was Carnation Instant Breakfast, not necessarily for dieters but more of a breakfast on the go for busy students, homemakers, and those on the run. Later they cashed in on the dieting market and came up with Carnation's Slender, sold as a weight-loss food.

Wanting in on the trend, Pillsbury brought out diet bars. "Diet Candy" was also a thing back in the day. One of the most controversial diet plans was called the Drinking Man's Diet, essentially a low-carb diet supplemented in part by a liquid lunch that consisted of alcohol. In 1964 the book sold two million copies.

Other drinking diets included Dr. Herman Taller's Safflower Oil Plan and another that asked one only to consume six glasses of buttermilk a day. The sale of diet pills was on the rise and even made Life Magazine's cover in 1968. Diet Pills such as Dexatrim had started to replace drinks, selling well throughout the 1970s.

Over a game of scrabble one evening, Linda and Joyce decided to go on a diet together. They thought the buddy system might help them both to stay on track. They had individually tried the Atkins Diet, The Sexy Pineapple Diet, and the Grapefruit Diet but thought the latest diet being flouted might be the ticket.

The Egg and Wine diet was first popularized in Helen Gurley Brown's book, *Sex and the Single Girl: The Unmarried Woman's Guide to Men*. The diet advocated three-five eggs per day plus a twenty-four-ounce bottle of wine. For breakfast, one egg and a glass of wine, for lunch, two eggs and another drink and then for dinner, a steak and the rest of the wine bottle.

With Linda being a non-drinker and working nine to five, she only lasted two days and had to opt out of the diet, as it just made her sick. She thought that perhaps that was how one would lose weight, throwing it all up. She laughed at the thought of it, as all food was far too enjoyable, and never in a million years would Linda force it out when she delighted in putting it in.

The Wine and Egg Diet bonus was that Joyce lost four pounds, and Linda lost ten, only for the lost weight to all come back on shortly after the diet ended, with an additional few more pounds on top of that. Medical experts eventually warned against the diet as being nutritionally unbalanced, unsustainable and, in the long run, doing more harm than good. The high alcohol content of the diet has been described as dangerous and a threat to the liver.

Linda's weight loss had developed a yo-yo effect. When she was happy and living her life with horses and a gorgeous cowboy boyfriend, her weight was manageable. When she was unhappy and lonely, she gained weight without her even noticing how it happened.

Linda and David had become an item, and there was only one thing that was getting in their way. That was their age difference. David was nineteen, and Linda was twenty-five. She was not bothered by it in the least, but over time, David was.

His mother and father were expectant for all their children to work the ranch and, when the time was right, find a mate, get married, and settle down to have children. Procreation was a vast topic of discussion with David and his mother, Joyce. Unfortunately, Linda rarely joined in the talk because she could not see herself as a mother—possibly a wife, but she still wanted a career and a life of ranching and everything Western. Linda was not afraid to be shovelling manure and fixing fences. In fact, she relished the work and felt it to be a fun and rewarding activity.

After a year of dating, Linda began to sense that something was brewing and not quite right with David. As she lived her dream life, David was becoming withdrawn, with other things obviously on his mind. He was not opening up to Linda, so she carried on hoping and pretending that everything was okay.

The Clinton May Ball was fast approaching, and the decorating and organizing had been going on for weeks. The whole town came together to spruce up the streets and deck out the businesses and community hall.

When the first ball was held in 1868 on New Year's Day, Clinton was a remote outpost. The historical event withstood the hands of time and has continued ever since. The historical photographs and documents depict and describe local ladies planning and ordering gowns from Victoria, San Francisco, and even Europe. Some women changed several times during the evening and were delighted as their male counterparts stood by their sides as debonair gentlemen in broadcloth suits.

Getting to the earlier balls was an adventure—journeys that went on for many days in conditions of drifting snow and treacherous conditions. However, after 1914 the PGE Railroad offered a far less complicated way for some attendees to get to the festivities. The balls first took place in the Clinton Hotel and then moved to the Clinton Memorial Hall as the event expanded in popularity.

This year Linda had purchased a whole new outfit. She felt sharp in her frilly Western blouse, dress pants, and shiny new bedazzled cowboy boots. She backcombed and loaded on the hair spray to her dark hair, just the way David liked it.

While she was waiting for David to pick her up, Linda felt the stirrings of excitement for the upcoming weekend. As she was admiring herself in the mirror, she heard David's familiar knock. Two soft taps followed by two louder raps.

She ran to the door, ready to embrace the love of her life, only to have the embrace not reciprocated. With head bowed, standing in the doorway, David looked sad and gloomy. Speaking faintly, just above a whisper, he said, "I have to break up with you. I cannot get over our age difference, and I can only see myself with a wife and lots of children. I know you and I both want different things."

Linda was speechless. Who knew that life could be so momentous? The morning can start like any other; by nightfall, things can occur that can change the course forever. She knew that it was unreasonable to expect to be happy all the time, but Linda had been on a perpetual high for the last year since meeting David.

And now he was gone. He just walked away and right out of her life. One year to the day of meeting him.

Linda quickly realized that everything would come to a grinding halt—togetherness, family dinners, riding, working the land, and weekend rodeos. The only earth-shattering romance Linda had ever experienced was over. Consequently, there would not be a May Ball and the gaiety that went with it. *How could she go now?* she reasoned. No way could she attend alone when the entire town knew that she and David were a steady couple. Now they were no longer an admired pair, a twosome, a team.

The spring air was abnormally frigid that following Monday morning, and it wrapped like a cold blanket around her pickup truck. Linda took the windshield scraper that her father had given her and, through tears, chipped away at the ice on the front, side, and back windows. After she put the key in the ignition, instantly the radio came on, blaring the popular hit love song, "How Sweet it Is to be Loved by You" by James Taylor. She abruptly turned the radio off and sighed.

In the frigid silence encapsulated in the cab of the truck, Linda was still in shock. She was chilled to the bone like the earth outside, and even her heart seemed frosted and numb. Her only solution was to get away.

After the breakup, on Monday morning, she quit her job at the bank. Reluctantly packing and loading up her truck, all she could think of was going home to her parents in Stave Falls, Mission. She reassured herself that Kamloops, Cache Creek, Clinton, Williams Lake, her friends and rodeos were only a few hours away. The Williams Lake Rodeo was coming up, and Linda planned on being there without her boyfriend of twelve months.

On the drive back to Mission, she reminisced of her time with David, riding the range, and their secret kisses in the barns. Linda had thought they would always be together, and she assumed they both felt the same way. They had soared to the highest heights, and now she alone was plunging to the deepest depths.

She recalled the scent of leather saddles, wool blankets, and dusty golden hay. All the times she had buried her face in a horse's mane and breathed in the smell of its dark, rooty nature, remembering how the flinty undertones could last for an entire day.

And then there was David, as Western as they come.

Smiling as she careened down the highway, she allowed herself to have one last memory of his loving, strong embrace under a jet-black night sky with a million stars looking down. They had both agreed and interpreted their brilliant twinkling to be a million approving smiles shining down on them.

The trip home proved to be a time of regrouping.

She wondered if she should have pleaded more for them to stay together, which also meant throwing all caution to the wind and becoming a woman she did not want to be. For the sake of not losing David, Linda questioned if she should have succumbed to a life of motherhood, house cleaning, endless loads of laundry, and big Sunday dinners, meals that traditionally only the household's women prepared and cleaned up afterwards. The bottom line was knowing she could not deprive David of fatherhood, grandchildren for his parents, and passing on the Coldwell name.

After sobbing for most of the drive, she caught her breath and finally stopped. Blinking her eyes and willing her tears to cease their insistent dripping, swallowing the burning lump in her throat, she made her first attempt to block David from her mind. Just outside the city limits of Mission, Linda gassed up and climbed back into her pickup truck. Still stifling the tears, she suddenly developed a raging headache.

Linda needed to make another stop. She purchased two bulk-sized red licorice bags, four small Jello Instant Pudding boxes, and a few chocolate bars—comfort food to look forward to once she got home and seemingly much more effective than aspirin.

You know you are finished grieving a breakup when you think about the person, and your memories bring peace instead of pain. Linda knew it would be a while before she could feel any kind of peace over David's decision to dissolve their relationship.

In the meantime, she would stay busy and not stand still to feel the stabbing pain and the breaking of her heart. Her gut told her that nothing would ever be as good as it was, and no one would ever make her feel like David had.

A few miles from her parent's property, she had another gut instinct. Even though she was miserable, Linda dug deep into her soul and felt a glimmer of hope that just maybe there could be good things on the horizon for her.

First and foremost, she would try to get her job back at the bank in North Vancouver and use her father's barn and fill it with horses.

Students from the Big Bar school house

Linda's apartment

Linda riding at the Grinder Ranch

Fun times at the Photobooth

Karen riding at the Grinder Ranch

Karen and Vince

CHAPTER THIRTEEN

Losing Love and Winning Big

"Learn to hear your inner voice, be led by your heart, and never stop giving back —
this way, you shall always walk the right path and shall never be walking alone."

-Aleksej Metelko

1975 was the year of fads and fashion statements—mood rings, pet rocks, and Rubik's Cube; bellbottoms, hip-huggers, and leisure suits. Everybody owned 8-track tapes, and disco was in full swing.

The song of the year was "Love Will Keep Us Together" by Captain and Tennille. Simultaneously, musical groups such as 10cc, the Bee Gees, Earth, Wind & Fire, and Queen were in the top 40 radio requests. Anne Murray and Oscar Peterson each won a Grammy. Paul Anka released "Times of Your Life," and Joni Mitchell, "The Hissing of Summer Lawns."

Hit films at the theatre, such as *One Flew Over the Cuckoo's Nest*, *Jaws*, *Nashville*, and *Dog Day Afternoon*, were popular must-see movies. However, the Western movie that everyone was waiting for was *Rooster Cogburn* with John Wayne and Katherine Hepburn, which was also the sequel to Linda's favourite film, the Oscar-winning *True Grit*.

The most-watched television shows were *Sanford and Son*; *Welcome Back, Kotter*; *Happy Days*; *All in the Family*; and *The Waltons*. For action and suspense, people tuned in to *Gunsmoke*, *Adam-12*, *Mannix*, *Kolchak: The Night Stalker*, and *Ironside*.

Margaret Thatcher was the first woman elected to lead Britain's Conservative Party. Pierre Elliot Trudeau was the prime minister of Canada. The United States president was Gerald Ford, and the Vietnam War ended on April 30, 1975.

The world was turning, and Linda felt as though she was standing still. She missed David but knew that she needed to keep moving forward, whether she felt like it or not. The night she arrived home, she noticed an envelope on the kitchen table. Inside was the ticket she had purchased for two dollars for the Lucky Leo Lottery. It was a charity event that she bought a ticket for every year.

The bank in North Vancouver was happy to take Linda back. Since her parents and little sister lived in the log home and both brothers would eventually be building houses on the adjacent properties, it felt like Walton's Mountain now with herself at home. In this favourite television show, an entire family lived together. Vince was happy as a clam, and Frances wondered why everyone in her life preferred the country to the city's excitement.

In the early 1970s, the national office of the Canadian Union of Postal Workers instigated an illegal strike for better wages. An arbitrator awarded female postal workers the same salaries as male employees. Also, in 1975, a forty-three-day legal strike occurred, which ended on December 2, 1975. Postal workers were promised job security and protection of full-time jobs. During the postal strike, a telephone call came through for Linda, stating that she had won $5,000.00 in the Lucky Leo Early Bird Draw. Linda had won the lottery with the ticket that was waiting for her when she arrived home.

The night before the call, she had a dream that she won something, so she was half expecting it when the call came through from the BC Lottery Federation. Because of the mail strike, they would not be mailing her a cheque and also because of the postal strike, Linda could not take time off work to pick it up, so her brother Ken picked up the $5,000.00 winnings for her in a cheque form.

The next day, Linda bought a brand new mobile home to put on the five acres of land her mom and dad had gifted to her. When the trailer arrived, everyone in the family marvelled at its newness and pristine style. It was complete with wall panelling, shag carpeting, front room bay windows, a three-piece kitchen, luxurious bathroom, and two bedrooms at one end, hers with a sliding glass mirrored closet—state of the art and top of the line.

Even though Linda was happy over her winnings and brand-spanking-new home, she was still hurting and chose not to share her heartbreak over David with anyone. So she bypassed the grieving process of their breakup and began to replace her pain with food, a pattern that had always worked in the past.

Many experts say that overeating is usually not about the food but more about our feelings and the desperate desire to run from them. Linda was from the generation where children were told to stop crying, or they would be given something to cry about. Girls especially were instructed to smile through thick and thin and were always expected to look pretty.

For most people, the challenging part about going through heartache is the feeling lousy part. But for Linda, food had become her safety net and saving grace. Therefore, the extended periods of feeling lousy never came, or they would be quickly filled with roast beef and gravy and Duncan Hines cake mixes.

As her weight crept up, Linda spent her time working at the bank, and when at home, she tended to the horse she purchased and at the same time, she won the Lucky Leo Draw. Happy Jack was the name she chose for her beautiful new horse.

Happy Jack was seventeen hands high. He was a white Appaloosa beauty and carried Linda's weight stoically. When riding the range or going on trail rides, Linda had often exclaimed that she needed a bigger horse, one that could carry her safely and adequately, mostly for the horse's sake.

Wanting to keep herself as busy as possible, she came up with a remarkable idea and created a riding club for all the neighbourhood kids, called the Rolley Lake Trail Riders, named after a lake in the area. She noticed so many young people riding their horses up and down Dewdney Trunk Road, and the idea came to her that by using all of her dude ranch experience, and also because her sister was new in the area, she could create an activity that would be an excellent pastime for Karen, her new friends, and other local people in Stave Falls.

Even with work, television, and organizing the riding club, Linda still found time for socializing. Bernie and Peter, her parents' neighbours, quickly became her friends too, regardless of what went on behind closed doors. Long before homosexuality was acknowledged or spoken about, it was apparent that Bernie and Peter were a couple. Still, everything about their relationship was hush-hush and never talked about by them or anyone else.

Missing her rodeo days in the Cariboo and evenings at the Arlington in Vancouver, Linda was thrilled to find out that her new friends enjoyed dancing. She, therefore, organized Saturday night trips across the border to a small Western-oriented town called Sumas, which was only a thirty-minute drive from the property.

With friends from the bank, as well as Bernie and Peter, Linda acted as the designated driver—reminiscent of driving all the cowboys who wanted to drink and not break the law or damage their vehicles, or worse, kill themselves or others.

Bernie was the more feminine one in his relationship, slim and well dressed in his usual Levi jeans, tucked-in dress shirt, beaded Western belt, shiny sequined cowboy boots, and a childlike, red straw cowboy hat, kept secure by a drawstring underneath his chin.

He and Linda had become best buddies and dance partners. Together they twirled and gyrated on the dance floor as a couple, with Bernie often requesting that Linda lead.

Linda's new confidante openly commented on her other dance partners and was happy to give her dating advice. Often when she was asked to dance, she would glance at Bernie and look for the thumbs up or the thumbs down, as the go-ahead indication that the guy was okay or not okay. Often the deciding factor was based on whether Linda's would-be dance partner was a hunk or a dud, and Bernie's indication sealed the deal as to whether she accepted or rejected the request.

Linda named one of her horses Sumas Dancer in honour of the fun times she had with her new friends in the small US town of the same name.

Karen was fourteen going on fifteen, and Linda was twenty-seven going on twenty-eight, sisters worlds apart but related by blood, their interest in horses, and their father's love. The timing was perfect for the riding club because Karen was in Grade 10 and had many friends in the area, all of whom became members of Linda's club. They held monthly meetings, had mini rodeos called Playdays, and Frances and Vince joined in the fun.

Vince had come across a set of bleachers during one of his lot clearing side jobs, so he placed the tiered seating arrangement next to the corral for the viewing audience. Just like a real rodeo, the crowds from the stands could cheer, hoot, and holler. At the same time, kids of all ages engaged in barrel races, musical sacks, and partnered events.

Frances made hotdogs and sold bottles of pop, with the proceeds going to the riding club. People from all over Stave Falls attended the monthly event. Young and old alike were encouraged to come out. If someone did not own a horse, Linda made a point of sharing the horses she owned.

Before winter that year, it had been decided the Rolley Lake Trail Riders would hold a year-end dance. Vince was enlisted to build a dance floor on Linda's property, adjacent to the barn and one of the trout ponds. Neighbours came from miles around to enjoy some foot-stomping dance tunes and the wind up for the club until next spring.

It was a time of family, friends, horses, and fun. From the outside looking in, everything was hunky-dory. It was at this time

Linda took up with a much younger man. His youthfulness and good looks reminded her of David. He was interested in horses and was young enough that Linda blatantly refused to get hurt. A fling was all she was interested in.

Winter turned into early spring, and one Sunday afternoon, after the trail riders had wrapped up their first meeting of the season, the shrill of Linda's telephone took over the silence of her trailer. She was just settling in to watch back-to-back episodes of *Barnaby Jones* with Buddy Ebsen and Lee Meriwether, followed by *Columbo* with Peter Faulk, when the piercing ring made Linda jump, almost not answering for fear of missing her shows. Curiosity got the better of her, and after picking up the receiver, she heard Betty's kind, familiar voice, wanting to know if Linda was coming up to Clinton for the May Ball and Rodeo.

Immediately Linda froze. She so wanted to go and yet was afraid of running into David. At the same time, she was secretly hoping to see him again, and that just like any romance novel, their eyes would meet, their bodies would embrace, and all would be well again. Throwing all caution to the wind, Linda responded, "Yes, absolutely, Betty, I wouldn't miss it for the world." With the ball still one month away, Linda could hardly wait.

In the meantime, she began dieting and needed to get the Rolley Lake Trail Riders ready for the Cloverdale Rodeo. They had signed up to be in the parade and had nominated a Miss Rolley Lake Trail Riders and two Princesses. The voting was a challenge since Linda's sister Karen was in the running, and it would not look fair if she were chosen. It turned out that she was not.

A pretty and down-to-earth girl named Norma now carried the title of Miss Rolley Lake Trail Riders. It was unanimous. Norma rode Linda's horse Happy Jack and was a poised and gifted rider, popular at both her school and the riding club.

The Cloverdale Rodeo and Country Fair in Cloverdale, British Columbia, was first held in September 1888 at the Surrey Municipal Hall. It was moved to the Cloverdale Fairgrounds in 1938. It is now held annually at the Cloverdale Fairgrounds during the Victoria Day holiday weekend, from Friday to Monday. Linda made a point of attending every year, dating back to when she lived in North Vancouver.

Even though rodeos are a historical part of Western entertainment, they are also a target for animal rights activists, who believe that all the rodeo events are physically abusive activities and terrorize the animals involved in the action.

However, due to the nature of the rodeo, bringing cowboys and cowgirls worldwide to compete, the controversy was never mentioned or discussed in the small circle of riders that Linda managed. The Rolley Lake Trail Riders were a group of teenagers with nothing much to do, getting together to enjoy their horses and, as Linda often referred to it, have some "good, clean fun." It was planned that after the parade, the whole gang would enjoy the rodeo, midway, rides, games, and greasy traditional fair food.

All the while, Linda could barely concentrate. She wanted to be there, but all she could think about was the following weekend in Clinton. She had missed last year's May Ball due to unforeseen and heartbreaking circumstances, but this time it would be different. Nothing could get in her way or stop her from going. Until then, there she was with a dozen teenagers in a parade—fresh-faced girls and a few select boys, with their horses all saddled up and ready to prance and show off.

Before the Cloverdale Rodeo and Parade, there had been great preparation. The riders had practiced their parade formation after school and on weekends. Eagerly they shopped for matching Western shirts, new jeans, and everyone spent time polishing their boots. The horses were perfectly groomed, and the lead-up preparations brought fun and unity for the Rolley Lake Trail Riders.

It was easy to see and feel everyone's excitement, and for Linda, that made the event entirely worthwhile. Besides, she knew that a commitment was a commitment, and Linda never faltered when she had a responsibility.

After the parade, she planned to be packed and ready to high-tail it up to Clinton to unite with her old friends and have a weekend of sheer fun. The motel in Clinton was booked, all her compadres had been alerted, and her suitcase had been packed for weeks.

Like air being released from a slashed tire, Linda's excitement came to a grinding halt and was completely deflated on the Wednesday before the long weekend. When she arrived home from work, there was a letter waiting for her on her doorstep.

Karen had a few after-school jobs, washing and delivering eggs to a few people down the street and collecting the mail from the rural route post office box. A rusty old lock held the mail in the confines of its rickety hinged door, and was often a struggle to open, but the excitement of receiving mail was worth the challenge.

It had become a ritual for Karen to drop Linda's mail off on her trailer's front porch. On this particular day, she made her way next door, over the homemade bridge extending across her father's trout pond, visiting her horse at the barn on the way, and dropping a beautifully handwritten envelope on her sister's doorstep. Thinking nothing of it, she made her way back across the bridge and home to settle into her favourite after-school program called *Phil Donahue* with her mom.

Linda's ego, hopes, and spirits were dashed when she opened the letter to reveal a newspaper clipping, with no note attached, just a grainy black and white photo of David appearing handsome and happy next to a woman Linda had never seen before. Underneath in bold font, all it said was, **To Be Married....** Linda did not bother to read the adjoining press release.

Something her dad had taught her was to never give up, and she could hear her mother's voice ringing in her ears, stemming back to the constant bullying from her tormentors as a little girl, telling her to hold her head high and walk with confidence.

Linda chose to do both. Leaving after the Cloverdale Parade, she kept her plans and headed to Clinton. Aside from her knight in shining armour officially being attached to another woman, Linda held her head high while wandering around the fairgrounds, watching the rodeo, and confidently dancing to live music with her friends to her heart's content.

She was dressed to the nines and made a point to be her usual friendly self with men and women alike. She felt happy and carefree just being there, aside from the slight twinge of nagging pain in her heart.

The longer she and David had been apart, the more perfect he had become in her memory.

The Saturday morning before the Clinton rodeo and May Ball, Linda was up early for breakfast and decided to check out the horses in the barns. Little did she know that she was very close to being arrested!

She had been persuaded to give up her motel room because one of her friends had brought a cowboy back to the room for a roll in the hay. Instead of a hayloft, they needed the comforts of a motel room, which meant Linda needed to stay somewhere else. This was not a problem, and there were no hard feelings because Linda knew many people and quickly made arrangements to stay with another friend.

The next day, the newly acquainted couple grabbed the bedspread off the bed to use as a blanket to cuddle in while they watched the rodeo from the stands. When the housekeeping service came to clean the room, it was noted that the lime green, floral-print bedspread was missing. After the front desk was alerted, it was determined that the paying guest was Linda Bonner. The small-town police were alerted by the motel manager and were sent in search of Linda and the missing bedspread.

Strolling around the fairgrounds, two officers spotted Linda, and when they approached her, they recognized her as Lynn, the friendly bank teller from a while back.

The motel owner who had accompanied the police said, "Dammit all anyway, that's Lynn! She ain't no thief!"

Linda was able to explain the situation, the bed covering was retrieved, and all was forgiven. Laughs were shared all around.

That night at the May Ball, the season's event brought out every cowboy, ranch hand, farmer, family, and city person from miles around. Folks of all ages were in attendance, and Linda was once again known as Lynn to all.

Partway through the evening, one of her friends spotted David sitting at a long table with his new fiancé. Strewn about them on the paper tablecloth were empty cups and beer cans, paper plates laden with white buttered buns, sliced ham, and half-eaten potato salad. Dirty napkins sat crumpled, and cigarette butts were smashed into the dried-up egg bits—all a typical sight at any country dance.

As the cigarette smoke wafted up into the rafters and blaring music made it impossible to carry on a lengthy conversation, one of her friends insisted she go over and ask David to dance, being completely unaware of the pain that Linda was dealing with. It was the last thing she wanted to do, but because of her happy-go-lucky nature and ability to push down her true feelings, she followed her friend's suggestion. Knowing her scarred heart and well-kept secret would never be revealed, off she went.

As one friend was dragging Linda over to David's table, the other friend pulled David up and onto the dance floor. The fiancé was none the wiser and seemingly not jealous. She smiled warmly as she threw a few cheezies in her mouth, followed by a swig of beer, entirely unscathed to see her husband-to-be dancing with his ex-girlfriend, Lynn, friend to everyone and loved by all.

Embarrassed but stoic, Linda accepted the waltz and trembled in David's arms. She wondered how suddenly they were together again—but not really. Biting the inside of her cheek to prevent herself from crying, she fought a paralyzed anxiety in her throat that prevented her from speaking.

Neither of them said a word.

It had only been a year since David had broken up with her, twelve months since she had fled Clinton, and 365 days of weight gain with only a month of effort to lose it all, or perhaps more realistically, at least drop a few pounds.

When the dance finished, Linda looked deeply into David's eyes, and she thought for just a fleeting moment she could detect a look of regret, of longing and wishing too that things could be different. Tipping his cowboy hat, David nodded and went back to his table and his soon-to-be bride.

If only she could freeze the moment, Linda thought. Or better yet, turn back the hands of time to a year ago when they were a contented, compatible couple. If she could have a second chance, she might have given in to marriage, pregnancy, cooking, and cleaning—the whole nine yards.

Instead, she let her mind wander and wondered if she would ever meet another man who was as caring, kind, handsome, and fun as David.

When the last horse trailer's gate was shut, and the hungover, prize-winning cowboys were all loaded up, goodbyes were had all around until the next rodeo and the next town.

Arriving back at the property in Stave Falls, her mobile home, horses, bank job, and family, Linda realized she had it pretty good. All she needed to do was fill in the gaping hole in her heart. She got busy doing that right away. Food, television, and something totally out of character, one-night stands—seemingly adequate tools to forget David, the only man she had ever loved.

Linda and David   *David Caldwell*

Linda and little Darin with Sumas dancer

Linda with David's niece at the ranch in Jesmond

Linda, David's niece and David

David

David and Linda goofing around

David working the ranch

Sept. 11, 1972

Dear Lynne,
      Just a quick this morning before I go to work. I wondered if you would pick me up a pair of navy pants, size 38" waist 30" leg. I was going to order them from the catologue but that usually takes about a month. Well I guess I better go, Charlie is sitting all excited to get to work. Where going to Mc Coulogh again today so I better go. See you friday.

                                    Love
                                    Dave

Clinton, B.C.
July 19/72

Dear Lynne;

Just time for a couple lines before I go to work. Haven't been up to much this week. Cut some hay monday but it rained nearly all day yesterday.

Did Jo-ann and Kenny go to Green Lake or what are they up to. I don't think Kenny was feeling to good on sunday. he a little rough.

Please excuse my sloppy writing but this writing letters at 7A.M is a little hard. My brain is still asleep.

Dad was over to Kamloops yesterday. Had to get some tractor parts.

Well this is a pretty short letter but I can't think of anything else so I guess I had better sign off. So be good and write some day when you get time.

Love
Dave

Clinton, B.C.
Aug 8/72

Dear Lynne

Thought I had better scratch off a few lines this afternoon before I forget and miss the mailman again. I've got the whole place to myself today. Everybody is away. Dads gone to Kamloops, Charlie & Carol are in town, so its pretty quite around here.

I just got home a few minutes ago. I've been out fighting fire since 6 A.M. over by Stable Creek. (making entry fees for Barnhartvale)

We got Henny's hay all finished last night so I guess he can go back to his mrs. any time now.

I have to go into town on friday so you won't have to come all the way out here to pick me up. So I will meet you in town around six o'clock at Marcels Places. If that isn't alright you can phone me some evening around 6 or 7 o'clock and let me know different. well I have some work to do so I guess I better get with it. So will see you friday night if I don't hear different from you. Be good.

Love Dave

Clinton B.C.
Oct. 12, 1972

Dear Lynne,

Figured I had better sit down and write to you right now before I forgot again. I haven't been doing much this week so far. I helped Gene move some cows today but that's about all. I think I'll go to town tomorrow and get my hair cut and a few other odds & ends.

Well I have sat here for the last twenty minutes trying to think of something to write about. So if I can't think of anything pretty quick I might as well give up. When it comes to writing letters and talking on the phone I never have to much to say. Well I've sat here for another twenty minutes and still can't think of anything to say so I might as well go to bed. If I think of any thing later I can tell you in person this week-end.

See you friday

Dave

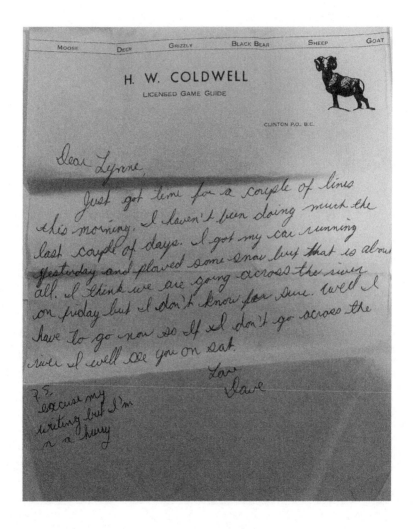

MOOSE   DEER   GRIZZLY   BLACK BEAR   SHEEP   GOAT

H. W. COLDWELL
LICENSED GAME GUIDE

CLINTON P.O., B.C.

Dear Lynne,

Just got time for a couple of lines this morning. I haven't been doing much the last couple of days. I got my car running yesterday and plowed some snow but that is about all. I think we are going across the river on friday but I don't know for sure. Well I have to go now so If I don't go across the river I will see you on sat.

Love
Dave

P.S.
excuse my
writing but I'm
n a hurry

Jan

Dear Lynne.

I thought it was about time I got around to sending yous, your truck key.

I haven't been up to much lately, just got done bear hunting last week. We got one big grizzly.

I didn't win anything in Clinton so I am going to Ashcroft this week-end. Carol & Charlie are going to Williams lake next week I guess.

I haven't seen any guests at @ yet so they haven't been to busy. Darcus hasn't found those three horses yet.

Well I guess I better close and get busy.

Lov
Dave

CHAPTER FOURTEEN

Keeping Busy

*"My wish for you is that you continue. Continue to be who you
are, to astonish a mean world with your acts of kindness."*

–Maya Angelou

Linda thought she was content but could not stop thinking about
the Cariboo. She greatly missed it, and her heart ached from the
very thought of it. Her weight was at an all-time high, and when
thinking about her future, she had a hard time thinking clearly.

Regardless, she continued to love food, and her dalliances with
willing men were no match for the way Swanson's Hungry Man
frozen TV dinners and instant scalloped potatoes made her feel.

When trying to make observations about her life, every
thought felt confusing and discombobulating. And then came
the bad dreams. When she least expected it, the nightmares and
flashbacks would invade Linda's sleep.

She had managed to maneuver around Alcide's temper, and
even though the pain over David's breakup was gut-wrenching,
nothing was as shameful and heartbreaking as her memory of the
attack in the barn a few years back. It was an incident her mother
never spoke of and encouraged Linda to do the same. Therefore,

she never confided in anyone and never divulged that she was not encouraged within her family to open up and talk about bad things.

Her parent's viewpoints were, "Don't rock the boat, keep your head above water, be nice at all costs, and never overthink. And for heaven's sake, smile!"

At night, in the confines of her two-bedroom trailer, when the television was turned off, and her mind was free of tasks, she was haunted by thoughts of that wretched night. The intimate violation. Sometimes it was glaringly vivid, the smothering heaviness of the men pushing down on her, their slurred laughter and lewd comments about her weight—the putrid, stale smell of alcohol on their breath and the sour, musky body odour.

The visions and aromas came back like they had happened yesterday. Linda had read somewhere that the senses of hearing and smell become more acute during an attack. When a body is in a predator's grip, the terror of death and severe injury take over. The body and brain are paralyzed by fear.

She often woke up in the middle of the night, barely able to breathe. Her nightmares caused her wrists to ache from the assailant's grasp as they pinned her down in the barn that night. But in the light of day, her wrists had no bruising and looked just fine.

Linda struggled with the thought of where the horrific incident took place—right there in the barn her dad and brothers had lovingly constructed. It somehow put a stain on the treasure that her family had created with her in mind.

Wincing, she would close her eyes tight and plan what she would make for dinner or recite her upcoming grocery list verbatim. Reaching for a cookie at her bedside table, all would be well as she crunched down, tasting the sweetness and feeling the crumbs powdery and soft on her chin. After making her way to the refrigerator for a diet pop, she would wash away the humiliation with each gulp. Climbing back into bed, she felt comforted and safe again, thankful for the snacks she had planted in drawers and cupboards throughout her trailer.

Going over it in her mind, she could not understand or come to terms with why she had never been attacked before. The men she knew, the ranchers and cowboys of every description, had always treated her so well. Everyone she had met over the years was a complete gentleman towards her. Even the hardcore drinkers never laid a hand or took advantage of her. It was an ever-present question in her mind—"*Why me? Why that moment? Did I do something to invite it?*"

Keeping Busy could have been Linda's middle name. In addition to working at the bank in North Vancouver, managing the Rolley Lake Trail Riders, and dancing on the weekends, she landed a job at the Pacific National Exhibition, a two-week event at the end of August every year.

Linda's banking experience and memorization skills were a huge asset working at the PNE. Her job was in the accounting office, greeting all the vendors to collect daily percentages of their sales. The wages were good, and the job fit in quite nicely with everything else she was doing, as her shifts were 4:00 p.m. until midnight, Monday to Friday. Right after her day ended at the bank, she would drive to her job at the PNE and then home to her trailer on the Mission property.

The city of Mission, BC, is on the Fraser River's north bank, backing onto the mountains and lakes overlooking the Central Fraser Valley eighty kilometres from Vancouver, BC. The township of Mission City began as a land promotion. Properties were auctioned off as part of the "Great Land Sale" on May 19, 1891. Hailed as a new metropolis, the growing and flourishing town was a regular stop for the Canadian Pacific Railway. The name Mission City was chosen due to the site's proximity to the historic St. Mary's Mission Oblate, founded in the 1860s. In 1954, Benedictine monks also obtained land near Mission, setting up their Westminster Abbey and Seminary.

The Strawberry Festival began in 1946 in celebration of the many berry farms, and the town acquired the rights to the Western Canada championship of the Soap Box Derby. They shared

Dominion Day with a significant loggers sports event, one of the largest in British Columbia. Mission's other primary industry was logging, and the town's several mills were noted for being the world's largest suppliers of red cedar shakes and shingles. Mission is also the home of a long-established professional dragstrip called Mission Raceway Park.

Next to the Mission-Maple Ridge boundary, below the Ruskin Dam, was a sizeable drive-in movie theatre, which was only a few miles from the Bonner family property. In addition to evenings at the horse auction in Matsqui, Linda also took some of the young people from the Rolley Lake Trail Riders to the drive-in movie theatre. She had many fond memories of her own, and this allowed her to relive a few. Plus, no one else had a car.

However, with progress comes change, and the theory of out with the old and in with the new was relevant even out in the country. The Ruskin outdoor cinema was to be torn down to make way for a mobile home trailer park. Just before the drive-in movie theatre was to close and show its last double feature, Linda loaded up her car and piled in as many teenagers as she could, reminiscent of the Cascades Drive-In back in the 1960s in Burnaby. Everyone was excited to see *The Outlaw Josey Wales* and *The Enforcer*, both starring Clint Eastwood.

Linda still favoured Western shows over anything else, which was to be put on the back burner when she met her next boyfriend. Arnie was the furthest thing from a cowboy and was more into cars than women. At least, that is the impression Linda got.

He was nowhere near as handsome as David, or even Alcide, for that matter. But he did have a Johnny Cash appeal with black hair parted on the side and thick mutton chop sideburns. He wore glasses and was often well dressed in a blazer and dress pants. Arnie was pleasant and someone to do things with, so Linda took the plunge to have a real, proper boyfriend again.

Up until that point, Linda had only ever been attracted to cowboys, ranchers, and hard-working types, but she decided that driving around in Arnie's 4x4 pickup truck would be easier on her back than riding horses anyway. It was also fun to be picked up in his 1969 Roadrunner after work.

Linda had never dated a car guy before. He was very meticulous and took outstanding care of his two vehicles. All the cowboys Linda had known had also loved their pickup trucks but had cared equally for their women and horses.

She figured that Arnie was so enamoured with cars that he might even dream about them when he was sleeping, which she understood because, for most of her life, she had dreamt about horses. When not driving his car, Arnie would talk about his car. When not talking about his car, he was doing preventative maintenance or repairing it. Something always needed doing—changing the oil, tires, fuses, and radiator hose were just a few duties that Arnie regularly tended to.

Not long into their relationship, Linda noticed that Arnie loved to point out other cars on the road. Just seconds after passing one, he was able to tell her the make and exact model, instantly knowing if the vehicle had four, six, eight, or even twelve cylinders. Afterwards, he would say to her how fast it could go from 0 to 60 mph. Linda listened and smiled as Arnie droned on, wondering if she sounded just as boring when talking about horses to other people. She doubted as much.

Their weekends involved driving around and attending car-related events. They only ate meals at the White Spot and the A & W because both had car-hop service. Linda enjoyed the drive-up meal service, as it was quite the going rage when she was a girl, a fun hang-out in the '60s with her high school friends. She remembered the waitresses sometimes wearing roller skates.

Arnie rarely left his vehicles, as he preferred not to leave them unattended, so a drive-in restaurant was always preferred. Linda never complained, and Arnie enjoyed her quick-witted sense of humour, especially since he did not have one.

However, she eventually acknowledged that she was not the star and centre of Arnie's life, similarly to her cowboy friends with their horses, but at least with them, she shared a common interest.

She doubted that she would ever be head over heels in love with four wheels like she was with four hooves.

After months of dating, Linda did not fall in love with Arnie, as in her mind, no one could hold a candle to David. When she found out that her new boyfriend was cheating on her, she came right out and told him, "I was not looking for a husband anyway."

In turn, Arnie introduced Linda to his other girlfriend and announced that he would be proposing to her. When all was said and done, Arnie's bride Carol and his ex-girlfriend Linda became friends. In retrospect, Linda was pleased that it was Carol and not her who tied the knot with car-loving Arnie.

Her long-time best friend Dennis was the only other person Linda knew who was obsessed with cars. He drove cars in the demolition derby at Callister Park by the PNE. Still friends through thick and thin, Linda marvelled at Dennis's ability to work on tall skyscrapers, washing windows in downtown Vancouver Monday to Friday, and then switching to driving in the demolition derby on the weekends, all while nurturing his love for alcohol.

Linda was proud of him, watching as he maneuvered his vehicle through the derby course, coming up behind an unsuspecting opponent. She admired his tall, lean frame, thinking it was no wonder that he still held the nickname "String Bean," derived from the *Hee-haw Variety Show*.

As far back as she could remember, Dennis wore his hair combed back and perpetually greasy. His only downfall was his unabashed passion for drinking. If it had not been for his addiction, Linda might have considered dating him.

But as Dennis would often exclaim, "It's only a drinking problem to other people, as I got no problem with it," and then he would break out into fits of laughter.

He would remind Linda of the backwards name game that she taught him and how his name spelled backwards described who he thought he was, "Sinned." This made him laugh all the more.

Regardless, Dennis was a pleasant, happy drunk, never angry or annoying to be around. Even though he had helped Linda get through some of her more challenging moments, they always kept their relationship platonic.

In the 1960s and early 1970s, the price of scrap metal was so low that people could not even give old cars away. Unlicensed parked cars took over Vancouver's city streets and got towed away at the owner's expense. During this time, the city was on the rampage to clean up yards and lanes littered with derelict, junky automobiles.

Simultaneously, the Satellites Motorsports Club came into the picture and offered a proposal to the City of Vancouver to start a demolition derby, thus making good use of these abandoned autos. Callister Park was a simple, fenced-in city block with a wooden grandstand across the street from the Vancouver Pacific National Exhibition Fairgrounds. It was an immediate success.

Demolition derbies were a fun, although dangerous, source of entertainment, with the most common injury being whiplash. It was a competition where older cars were deliberately driven into each other until only one car was left running. The sport's popularity grew throughout the 1960s, becoming a standard event at country fairs throughout North America, and the Vancouver Pacific National Exhibition was no exception.

In most demolition derbies their were five to seven events with drivers competing for prize money. Sometimes their were extra featured events including rollover contests, "powder puff" heats with female drivers, and a paper bag race where the driver's head was covered while taking directions from a co-pilot.

DJs such as local announcers Red Robinson and Al Jordan, promoted the derbies on the radio and showed up to compete during the derbies. DJs used sledgehammers and axes to face off with each other to determine which one could inflict the most damage to the derby cars. This was great entertainment for all ages and proved to be a real crowd pleaser.

The Callister Park derbies initially lasted for five years, but there was such a high demand from spectators and derby drivers alike for the popular sport to be reinstated that after two years, it was brought back. The new location was across the street at the PNE.

The derby bowl was shared by loggers putting on a woodcutting show at the annual fair. Both events were popular with Linda's family because her dad had competed in loggers sports many years prior when he first came to BC from Saskatchewan, while he worked in the logging industry. Because the whole family knew Dennis, they made it a point to attend on the days Dennis was driving.

It was mandatory that all drivers wear a helmet, have a working seatbelt, and obey the track officials at all times. Failure to do so would result in disqualification. The competing cars were stripped of all glass, body moulding, and exterior lighting. All doors had to be chained, welded, or wired closed to prevent them from opening during the derby. The list of rules was extensive.

Roz Kelly, aka Pinky Tuscadero, an occasional love interest to the most famous character Arthur Fonzarelli from the sitcom *Happy Days*, was a female professional demolition derby driver. She inspired Dennis to try to persuade Linda to drive his cars in the women's Powder Puff Derby.

Turning him down, Linda joked that she was too large to climb through the window, as it was the only way to get in and out of the car, and she would be trapped, possibly going up in flames with the vehicle. They both laughed in unison at the thought of it. In reality, the visual was not amusing at all.

One Saturday in late August, Linda had made arrangements to see Dennis at the derby. He was not expected to be driving until later in the afternoon, so they planned on going to the horse races first, betting on a few horses, eating a few hotdogs, and then Linda would watch Dennis compete in the derby. Linda had fond memories of attending the racecourse as a little girl with her parents, so she was comfortable stepping up to the wicket to place her bet like she had seen her parents do many times before.

While Dennis was ordering two rum and Cokes, one for himself and the other one for himself, Linda checked out the race card, placed her bet, and found them both seats. As soon as she heard, "And they're off!" Linda jumped to her feet and started chanting and rooting for her mare.

When the race began, Linda's horse was immediately boxed in but broke free and was suddenly neck and neck with another.

"And down the stretch they come," cried the announcer over the loudspeaker.

Worrying that it would be a dead-heat (meaning the prize is split between two horses), it ended up being a photo finish. Linda was sure her horse had come first, but the race-day judge needed to consult a photo before the winner could be determined.

Sure enough, Linda's chosen racehorse that day won. The three options on the card for betting were win, place, or show. She had put $2.00 on Galloping Gilda to win. The prize was $1,700.00. Dennis and Linda jumped up and down, hooting and hollering. After wolfing down their hotdogs, they collected Linda's money and left.

Next up was Dennis with his car at the derby. Not feeling any pain by that point, thanks to his two rum and Cokes, Linda was amazed that he never got booted out or, worst-case scenario, injured. He was tough as nails and always felt that he would be in worse shape if he didn't drink.

Dennis also won, being the last car still running, to add to Linda's excitement of winning big at the races. That night they celebrated, and as usual, Linda drove Dennis back to his place, hoping he would not pass out en route, and making sure he got to bed before she left. Another sign of progress and an end to an era was when the demolition derby was eventually eliminated.

The PNE was not only a summer job for Linda and home to the demolition derby and horse races, but it was also where the Vancouver Pacific Coliseum was situated. The Coliseum was an indoor arena whose original primary use was to attract an NHL franchise. The construction was completed in 1967, but Vancouver's bid for a national hockey league was at first rejected, until 1970, when the Canucks hockey team came to be.

The Coliseum was also the best place in the lower mainland to see a music concert. On December 21, 1976, Linda again loaded up her car with teenagers, but this time she took Karen and a few of her friends to a rock concert to see the Beach Boys' live performance at the Vancouver Coliseum.

It was Karen's first concert ever, so Linda was sure to warn her of all the pitfalls. With their seats as high up as the rafters, often referred to as the nose-bleed section, Linda was certain they would not get trampled. They would be safe there if concert-goers decided to swarm the stage, evocative of the Beatles concert Linda had attended many years before at the Empire Stadium.

However, Linda was taken aback by the pervading aroma of marijuana, not a practice that she or any of her friends ever partook in. Therefore, as the second-hand smoke wafted up to them where they were seated, she insisted that Karen and her friends cover their mouth and nose to prevent getting stoned or high or whatever horrible thing might happen to them from breathing in the mood-altering drug. Karen rolled her eyes but obeyed her sister's wishes anyway. All had fun, but Linda felt it was a narrow escape from allowing her little sister to become influenced by a rough, drug-induced crowd.

In 1978 Karen graduated from high school and moved to Vancouver upon their mother's suggestion, which brought an end to the Rolley Lake Trail Riders. In Frances's own words, she wanted Karen to have a big, beautiful life, one of adventure, successful eligible bachelors, and fun. In her mind, it would not be attainable on fifty acres of land in the middle of nowhere.

Perhaps this was more of what Frances wanted for herself. Nevertheless, seventeen-year-old Karen was seemingly ready and willing to leave the nest.

Inevitably, both sisters had grown apart. With their thirteen-year age difference, Karen had lost interest in her sister's Western ways and started to find a few interests of her own, primarily spandex on the aerobics floor and in the discotheque.

With less to do, Linda began to spend more time working on her contests. In the 1960s, Linda was influenced by friend and neighbour Anna Hocevar's knack for entering and winning contests. So much so that Anna sat down with Linda many years prior and taught her everything she knew.

Sitting with a pen and notebook in her late teens, Linda had scribbled down Anna's pointers.

- Always address the envelope precisely the way it is stated on the entry form.
- Use long envelopes instead of small.
- Add stickers or draw something silly on the outside of the envelope to attract attention.
- Listen to as many radio stations as you can.
- Keep track of all radio station phone numbers and have them ready at your fingertips.
- Keep calling until you win.
- Think positive. If you enter a contest thinking you will never win, then you won't. Expect to win.
- Call into radio contests early in the morning or late at night to increase the odds.
- Always be as enthusiastic as possible. If the radio announcer hears a flat soft voice, they will tell the caller to try again. Louder, friendly people have a better chance of not getting passed on.
- Most importantly, follow the three Ps: patience, persistence, and a positive attitude.

Anna was an avid bingo player but had limited finances and could not afford many bingo cards. Therefore, to challenge herself, she would play her cards upside down, utterly unheard of but unique and intriguing just the same. Linda's first big win came on her dad's birthday, August 13, 1969. She won a thousand dollars on B-13.

One of her clients at the bank was eighty-year-old Mr. Buck, a kind, lonely widower who got to know Linda from his visits to the bank. He was one of many who waited off to the side until Linda's wicket came available. Through light chit-chat, he eventually asked if he could take Linda for dinner one Friday night. This turned into a once-a-month routine, not as a love interest but more as a companion.

Even though Linda always looked older than her age, with North Vancouver still being a relatively small town, people started to talk and wondered what either one saw in the other. They asked if Linda was a gold-digger or if elderly Mr. Buck was into something weird and kinky.

Linda turned a blind eye and had an excellent relationship with older people. She felt comfortable around them, was not judged, and her sense of humour often brought them joy. This warmed Linda, and that was all.

Mr. Buck was a stately gentleman with silver hair and a matching grey mustache. He had impeccable clothing and manners. Adoring Linda's healthy appetite, animated personality, and gift of the gab, he insisted they eat at his most treasured restaurants, as only the best would do.

The Tomahawk, The Seven Seas, Frank Bakers, The White Spot, and The Cannery were Mr. Buck's favourite places for steak and lobster or hamburgers, both of which were his chosen meals. Again, Linda would be the designated driver so that Mr. Buck could enjoy his whiskey sours.

After dinner, it would be a night of bingo with his extraordinary bank teller friend, Linda Bonner.

Linda always felt lucky at contests, but she never fell for the usual lucky charms evident on the many bingo tables. Even though her mother would only play bingo cards that displayed the numbers thirteen and seventy-five, Linda was not superstitious at all.

Many bingo players find inspiration and hopefulness in a variety of baubles. Some bring elaborate shrines in hopes of getting good luck. Not uncommon items to see on varying tables of avid bingo players, were a selection of lucky charms, family photos, stuffed animals, a furry rabbit's foot, troll dolls with wild, colourful hair, key chains, heirlooms, and even cremation ashes.

Another avenue to bring good luck were talismans relating to people's faith; cards of the Virgin Mary and various saints, a Bible, a rosary, or prayer dolls.

For many bingo players, the superstitions would go beyond charms to where they sat, which dauber they used for games, and who they bought "paper" bingo cards from. Some believed in touching the head of a red-haired person. Sitting next to twins or a pregnant woman was supposedly the luckiest.

For bingo players, even today, "good luck" has a variety of meanings and interpretations. Sometimes the players genuinely believe the item or items contain positive energy that will attract winnings; other players have an "It can't hurt, so why not bring it?" mentality. The atmosphere in most bingo halls across the country is one of fun, with game-loving people who do not mind sitting for an entire evening.

Attending bingo games, listening to radio contests, playing in card tournaments, and filling out mail-in rebates—no matter what, Linda would perpetually win, anything from trips, cash, trophies, household items, clothing, groceries, and jewelry, to a year's supply of toothpaste, toilet paper, gasoline, and canned beans, in addition to toys, stuffed animals, games, and puzzles.

If marketing and advertising strategies suggested cereal box tops or labels of any kind, Linda enlisted friends and family to save them with her and for her. Pop bottle lids, soup labels, and matchbook covers, when mailed in, brought an assortment of items to Linda's doorstep. On most occasions, she would give her prizes away. Therefore, Christmas presents for her siblings, friends, and co-workers would often be her winnings—decoder rings, sea monkeys, and cubic zirconia imitation jewelry.

On a CKNW Power Play contest, she won a trip to Mexico. Not fond of air travel or the beach, and having just started a new job, Linda quickly transferred her winnings to her mother. She had entered under the name L. Bonner, and her mom went as F. L. Bonner, so no problem when collecting the proceeds. Linda took pleasure in giving.

The trip was for two, so Frances invited her friend Mary Benson. In retrospect, Frances wished she had brought her husband, as Mary spent most of her time getting soused at the bar and flirting with the staff. Frances knew her husband would have insisted on dancing the night away and engaging in daily adventures. Regardless, Mary was appreciative and brought Linda back a hand-tooled Western purse with two hundred dollars cash inside.

On nights alone in her trailer, Linda would enter contests, address envelopes, and submit what was requested, all while watching reruns of her most-loved shows on television, most of which had a Western flavour.

The hit variety show called *Hee-Haw*, presented by Buck Owens and Roy Clark, was a famous American television show. Entirely Western in theme, it featured country music and humour, with the fictional rural town of Kornfield Kounty as the backdrop. It was well known for its corny (no pun intended) humour and its scantily clad women, called the Hee-Haw Honeys, in stereotypical farmer's daughter outfits.

Hee-Haw was inspired by another variety show called *Rowan & Martin's Laugh-In*, with the significant differences being that *Hee-Haw* was country and *Laugh-In* was pop-culture. It replaced the popular variety show called *The Smothers Brothers Comedy Hour*, a program that appealed to young contemporary youth. With dancing, political satire, humour, and major musical acts such as Buffalo Springfield, Pete Seeger, Cream, and The WHO.

The Smothers Brothers' success brought with it continual conflicts with network executives over content, which led to the show being abruptly pulled from the schedule in violation of its contract. Apparently, seductive young women in Kornfield Kounty took precedence over political views and newsworthy satire.

Not only did Linda love *Hee-Haw*, but she had a few connections of her own. Back when she was practically living at Laura Lynn in North Vancouver, Buck Owens stopped by to ride one of the horses and use the riding arena and horses for one of his movies.

He wrote, produced, and sang *I've Got a Tiger by the Tail,* by Buck Owens and the Buckaroos. Linda repeatedly played his claim-to-fame country song on her record player.

Despite Linda's enjoyment of her life on the coast, the Western world never ceased calling out to her. Coupled with her ability to turn lemons into lemonade, Linda had a money-making idea brewing in her mind, perhaps opening up an opportunity to get back to the Cariboo.

Auntie Bonnie visiting from Minneapolis, niece
Jeanette and Linda at the farm in Stavefalls

Linda and Arnie

Jack in the coral at the farm in Stavefalls

Dad and Karen on one of their trips

Karen with Ginger, Spice and Crackers the dog

CHAPTER FIFTEEN

You're Big, and You're Beautiful

"People will make mean comments. People will say that you're fat, that you're this, that you're that. You just have to be comfortable in your own skin."

–Anonymous

In 1979, wanderlust was at it again. Linda was ready to move back to the Cariboo. She wanted to pack up and permanently leave Stave Falls, Mission, lock, stock, and barrel. The area had served her well, but after much recollection, Clinton was where Linda was at her best. She had kept up with all of her friends over the years and continued to make weekend trips to attend all the popular rodeos and dances. She missed the Interior and revelled in the dry, crisp winters and equally dry, warmer summers.

Since having been bucked off and thrown from two different horses at two different times in her life, Linda could not ride like she used to. Subsequently, she had put on more weight, primarily due to pain and lack of exercise, although, in the back of her mind, she also knew that loneliness and unacknowledged pain from her past had something to do with her ever-increasing appetite.

Food just undeniably brought her comfort. Linda was fed up, having tried every diet in the book, and after losing ten or fifteen pounds here and there, she always seemed to gain it back, and then some.

Like an epiphany, Linda woke up one morning in her trailer and said out loud to no one but herself, "No more!" Taking the bull by the horns, she was ready to celebrate her size. She was big and beautiful, and she knew it.

Despite her positive confession, sometimes, before things can get better, they become far worse.

Linda always had many suitors, and she frequently was asked on dates. Dave Strain was a good friend and a potential boyfriend. He was a barrel of laughs, but things never became serious, and Linda realized early on he was not a person she wanted to spend the rest of her life with.

Dwayne Jones was a casual boyfriend but accused one of Linda's friends of stealing his wristwatch when it was sitting on the back of the toilet seat the whole time, strange and yet laughable for storytelling purposes. She quickly broke up with him after the accusation.

Despite not meeting the man of her dreams, there was always something to do and someone to do it with. She was treated well by many and enjoyed dinners out, dancing at the Blue Room or Friar Tucks, and attending rodeos.

Be that as it may, the lesson Linda learned from dating her next boyfriend could not be found in any medical journal or taught in any psychology manual. However, the advice columnists Dear Abby and Ann Landers would have indeed said, "Run for the hills and don't look back!"

Dale was a gorgeous man of First Nations descent. He enjoyed dancing, playing cards, and rodeos. Some might call him a man's man and jack-of-all-trades, while others would say he was a gentle giant or a tall, dark, and handsome dreamboat.

To Linda, he was kind and comical and always up for some fun until the alcohol came out, at which time he became the fictional characters, Dr. Jekyll and Mr. Hyde. When Dale occasionally drank alcohol, he could not stop until every bottle was drained. It was never just an evening drink to unwind. Instead, he would ingest copious amounts of the poisonous drug.

Linda learned through trial and error when Dale was about to reach his breaking point, and his physical characteristics were always the first indication. His feet would start to shift, whether he was sitting or standing. Next, he would repeatedly drag his hands through his hair and then begin to rub the back of his neck. Mixed with poor listening skills and an inclination to jump to conclusions, he became a ticking time bomb.

Linda referred to this as his transformation period, from a lovable teddy bear into a cantankerous grizzly bear. The usual fun-loving, kind man would explode with name-calling and sometimes physical outbursts. The more intoxicated he became, the more hurtful were his words and actions.

Most times, Linda was able to steer clear of his flip side. Every singles record album had a famous hit song on one side, with the flip side often being a song with less appeal. Dale turned into the other side of the record that nobody liked.

Sometimes, however, Linda got caught in the crossfires, which entailed name-calling and putdowns such as, "You are fat and ugly!"

She was always good with a comeback, and she tried to say something creative like, "I may be fat, but I sure am not ugly!" But whatever she said only fell on deaf ears and magnified his temper.

Linda figured out it was best to stay silent or get in her truck and leave until he could sleep it off. The next day he would display remorse, that is, if he even remembered the night before. She would forgive him, mostly since she knew deep down inside, he wasn't always mean. She had fallen for him.

However, being a non-drinker, Linda could not understand Dale's need to overindulge. She wondered why he could not just have a few and gathered he was pushing down some pretty fierce demons that plagued him. His saving grace was all the times that he was sober. In her mind, those times outweighed the few times he was drunk and intolerant to be around.

And then came the incident when he went too far.

Linda and Dale had driven down to see her family. It was Christmas time. The tree was decorated, and presents were wrapped. There was fresh snow, so Karen and her friends were out snowmobiling with their dad. Frances was in a good frame of mind, watching soap operas and game shows, with a pot of Vince's favourite homemade soup on the stove.

It had been a great day, there was no alcohol in sight, and the mood was light. Out of the blue, Dale decided late in the afternoon that they should all go to the horse races in Vancouver. Frances and Vince opted out. Then Dale changed his mind and said he wanted to see his buddy in Langley. Against Linda's better judgement, she drove him.

Linda's dad enjoyed a cocktail occasionally after work, especially in the heat of the summer. One drink was his maximum, and it was often ice-cold lemonade with one shot of vodka. He referred to it as a Vodka Collins. Frances was a non-drinker, but she would split a beer with Vince or accept his offer of a specialty punch-like drink with very little alcohol once in a while.

With the term "eat, drink, and be merry" comes a lovely heartwarming, festive thought. Linda chose to repeat the well-known phrase as "eat, drink, and be scary," which described Dale when he decided that it was party time.

Eventually, a day of fun became a night of horror. Dale started drinking the minute they left Linda's parents' place and continued throughout their visit with his friend, during dinner, and driving home. There was nothing Linda could do about it. She hoped he would pass out or go straight to sleep when they got back to her parents' place.

The yelling, name-calling, and aggressive behaviour began on their return as they were sitting on the Albion Ferry, crossing the Fraser River in Linda's truck.

When they finally arrived at her parents' home, everyone had gone to bed, but Dale was not ready to call it a night. He demanded that Linda get him more liquor. He insisted that her dad must have a stash somewhere. When Linda refused, Dale yelled obscenities and pushed her.

Hearing the commotion, both Frances and Vince stormed out of their bedroom. Linda's mom had a flashlight and was ready to strike Dale over the head. Vince stepped in and put Dale in a stronghold and somehow got him to the ground. Karen was in her room and heard the raised voices but was afraid to step out into the hall.

Dale screamed to Vince, "Why don't you go back in your bedroom with Frances and make more fat babies like Lynn?!"

Vince dragged Dale outside by the scruff of the neck and managed to get him into his pickup truck. It was late, the roads were icy, but Dale was no longer welcome in their home. Vince drove him to the bus depot and bought him a one-way ticket for Clinton. Dale sobered up some, but he was still three sheets to the wind. In no uncertain terms, Vince told him never to return and to stay away from his daughter.

That night was an eye-opener for Linda when her parents jumped to her defence. A lightning bolt struck her in the heart and extinguished her love for Dale. It was then that she realized she was with the wrong man.

In her family, words were never spoken that were derogatory, abusive, or hurtful. Many strangers had called her names but never a loved one. She initially felt embarrassed over the whole episode but then was flooded with extreme gratitude and love towards both of her parents for supporting her. Arriving back in Clinton, she broke up with Dale and never looked back.

Everything was about to change for the better.

In the 1970s, fashion became more about loving our bodies than trying to hide and conceal them. Even though the first plus-size retailer came onto the scene as far back as 1904, it was not until the late 1970s that "plus-size" became the descriptor of choice for sizes fourteen and up. Even high-end fashion designers started getting in on the trend—names such as Valentino and Givenchy.

In North America, the popular stores to purchase XL, XXL, and XXXL clothing were K-Mart and Woolco, big box stores that sold clothes for larger gals that were cheap and practical but not necessarily fashionable.

The 1970s also brought the first larger, non-traditional models. Former plus-size model Mary Duffy owned Big Beauties/ Little Women, the first agency specializing in plus-size and petite models. Pat Swift, a plus-size model, founded Plus Models and, by the 1980s, represented over sixty-five models, grossing over two million dollars in revenue.

Linda was aware of the "Fat Revolution," when women worldwide banded together to fight weight bias and discrimination in the fat acceptance movement. Frances, being an avid reader, had told Linda about fat activists in New York who held a "Fat-In" where they ate ice cream and burned Twiggy posters. They also met to stage plus-size fashion shows and raise funds to promote awareness of fat issues.

By 1980 *Big Beautiful Woman* magazine began publication and was one of the first publications in the US catering specifically to plus-size clothing consumers. People were changing their tune on body image, and the media was catching up.

Full figured woman, the hourglass shape, queen size, voluptuous, and big busted, were all terms Linda had grown up with, primarily when other people referred to her. As a child and young teen, the names were far worse. Constantly bullied for her size, Linda had endured the name-calling, and by the time she was thirty-two, she'd had enough. She was big and beautiful, and she knew it.

It was time for Linda's seed thought to blossom. After much discussion with her parents, they agreed with Linda's pronouncement, and to help their eldest daughter, the three of them came up with a plan. Her mom and dad offered to purchase her mobile home and five-acre land plot so Linda could live in the Cariboo permanently.

Linda had been in discussion with a friend who knew retail, and with Linda's financial backing, they decided to open a clothing store for bigger women. Both women knew there was a need and a market. The name they chose was Freedom Fashions, with a butterfly motif to represent the store. It was decided that the plus-size clothing store would be in 100 Mile House, where Linda's new business partner lived, and only a thirty-minute drive from Clinton, where Linda lived.

100 Mile House is a town located in the South Cariboo region of central British Columbia, Canada. It was originally known as Bridge Creek House, named after the creek running through the area. It was later referred to as 100 Mile House during the Cariboo Gold Rush, where a roadhouse was constructed in 1862 at the 100-mile mark, up the Old Cariboo Road from Lillooet.

The surrounding area features hundreds of lakes for boating and fishing, including 101 Mile Lake, 103 Mile Lake, Lac La Hache, Canim Lake, Horse Lake, Green Lake, Bridge Lake, and Sheridan Lake.

And for some reason, obesity was on the rise. When Linda was a girl, her mother purchased clothes for her from the teen section. When she was a teenager, she had to wear adult women's clothing, and when she was an adult, Linda shopped at K-Mart and Woolco for matronly-looking clothes in extra-large. As fashionable as Linda tried to be, she felt the selection of clothes for her age and body size were not up to speed with how the rest of the world was dressing.

The grand opening of Freedom Fashions in 100 Mile House was a huge success. They handed out flyers, advertised in the local newspaper, and through word-of-mouth, everyone was talking about the new store.

Linda started to respond to people who said, "You have such a pretty face," with "Thank you, so do you." She had learned that what people say can come from their own backstory. Sometimes Linda thought that prejudice was a way of gaining superiority, mostly words that hid people's hostility towards her and, for some, a desire for her to fail.

All the supposed constructive comments Linda had heard over the years played a crucial role in her new thinking. She was discovering that part of the problem, especially for women, was that they were often judged by their physical attributes. How they looked was connected to their success and level of perceived attractiveness.

Another part of the problem, and a contributing factor to the prejudice, were people who did not understand complicated conditions like obesity. Exercising when you are heavy is arduous, and when not performed correctly, can result in injury. Countless doctors had tried explaining to Linda the related medical conditions resulting from excessive weight gain—hypothyroidism, insulin resistance, polycystic ovary syndrome. As well, Cushing's Syndrome was a condition that could sometimes be a cause of weight gain. The fearful part was not cosmetic but rather issues such as heart disease, diabetes, high blood pressure, and certain cancers.

With it all, came low self-confidence that brought on even lower self-esteem. Linda had grown tired of being fed fear and judgement from others. Some people she ignored, while at other times, she turned heckling into a joke as quickly as any stand-up comedian could, packing a punch with every barbed insult.

"We are big and beautiful, so let's dress that way!" was one of their first newspaper advertisements and slogans for Freedom Fashions.

Before the opening, Linda and her business partner went on a buying spree. Tailored suits, frilly blouses, stylish blue jeans, capes, coats, jean jackets, scarves, bold jewelry, knee-high boots and sequined caps. Linda's favourite items, something for underneath it all, were sexy lingerie—red camisoles, black nightgowns, yellow lace panties, and other unmentionables.

From 100 Mile House, it was more than a one-hour drive to any other big department store. Freedom Fashions offered female consumers comfort, style, high fashion, and convenience.

They hosted evening events for men to purchase attractive clothing for their wives, girlfriends, sisters, and mothers. With every purchase came an ice-cold beer.

Besides the store's success, Linda's hobbies of entering contests, sorting coupons, playing bingo, and competing in cribbage tournaments took up most of her time and were a great pastime. Winning cash prizes, trips, and trophies resulted in photos in the local newspaper. She was known as Lynn with the Luck.

Linda started to shop for seniors and shut-ins, somewhat of a volunteer position that she created. She excelled in helping others, but first and foremost, if there was a deal to be had, Linda was the gal to get it. She never paid full price for anything! And was proud of it!

Her most spectacular claim to fame was when she spent three hours of precision shopping with coupons and received over $200.00 worth of groceries for $8.47. She joked about how lucky she was with numbers, as she was born on the eighth month in 1947—which produced the number $8.47

In those days, some stores had a triple coupon offer. As an example, if the product were priced at $2.29 and you had three $1.00 coupons, you actually could get paid eighty-one cents for the product. Her shopping for seniors was a hobby and a good deed all in one fell swoop.

Just when things were going full steam ahead, the store was doing well, and Linda was enjoying life, the apple cart was upset yet again. Everything was about to change. When news came that Linda's dad was diagnosed with an inoperable brain tumour, while at the same time her sister was racing to the chapel to get married, Linda was certain of three things:

She hardly knew her sister's fiancé and needed to change that; with the terrible news about her dad's cancer, she wanted him to see her healthier; and if she could drop a few pounds, she wanted to start riding horses again.

Linda knew that her knees and back would benefit from a significant weight loss but more importantly, because of her adoration for her dad, and if he was truly leaving this world, she so wanted him to see her thinner and healthier. He had always been conscious about his own weight and maintained the best shape possible.

Linda still felt great about who she was, but perhaps that was why she was ready to do something drastic.

Weight loss surgery began in the 1950s with the intestinal bypass. It involved anastomosis of the upper and lower intestine. The laboratory research leading to gastric bypass did not start until 1965. By 1986, shortly after Linda's father was diagnosed with cancer, the procedure was called gastric segmentation.

The surgery was not recommended as a weight loss procedure but as an alternative for an individual who had a lifetime of obesity, whose health was in danger and who had tried countless times to lose weight. The bonus was a substantial weight loss.

There were also strict guidelines to be accepted for the surgery. Linda would need to be part of a screening process that involved extensive interviews. It was demanded and enforced that each applicant be in top form mentally and emotionally. Numerous health care professionals would evaluate her. After doing the groundwork, Linda understood the operation's complexity, pros and cons, health benefits, and upkeep.

Healthwise, Linda had begun struggling with excessive sweating, shortness of breath and was easily fatigued; her back and knees hurt, and her periods had become irregular. Worst of all, she had become borderline diabetic.

As far back as she could remember, Linda thought of herself as Daddy's little girl. Even though her younger sister, Karen, had taken over the title, Linda still wanted to please her dad. She never took him for granted.

Linda was well aware that all four kids invariably came first and was grateful that her dad had always supported her horse dream, beginning with her first wanting a horse for Christmas at the age of four and then seeking out riding stables on every family vacation, to eventually helping her start her own riding stable many years later.

To Linda, her dad was her hero—handsome and fit, generous and kind, funny and hard-working. Vince was seventy-one years old and could still jump over fences like a spring chicken, throw one hundred-pound bales of hay into a truck, work the mechanics on a bulldozer, change a tire, and touch his toes. If not in one fell swoop, then at least all in one day.

The brain tumour came as a shock to the whole family. Vince had started to have dizzy spells and slurred speech, so Karen and their brother Doug's wife suggested that Vince go to the doctor. He had already had a cat scan a year earlier. At that time, a small mass the size of a dime had been detected resting on the frontal lobe of his brain. Now a year later, upon further investigation, they closed up Vince's scalp with the report that his tumour had grown in and around vital parts of his brain, therefore making his tumour inoperable.

In 1986 Linda was thirty-nine years old. World events at that time involved stories about the Space Shuttle Challenger being destroyed shortly after it launched from Cape Canaveral in Florida in January 1986. Tragically, all of the astronauts on board were killed in the explosion. In March of the same year, Halley's Comet reached the earth's closest point during its second visit to the solar system in the 20th Century.

"Hands Across America," the most extensive public charity event, was held in May 1986. The publicity campaign asked Americans to join hands in a human chain across the country. Those who participated were asked to donate ten dollars through local charities to help people in poverty. Approximately six-and-a-half million people participated.

It was a time of change, strengthening humanity, and helping others. The song "That's What Friends Are For" by Dionne Warwick, Gladys Knight, Elton John, and Stevie Wonder was number one on the billboards.

The Oprah Winfrey Show debuted nationally in September of 1986. It soon became the highest-rated talk show in the United States. Western movies had been few and far between, and in 1986, comedies were the going trend. *The Three Amigos* with Martin Short, Steve Martin, and Chevy Chase was popular at the box office, followed by *Crocodile Dundee* and *Ferris Bueller's Day Off*. For adult adventure, *Top Gun*, and for the kids, *The Karate Kid*. The war film *Platoon* won Best Picture at the Academy Awards.

Expo 86, the world's fair, was held in Vancouver, British Columbia, from May 2 until October 13, 1986. The theme was "Transportation and Communication: World in Motion—World in Touch." It coincided with Vancouver's centennial and was held on the north shore of False Creek.

In late 1986, Linda had been called down to the hospital in Vancouver for her long-awaited extensive interview. At the beginning of 1987, she had been approved. Her gastric segmentation surgery was scheduled for June.

Karen's wedding took place on April 10, 1987, only two months before Linda's surgery and five months before Vince's death. No one knew that the end was near. All seemed to be in denial, hoping and praying he would beat the odds.

Linda chose a yellow silk blouse and brown dress pants from Freedom Fashions for the wedding. She wore sparkly earrings and was sporting a new perm.

It was a lovely celebration and a fun time for relatives, family, and friends. Many people Linda had not seen in years.

Karen's soon-to-be husband, Dale, was kind and friendly. Linda liked him and his extended family. She danced and carried on like a thin person, even though deep down inside, she felt large and cumbersome. Her back ached, and she was having trouble standing. *If only I could have had my gastric segmentation before the wedding*, she thought.

Seeing her dad at the wedding was shocking. His usual handsome, chiselled features, washboard abs, and head of black curly hair were very much altered. His mid-section had widened, his face was puffy, and his shiny, thick black hair was thin and in patches. He had been undergoing chemo, and the effects were showing, leaving behind a fragment of the man Linda had idolized her whole life.

What bewildered Linda the most was her dad's inability to speak. His colourful stories had ceased, and his loud, gregarious laugh was no more. Looking into her father's eyes, she could see his pain and noticed how his once-bright hazel eyes were dimming.

With her father's illness and imminent death, unbeknownst to Linda, her mother was not coping well. Having struggled for years with mood swings, she appeared extroverted, loud, and sharp at the wedding, on edge and teetering like a cartoon character on a cliff. Would she tumble off, or would she not?

Except this was not the funny papers. Even though Linda was happy for her sister and ecstatic about the eventual weight loss, she suddenly could not stand to be around her mother, and her heart broke for her dad.

With so much on her mind, Linda did not have the patience or understanding for her mother's outlandish behaviour. She had changed, and avoidance of her mother's moods was the only response she could muster.

The wedding came and went, the newlyweds left for their honeymoon in Mexico, and Linda left for her home in the Cariboo and all that she loved.

On June 12, 1987, with trepidation and excitement, Linda was back on the coast and waiting to be prepped for her surgery at Saint Paul's Hospital in Vancouver. In her handbag were the many pages of guidelines, food restrictions, and warnings on everything that could go terribly wrong if she did not adhere.

As she sat in the waiting room for the clerk to call her name, Linda ran into an old friend who worked in the admitting department. She had been one of the old neighbourhood kids that lived next door growing up in North Vancouver. They had not seen each other in years and were mutually delighted to be connecting with one another.

Carol was a petite and pretty blonde, fashionably dressed in a bright green suit with matching green high heels. She stood out to Linda against the drab pale blue walls of the hospital. Linda had fond memories of backyard games while their mothers hung their laundry next to adjacent back porches and visited. She could still visualize the flapping floral bed sheets, crisp pillowcases and hard, rough towels—all blowing and billowing out from the clothesline.

Snapping Linda back from her childhood memories, Carol asked why she was at the hospital. When Linda explained gastric segmentation Surgery, Carol gasped, covered her mouth and shook her head. She told Linda how beautiful she was and asked if she could get out of the surgery. She stated that people had died from the upkeep and maintenance afterwards, if not directly on the operating table.

Linda could see the look of concern on Carol's face and hear the worry in her voice. But in Linda's mind, it was all too late to cancel. Carol's response was too much information for her to grasp only moments before she was to be sedated. Besides, it had been a year of research, interviews, and decision-making. There was no turning back.

Linda half-heartedly explained that she was going through with it, and that was that. Besides, all the papers were signed, and her mother was waiting out in the parking lot. Linda thought that her mom would have enjoyed a visit with Carol, but with her being so terribly out of sorts, Linda was pleased that she was not there. And now, the query from her childhood friend had rattled her.

She momentarily thought of her other old friend Dennis and how he had always been there for her, supporting other big decisions she had to make.

As she stared up into Carol's face, she wished Dennis were staring back at her instead. She could imagine him, tall, skinny, and handsome but reeking of booze. He would be driving around in his white 1960 Pontiac Parisienne convertible, with a pretty girl sitting next to him in an eye-catching scene, with the top down and shiny red upholstery glistening in the sun, the girl's hair billowing like her mother's laundry on the clothesline.

In this tense moment of consternation, Linda recalled a time when she and Dennis had pulled up to a McDonalds out in Surrey. After he went in to get their food, a rowdy bunch pulled up alongside in an old beater car. When they opened their car door to get out, they dinged the side of Dennis's pristine, well-cared-for automobile. Linda rolled down her window and exclaimed, "Hey, you hit my friend's car! Please be more careful."

Without apologizing, the fellow jumped out of the driver's side, pulled out a switchblade and lunged towards Linda. He pointed the knife towards her throat. Once Dennis caught sight of what was going on, he darted out of the McDonalds with food flying everywhere. He had that guy in a headlock so fast he did not know what hit him. When Dennis finally let him go, the motley crew took off without their Big Macs and super-size french fries.

As Carol walked away, Linda thought how strange it was that her thinking was all over the map. She weakly waved goodbye to Carol just as a nurse was calling to her. Linda wondered where Dennis was at that exact moment as she was about to go under the knife again. This time, Dennis could not save her.

She had read the procedure repeatedly and could recite it back verbatim to anyone who cared to listen...

...a surgical procedure involves the placement of an adjustable belt around the upper portion of the stomach using a laparoscope.

...the belt ultimately restricts the size of the stomach and the amount of food it can hold.

...in doing this, a signal of fullness is sent to the brain.

Linda had filled out questionnaires and written pages relaying the history of her obesity: failed weight loss attempts, years of bullying, and now the deterioration of her health. She admitted to having a complete understanding of the procedure, and she signed documents stating she would adhere to the lifestyle changes.

She was informed that if she had difficulty understanding the procedure, was emotionally unstable, or dependant on drugs or alcohol, she would not be approved for the surgery. If she had any underlying medical conditions that made her high risk for surgery, such as heart or lung conditions, she would be refused the operation. But, like an exam at school, she had passed with flying colours.

Just before dozing off after the anesthetic, Linda felt tired and confused, desperately hoping she had made the right decision. The procedure was performed under general anesthesia and would take one–two hours.

Frances sat double-parked in her car just outside St. Paul's, and she was not in any shape to be caring for Linda after surgery, assisting her dying husband, or figuring out her mood disorder. Her manic behaviour had reached an all-time high. She felt unhinged and entirely out of touch with her family and the fast-spinning world around her.

She could not remember driving her car from Mission to downtown Vancouver, and to make matters worse, after Linda's surgery, they would be heading over to North Vancouver in rush hour traffic so she could purchase a house. With Vince at death's door, she wanted him closer to a hospital. In case of an emergency, the thirty-minute drive from Mission to Maple Ridge would not do. Besides, she needed her husband to enjoy the last few months of his life in the place where she had the fondest memories.

Frances sensed that her behaviour was rather irrational, yet she was so energized and felt as if nothing could stop her. Grand ideas and farfetched plans seemed effortless, and yet her coping skills were laborious.

Without telling anyone, she had done her fair share of research into Linda's weight loss procedure as well. Frances had always been squeamish when it came to anything medical. It had been Vince's job to bandage the children when they had a scrape, so she skipped to the end of Linda's handouts and researched side effects and risks. The paperwork explained how it was expected that Linda would have nausea, vomiting, indigestion problems, and constipation. The risks were far worse. The mortality rate was 1 in 2,000, with the possibility of the band slipping or eroding into the stomach. Other complications could include infection, bleeding, and intense abdominal pain.

By the time Linda was wheeled out to the car, and all was said and done, rather than comfort her daughter and check in with how she might be feeling, Frances made Linda get in the back seat. She then sped off towards the Lions Gate Bridge and her impending appointment with the realtor in North Vancouver.

Linda sat quietly. When she got in the car, she immediately knew that her mother was unbalanced, if not downright unhinged. She took it personally and started to cry. Instead of reassuring Linda, her mom vehemently spat out the words, "Well, you got yourself into this mess, and there is nothing we can do about it now. No sense crying about it!"

At this point, Frances knew that her mental and emotional capacity was on overload, and her nerves were like loose wires crackling in an electrical force field. She felt angry and annoyed with everyone, and worst of all, she could not fathom what her daughter was doing to herself.

With her mom's inability to express empathy, Linda folded her arms and hugged herself. Sure enough, they were stuck in rush hour traffic on a sweltering June afternoon. With her mom driving at a snail's pace, Linda soon began to feel nauseous and sweaty, and also experienced very severe stomach cramps, just like the forms had indicated would happen. By the time they reached the realtor, Linda was on the verge of passing out. She needed water to drink and a bed to rest in. She stayed in the car while her mom went for a tour of the house that was for sale.

Finally, after about two hours, they were ready to drive again. Rush hour traffic was such that they did not arrive back at the Mission property for another two hours. Frances had purchased the house on Jones Avenue that afternoon in good old North Vancouver without telling a soul.

Linda went straight to bed, but she knew that she could not stay with her parents to recover in the morning. She and her mother were like oil and water. If Linda said up, her mom said down. Black was white, and hot was cold. Besides, she was hoping to go back to work in a few days.

Meanwhile, Frances had not slept in days, which was one of the many by-products of her manic state. When Linda announced that she would be driving home to the Interior the next day and bringing her father with her, Frances was outraged.

Unable to think clearly, Frances was worried for her daughter but could not convey her concern. Instead, her anxiety came out in the worst way. She could only imagine her husband and daughter both tumbling off the highway in a fiery car wreck and dying, or maybe Vince's head would explode, and Linda's incisions would rip open. Everything in Frances's brain was blown up and out of control.

Before he died, Vince wanted to see his brother, who lived in the Okanagan. Rather than sit down and reasonably figure out a plan, Frances yelled for Vince and Linda to get out. She said, "Good, you can take your father to see Hank, and together I hope you both die in the process. Now I think you should leave. Go. Get out!"

Once again, everything came out as an abomination.

Linda and her dad were bewildered by what used to be a practical mother and pleasant wife. They were both sensitive, both not well, and were very hurt by her harsh words and incredible insensitivity. They could not see her illness, only experience the outrageous effects of it.

She, in turn, was wild-eyed and illogical. Unfortunately, the family did not know the tremendous remorse Frances had when her escalated moods subsided, and her out-of-character temper tantrums had ended. Her manic episodes came upon her instantaneously. As if uncontrollably, she tumbled down the rabbit hole, and like Alice in Wonderland, she became small and left in a heap at the bottom—with no "drink me potion" to help her. She did not know how to climb back up again. There were no ropes and pullies or someone reaching out their hand. That person, the unbalanced and mean one, became a stranger to even Frances.

When reality set in and the manic episode had ended, she spent two or three days recovering from the outrageous behaviour that distanced her from everyone. The people she loved the most grew to despise her.

She regretted her outbursts but told no one of her regrets, and she never apologized. Rather than fix collateral damage, she swept it under the carpet, just like she had learned to do with all the years spent dealing with her mother's and sister's patterns. When the waters calmed, when she could momentarily gain control of her thoughts, she would dig deep, looking for her old self again, at least until the chaos returned.

She felt like a puppet, with someone else controlling her strings. *Who was it, and why were they so cruel*, she wondered?

Brother Ken and Linda

Ken and Linda

Back row, Ken, Marjorie, Cindy, Linda, Uncle Hank, Auntie Leona,
Karen, Dale, Auntie Dottie, Uncle Eddy, Louise. Bottom Row,
Aunt Edith, Auntie Bonnie, Frances, Jeanette, Vince, Doug

CHAPTER SIXTEEN

Endings and Beginnings

*"Happiness consists more in conveniences of pleasure that occur every
day than in great pieces of good fortune that happen but seldom."*

-Benjamin Franklin

Linda could not lift, and her dad could not speak. They made a
great team. After Vince had loaded up Linda's truck, he settled
into the passenger side while Linda took the wheel. They took off
on what was to be a memorable road trip.

Her pain had subsided considerably, and without the wrath of
her mother, she felt a lightness of being. The long-awaited surgery
was over, and her dad was sitting next to her. As far as she was
concerned, this was a win-win situation, as there was no one else
she would rather be with.

It had been decided that Linda would drive Vince to go
fishing for a week with his brother in Blind Bay. She would stay
recuperating with Hank's wife, Auntie Leona. Vince's brother and
his wife lived one block from the lake and looked forward to Vince
and Linda's visit

Blind Bay is located on Shuswap Lake's southern shore, twenty-
nine kilometres northwest of Salmon Arm and six kilometres east
of Sorento. Beautiful Blind Bay is so named because of the angle at

which the bay joins Shuswap lake. It can easily go unnoticed since it is almost concealed from sight. Shuswap Lake offers more than 1000 kilometres of shoreline to explore amidst spectacular scenery and a pristine environment.

The lake takes its name from the Shuswap First Nations of the Great Salishan Family, or the Secwepmc, one of the most prominent First Nations bands in British Columbia's Interior, once numbering over 5,000. Most were fishermen and hunters, spreading out and roaming in bands through the vast land of lakes and forests, thousands of kilometres to the east, west, north, and south.

During the drive, Linda played some of her dad's favourite songs on her 8-track cassette player. Vince listened to the melodies, and although he could not sing aloud, he could hum along and would point and gesture to the scenery along the way. Both sights and sounds transported him to all he had once known and loved— happier times from days gone by. He felt impacted and embraced by music and memories.

In his mind, he reminisced, and outwardly he smiled about the past—Okanagan road trips with Frances, the fruit stands, camping, and horseback riding. The warm summer evenings and lazy afternoons, gazing over at Frances with her nose in a book, always made him feel proud of his wife's intelligence and her enjoyment of reading. Swimming and boat rides, card games and cribbage, meals of canned meatballs and Kraft dinner, cucumber sandwiches, fresh berries, instant coffee with Coffee-Mate—all beautiful memories that satisfied his soul and warmed his heart.

Vince did not cry or feel mournful on the road trip with his eldest daughter, but he eagerly took in the lay of the land while his daughter drove, deep down knowing that this would be the last time for such a trip. His fond memories cradled his heart and enveloped his body with each passing mile.

Vince and Hank could have been body doubles for the movie actors James Garner and Henry Fonda, Vince with his dark hair and upbeat personality, and Hank, tall and slim with a calm demeanour and dry sense of humour.

As adults, grown men with their dysfunctional childhood behind them, the two brothers got along famously. Over the years, their personalities grew to fall in place and complement one another. Vince did the talking while Hank listened, every once in a while throwing in a witty quip, comment, or anecdote.

This time around, their visit would be different. Hank would take the lead and do the talking, maybe not as frequently as Vince once had. Vince would listen, as his inability to speak would keep him silent. At first, Hank grappled with the idea of time alone with his brother, and then without realizing it, they settled into a rhythm.

Hank was excited to share some of his fishing spots with his younger brother. How odd it felt to be in charge. Even though he had always felt older and wiser, it had been Vince's charismatic personality and gift for storytelling that kept Hank engaged and, more times than not, relieved not to be the one responsible for holding down the conversation. With the change of status between them, Vince came to enjoy and appreciate the calm, gentle tone of his brother's voice and his slow, systematic way of speaking, methodical, neat and tidy.

Auntie Leona greeted Linda with open arms. She immediately got busy going through Linda's surgery information. She read that Linda could return to work in one week and to general activities in approximately six weeks and that Linda needed to have water and eat baby food in three-ounce serving portions every three hours. The amount and timeline were crucial.

While Vince and Hank were fishing daily, Leona took care of and pampered Linda, who, in turn, delighted in the attention and felt loved. They talked about her surgery and the clothing store and shared fond memories of when Linda was a little girl.

Ever since Hank and Leona married, Leona and Frances became friends, even though Hank's former wife was still involved with the family. They liked each other as two close sisters would. Even Gladys, the previous wife, was occasionally included in the mix. Everyone just got along. When Linda shared about her mother's mental health issues, Leona fell silent. Neither of the women, aunt or niece, knew anything about manic depression or bipolar disorder. They struggled to form an opinion or an understanding, so they left the topic of Frances's outbursts alone.

Every morning after Leona's porridge, sizzling home-cured bacon, fresh farm eggs, and homemade toasted bread, the brothers packed up their tackle box and lunch pail to walk one block to the lake, just like two little boys heading off for a day of unbridled adventure.

The Shuswap Lake was remarkably calm that time of year, and even though it was the middle of summer, the speed boats and water skiers were unusually absent. The lake was graceful as the sun danced on its surface. With the untouched waters shining and glistening, that week was an ethereal and almost spiritual experience for the two men as they fished side by side. They noticed each other's presence with a clarity neither had experienced before.

Hank would occasionally ask how Vince was doing or share his political views on the NDP government, feeling somewhat giddy at having a captive audience. Mostly, though, the only sound that could be heard was the freckled trout leaping for flies and splashing back into the tranquil lake. There was mending, sewing, and cementing brotherly love that week, and both men felt it deeply.

When the week was up, Linda got in her vehicle and went back to Clinton, while Hank and Leona drove Vince home. When they arrived at the property in Mission, Frances was there waiting. She embraced her husband like he had been gone for months. No words were exchanged.

The two couples had shared many pleasant times over the years and had a lot of great memories. They were family, but also friends, and now they were together again under the saddest of circumstances. Even though they had a vague understanding of each other's struggles, the topics of marriage, money, raising children, death, and unbalanced behaviour were never brought to the surface for discussing and sorting. Instead, they laughed at days gone by, played bridge, and shared a social meal. Frances made her specialty: roast beef, mashed potatoes, and broccoli with cheese sauce.

The four of them were good-natured and good-humoured, and then they parted ways. Each went back to their idea of normalcy. That was to be the last time Hank and Leona would see Vince alive.

After Hank and Leona left for Blind Bay, Frances's eagerness to move back to North Vancouver brought her a glimmer of hope. The packing up would be arduous but necessary. The furniture and some belongings would stay behind. Doug, the eldest son and next-door neighbour, would watch over the property as it lay vacant for a time, partially empty and waiting.

As an assiduous current seemed to ignite Frances's brain in regard to packing and moving, there was also an underlying dread beneath her high spirits, waiting, lurking. As always, she would push down the reality that a dark day of depression was coming. It was almost as if she would forget that her emotions would not forever be on the upswing. Instead, she focused on the task at hand, moving and getting herself and Vince away from the property.

Frances would sidestep the realities of her husband's brain tumour, the doctor's appointments, specialists, and cancer treatments. Instead, she would be fueled by the past, her romantic courtship with Vince, years of marriage, four children, and happy memories: neighbourhood block parties, PTA meetings, curling at the North Shore Winter Club, and road trips to the Okanagan.

Frances felt like a bat out of hell flying backwards in time. She would try her best to behave reasonably, but every car horn, voice, and sideways glance seemed to be amplified—louder and more furious, sharper, preventing her from slowing down—and she could not seem to get the sting out of her words.

If she could only calm herself, then she would be able to think more clearly. Instead, the inevitable hurled towards her at breakneck speeds. It was coming—death and endings, all rolled up into one nice, neat package. Better not to think at all, she decided.

Frances had made arrangements for Linda's younger sister Karen and her new husband Dale to move into the Jones Avenue home. She suggested the couple take the upstairs while she and Vince would move into the fully contained basement suite.

Being the youngest child in the family, Karen grew up the centre of attention, like a new puppy added to the household and concurrently left out of the more in-depth, serious conversations. The upheavals that family life generated and the underlying strife were kept from her. What fell to Karen was not the burden but rather a lightness of being. Therefore, she maintained calm, people-pleasing patience and never questioned what she was oblivious to.

Now, as an adult living under the same roof with her mother and father again, Karen struggled to understand what they might be going through, often coming up short with ineffective strategies for coping. She survived by scurrying off to exercise classes and appeasing her mother while doting on her father.

Besides living somewhere above the clouds, Karen never took the calamity personally, not as Linda did. It had been ten years since the Rolley Lake Trail Riders, which meant ten years of two sisters growing apart. Karen felt removed, unaware of the complexities and cause and effect of Linda's torment and the years of bullying she had endured.

Even though they were worlds apart, they shared similar, yet different, childhood memories. Karen's upbringing consisted of her father's stories, games of charades, bulldozer rides, and trips to faraway places. Linda's, on the other hand, involved undivided attention and endless searches for horses, ranches, and trail rides.

Earlier on, after Linda left to become a cowgirl, Vince took the boys camping and fishing and coached their sports. The rest of the time, the two brothers were off at school.

Meanwhile, little Karen was alone with their mother, whose mood swings were just beginning to pick up speed. She spent hours by herself playing dolls or was a sidekick to her mother, traipsing all over town, not knowing any other way of being. Afternoon matinees, shopping sprees, talking to strangers—as a passive child, she happily went right along with their mother's shenanigans. What her mother thought comical, Karen did too.

At times it struck Karen as peculiar that she, Linda, Doug, and Ken were raised by the same parents under the same roof, yet unintentionally were compartmentalized by their parents, which would explain their diverse perspectives on how they were raised. Now despite their polar opposite lives, they were all imploding with grief at their current circumstances.

In 1987, with Vince close to death, Karen had a new marriage and yet was smack dab in the middle of it all while everyone in the family was elsewhere.

After recuperating with Auntie Leona, when Linda returned to her home in Clinton, she delved back into her coupon collecting, contests, and shopping for those who could not drive to nearby Kamloops for groceries. Freedom Fashions was doing well, and Linda began to be more of a silent partner.

The weight on her body began to melt off. However, the rules, regulations, and food options were almost impossible to adhere to. She had been warned that even one piece of raw broccoli could rip open her intestine that had been elasticized to make for a smaller space. Due to the small amount of food allowed, with nothing fresh and all of it pureed, Linda had to travel weekly to the hospital for enemas. She was in a state of survival. Sometimes she wondered if she had made a terrible mistake.

In addition to her health concerns, healing, and recovery, she was constantly on edge, waiting for the inevitable phone call to come, the ring that she dreaded, the call that would bring an end and finality to her hero.

In early September, it came. The ear-splitting ring was ominous. Frances said very little but suggested that Linda not waste time getting to the coast, as her father had just been admitted to Lions Gate Hospital in North Vancouver. The end would be soon.

Simultaneously with the news of her father's looming death, Linda received another phone call. This one came from her accountant, stating that Freedom Fashions was on the brink of bankruptcy due to her business partner's sketchy management of the store. All Linda could do was pack, drive, and pray that bad luck would not come in threes as the old superstition suggested.

Upon arrival in North Vancouver, Linda realized that her mother was not coping well. Linda set up a lazy boy recliner, available to all of the family members, in the palliative care ward at Lions Gate Hospital. She often stayed there overnight.

Nurses were kind and caring, but no calendar or agenda could predict when Vince's time would come. The clipboard that hung at the end of his bed had no hidden code or messages of everlasting life. When he took his last breath, Linda was not there. She had gone back to the Jones Avenue home momentarily to shower, rest, and regroup.

When it happened and death came knocking, Frances was holding Vince's hand. He inhaled sharply, and his lungs filled with one final gulp of air. The father of their four adult children, and friend to all, was gone. She tried to revive him. With extra-human strength, she pulled him up to a seated position and pounded him on the back.

It did not work, and he passed silently on September 25, 1987, just one month after his seventy-second birthday.

Frances had fleeting memories of special moments they had shared over the years: waltzing in the Copper Room at the Harrison Hot Springs Hotel—they had danced well together; Vince cracking crab legs so she could easily pick out the succulent sweet flesh, and then him joking, "Hey, aren't you going to save some for me?" followed by her crying from embarrassment and Vince feeling terribly bad; his many repeated stories that she began to tune out over the years—how she wished to hear them again.

Now what?

After spending night after night at her dad's bedside, Linda had briefly gone back to her mother's home. She hadn't planned on staying very long, but she fell into a deep sleep and was awakened by a dream, an image of her father standing at the foot of her bed. He was smiling and waving goodbye. He whispered that he loved her.

Linda was not frightened but rather was alerted to the fact that he must have died. What followed was chaos.

Linda fled for the hospital and could not find a parking spot. She stopped outside the police station, which was next door to the hospital. Crying out to an RCMP officer standing on the sidewalk, she yelled, "My father just died, and I cannot find a parking spot!" The kind policeman said, "Throw me your keys. I'll park it for you!"

She arrived as her sister and mother were coming out. Frances said, "No use in going up. He's dead."

Feelings were overwhelming and sat in the pit of everyone's stomach. The entire family was devastated. Unspoken words wedged them all apart, like huge spaces and gaps that could not be bridged.

Linda became angry. She wondered why she felt like an outsider when she was there first. She was so loved and nurtured as a baby, always protected and the apple of her father's eye, yet treated like a grown-up by her mother.

She relished in reflections of her childhood and could only think of the good times. At the same time, she felt trapped and confused with the reminder of mortality.

On the day of the funeral, Linda found out there was no money left in the store's business account. She had gone to the bank, as she planned to purchase some snacks for the wake, and her personal account had been drained too. A few days prior, Frances had invested money to bring the store back, to get it above water again. But like a sieve, her cash was depleted as soon as it was poured in. Freedom Fashions had been successful. Improper management was taking it under.

Despite her mental state, Frances tried to put her family first. Unfortunately, she confused them all with her frenzy and her unbalanced flare-ups. In the depths of her heart, there was great love, but it was smothered behind her imbalances, making it nearly impossible for others to see it.

After the funeral, Linda was anxious and antsy. In the late afternoon, she left the wake to race back to 100 Mile House, mainly to take note of the damage and try to figure out what to do next with Freedom Fashions. She hoped she could rescue the fashionable plus-size store.

Visualizing the plaid coats, jewel-studded blue jeans, and frilly undergarments hanging on the racks in the darkness brought her great annoyance and uncertainty. Foreseeing empty change rooms and a padlocked front door brought Linda to an overwhelming state of exhaustion.

Her father's spirit gave her composure as she left North Vancouver. His presence seemed to encapsulate her vehicle. Linda was certain he was there with her, a warm, bright sensation of comfort.

She still appreciated long drives. The highways and byways with their hills, twists, and turns brought a sense of unravelling to her tightly wound thoughts. A calming and sorting process took place as her vehicle obeyed her demands and hummed along.

When Linda got to Spence's Bridge, approximately three hours into her drive and closer to her destination than where she was coming from, she was engrossed in a perpetual state of thinking and reliving her past, combined with figuring out her future, and she decided to pull over for a drink.

Usually, Linda would drive right through and never consider purchasing an expensive product when she could get it in bulk somewhere else, for less. Nevertheless, she was unusually thirsty and desperate for a beverage.

A strong force told her to get off the road and stop—something indescribable, pulling and tugging at her with great urgency. Her mouth had become dry and dehydrated, making it difficult to swallow, so she embraced the urgency.

Within minutes of leaving the highway, a landslide happened, just ahead of where Linda would have been travelling, on the same road towards Ashcroft. In an instant, she had sidestepped the third link in the chain of bad luck with, she sensed, her father's guidance.

While she waited for the road to be cleared, seeing the earth-moving equipment brought an instant reflection of her dad and his excavating business. It brought a pang of regret to her heart, remembering that when she was younger, he had wanted her to be a cat operator alongside him—father and daughter, clearing land together.

She smiled at the thought of it, and then her views shifted. Momentarily she was happy to be rid of her family. In retrospect, the funeral had been harrowing. Her mother's toxic behaviour was almost unbearable. She had nothing in common with Karen anymore, and both of her brothers were with women she could not relate to. She loved them and would defend them at all costs, but that was about all. At least for now.

With Dad gone, who will be the glue to keep the family together, she wondered?

She then thought of the Coldwells, another family she had loved. A different family, one that had horseback riding, hunting, and card games in common and working the land, shared meals, laughter, and love. A family that she missed and longed for.

After the first meeting with a lawyer, Linda locked her business partner out. She had abused their contract, not to mention their friendship, and Linda learned it was her legal right to take action.

While she was overwrought with grief at her dying father's bedside, the partner whom Linda had trusted was charging the Freedom Fashions business account for personal items. Many dishonest acts had been committed in Linda's absence. Linda took over and tried to make a go of it. Her mom tried to help. However, unbalanced, flying-off-the-handle types of people can rarely make a go of anything.

Frances eagerly kept putting money into Linda's account and even drove up to 100 Mile House to work in the store, which turned into a disaster and did more harm than good.

Frances was up, high as a kite. She was excessively laughing and manically jovial. The small town of 100 Mile House thought the circus had come to town. Some were drawn to Frances, while others were driven away.

Eventually, Linda shut the store down on the advice of her accountant. She took the surplus of unsold items to Clinton and opened a makeshift store at the suggestion of a dear friend who had a substantially sized home. They turned the remains and leftovers into a clothing party of sorts and had no problem selling and outfitting plus-size women with capes, gowns, and accessories in the unsuspecting western town.

. Checkered pantsuits and fluffy, hot-pink coats could be spotted on Clinton's streets like exotic birds. Unusual sightings and glimpses of the beautiful, bold women caused heads to turn and smiles of admiration to form on the faces of many rugged cowboys. The dream was shattered, but it would live on in sequined fabric and cotton and wool garments for many years to come.

By winter, Linda had lost one hundred pounds in only nine months. Her food consisted of a jar of baby food ingested slowly three times a day while sipping water constantly.

She missed her late-night snacks and social gatherings at friend's ranches and restaurants. Roast beef dinners, burgers, and french fries had little meaning and enjoyment due to the lap-band surgery. She was primarily full all the time, and the food that graced her palette tasted like dust.

With the weight loss, though, her back felt better, her knees worked better, and her clothes fit better—all positives. She was also able to ride horses again, but the downside was living in constant fear.

Linda was worried sick about what was going on inside of her shrinking belly. There had been numerous strict warnings of the hazards too much food would cause, how anything other than pureed food could be the death of her.

She had made a friend—another woman undergoing the same procedure—whom Linda met in the waiting room at Saint Paul's hospital in Vancouver. They exchanged phone numbers, and since it had been highly recommended to have a support system in place, she was pleased with her new acquaintance.

Linda got in the habit of calling her new weight loss friend weekly. Sadly, the last time she called, the person on the other end of the line said her lap-band buddy had died. The shocking news shook Linda to the core and caused an adverse effect.

She slowly began to slip.

Linda started her road back to real food with ice cream. The sweet, heavenly flavours brought a sense of joy to her tastebuds. She validated the spoons full of icy vanilla and strawberry melting goodness by savouring every mouthful, eating more slowly than she had ever done before. Her weight crept up little by little. All the compliments ceased, and comments about her increasing body mass returned.

Linda was still attending rodeos and dances and remained the life of the party. When one of her dance partners suggested that it wouldn't hurt her to lose another twenty pounds, she laughed it off, stating to the rude, outspoken man, "Many of my gorgeous boyfriends prefer me just the way I am, men who are far more attractive than you," she added with a dazzling smile.

Linda was often astounded at the uncaring blanket statements and rude remarks people made without knowing who she was. They were not therapists or dear close friends but unacquainted busybodies. How could they think their opinion mattered?

Always baffled, she realized that stranger's remarks still hurt her feelings, although she realized that her thick skin protected her, and her sense of humour always acted as a shield of armour.

The disrespect from others invariably brought Linda back to what was important—the friends she had made over the years and the people who loved her for who she was. One, in particular, was her close friend Jimmy Bourgeois. They instantly became fast and furious friends when they first met at a rodeo in 1966. They called themselves birds of a feather who flocked together.

Jimmy was handsome and kind and of First Nations descent. Their relationship was, and continued to be, strictly platonic. They hung out and knew a lot of the same people. Sometimes Jimmy accompanied Linda on her drives to the coast. He helped her out, and she helped him out. They shared boyfriend and girlfriend stories and struggles and got along famously.

On one trip, early on in their friendship in the late 1960s, Jimmy had accompanied Linda back to her home in North Vancouver. They were travelling down Kingsway in Vancouver when a Harley-Davidson motorcycle pulled up alongside them at a streetlight.

The rider was outfitted in head-to-toe leather gear, but what struck Jimmy as comical was the attached sidecar and the passenger within. A huge man was wedged inside, with his bulging body overflowing the confined space. What struck Jimmy as most humorous was the jewelled crown on the man's head, so out of context to the usual image of a motorcycle rider, revving engine, and tough-guy scowl. Jimmy burst out in laughter at the strange sight and wondered how the motorcycle could remain upright.

The biker noticed his eruption of amusement and took a dim view. He proceeded to follow them. Quick-thinking Linda pulled into a police station, and the motorcycle high-tailed it out of there. The next day, Linda found tacks that had been neatly placed under her car's wheels outside her childhood home in North Vancouver. They wondered if this action was related to being followed the day before.

There was another motorcycle incident shortly after she and Jimmy were followed. Sometime before 1970, the Burnaby Cat Walkers, a motorcycle club, came to Clinton. Rumour had it that they were there to take over the town. Dozens of choppers in all forms with their riders, who also came in all forms, pulled into town with a set of ideals that celebrated freedom, nonconformity to mainstream culture, and loyalty only to their own kind.

Linda and Jimmy immediately noticed the man in the lead as the sidecar passenger who wore the crown a few years back. Years later, they found out the man's name was Brian Binns, and he was quite a lovely man. Lots of friends and no enemies whatsoever, or so the record stated.

All in all, bikers and cowboys were not a great match for one another, but everyone thought it would be a great theme for a movie—the day the bikers came to take over Clinton, BC.

After Freedom Fashions closed down, Linda became a nanny. Children loved her jokes and cuddles. Bouncing them on her comfortable knees, she sang them Beatles songs and laughed at their antics. She cooked them Beefaroni from a tin, and Pillsbury doughboys leaped out from a tube to create hot, flaky crescent rolls.

They adored her adventurous spirit, stories, jokes, and horse sense all combined. Linda played school with them and turned learning into a game. She taught them about money and paying bills and gave them little math assignments. The local schoolteachers loved getting Linda's daycare kids over the years because they all knew their ABCs, could print, and do basic math calculations.

All in all, Linda was Auntie Lynn to many and fondly looked forward to early mornings, days, and afternoons with the Thomson, Nelson, Bourgeois, Guerin, and Grinder kids. After Jimmy and his wife divorced, Linda became his number one babysitter and caregiver to his children while he was working at the mill. He paid her well, and Linda fell in love with his children, as she did with all of them, although she enjoyed knowing that she could get back to her contests, Western shows, and card games at the end of the day.

Jimmy had gotten to know Linda (Lynn to him and others) so well that he noticed the times when she appeared to be slightly lacklustre or even lonely on occasion. So, he took it upon himself to arrange a date for Linda with an older widowed man he knew.

She had met him years earlier, as one would make an acquaintance, but they were both doing different things at the time and with other people back then.

The man was a handsome fellow with a dry sense of humour who enjoyed the rodeo and a card game or two. His name was Doug Brown. Just the mention of his name gave Linda a funny sensation in her heart and stomach, a wonderful feeling that was warm and fuzzy and reminiscent of many years prior.

Fran and Vince at Karen's wedding

Karen and Vince on one of their trips

CHAPTER SEVENTEEN

Romance and Reno

"In the journey of finding love, I focus on loving myself first."

-Angel Moreira

Dennis, David, Dave, Dwayne, Dale, Dan, Donald, and now Doug. The letter "D" in a name is said to represent determination and diligence. People with D as the first letter want security and have a systematic way of solving their problems. D people offer sound advice and are very empathetic, they always seem to know what is right, and everyone wants to be in their presence. They are pragmatic and learn how to get things done. D in their name indicates they can see things others usually ignore.

Which is precisely why, when a co-worker at the mill asked Doug, "Why would you want to date someone fat like Lynn?" Doug's response was, "Oh, I hadn't noticed. All I see is her beautiful, caring eyes, gorgeous smile, and fun, happy nature." The said co-worker slunk off, knowing he had been cruel and possibly wrong about Doug's new lady.

When Linda had met Doug years earlier, she immediately felt an attraction for him. However, he was married to a wonderful woman twenty years older than him named Anna, who had eight children, some of whom were close in age to Doug. They married when Doug was thirty-nine, and she was fifty-nine. At that time, Linda also was with someone else.

Linda would never be a homewrecker, so she admired Doug from afar and carried on with her busy life. However, there came a time when Jimmy knew that Anna had passed, so when he suggested to Linda that Doug was now available, and since Linda was too, she went right to work figuring out a plan.

A couple of days later, she dressed up in her finest blue jeans, Western belt, pink blouse, and dangly cowboy boot earrings and drove over to where Doug was living.

Clinton being the small town that it was meant that everyone knew where everyone else lived, what they drove, how many kids they had, where they worked, and what they were having for dinner. After knocking on his door with confidence, she was invited in. Linda suggested a game of cribbage. Doug was shy but happy for the company, so he gladly accepted. As he set up the crib board, Linda put a batch of chocolate chip muffins on the table. She had a way of doctoring instant muffin mixes so they almost tasted homemade. These had a sprinkling of cinnamon and milk instead of water added to the Quaker Oats mix.

In making conversation, Doug mentioned that he needed to drive into Kamloops on the coming Saturday. Fast-thinking Linda asked if she could catch a ride and be dropped off at the bingo parlour. She suggested he conduct his business and then pick her up afterwards, and perhaps they could go for dinner on the way back to Clinton.

When Saturday rolled around, Doug arrived in his 1980 Chevy pickup truck. As a gentleman, he parked, turned off the engine, and went up to Linda's door. Linda answered the door with excitement, eagerly taking in the wonder of Doug's gentle face. The first thing Linda noticed was his straight, white teeth and broad smile, which seemed magnified by his dark, rugged complexion. During the drive, as they listened to the country radio station, Conway Twitty's popular song from 1989, "She's Got a Single Thing on Her Mind," came on, causing Linda and Doug both to blush and then laugh out loud.

After getting dropped off at bingo, Linda could hardly see the numbers under the B-I-N-G-O or concentrate on the caller. She had not felt butterflies and the stirrings of love for almost twenty years, at least since she had been with David. She could hardly wait for the game to end, even though she won fifty bucks in the interim.

Soon enough, Doug was there right on time to pick her up. Linda felt fabulous being picked up by such a handsome older man. On the drive back to Clinton, Linda found out that Doug was fifty-eight. Being fast with numbers, she realized that he was not all that much older than her forty-two years, mostly since she had dated far younger men back in the day. She knew that connecting with Doug was a step in the right direction.

At the 20 Mile Café, while sitting across from Doug, she observed more endearing qualities to the quiet, sweet man across from her. Doug was impeccably dressed in a light-brown Western shirt, GWG blue jeans, and a bucking bronco belt buckle that pulled the whole outfit together. Besides his attire, what Linda admired most was Doug's deep-set, brown eyes that held a mischievous twinkle.

He found Linda's energy and dynamic personality amusing. Not in a mean or disrespectful way, but more of a proud, "I'm so glad that I am with this woman" sort of way. Linda gladly reciprocated. With Doug not being a huge talker, Linda jumped right in and spoke about herself, her family, and what she did for a living. When she recanted her love affair with horses, Doug's eyes lit up, and he began to open up and share about his love for the rodeo.

She asked him questions about his life and his past. When he confided in her that he used to smoke three packs of cigarettes a day and drink plenty of whiskey, Linda was taken aback. He followed by saying what a perfect match they were because he no longer had those nasty bad habits and how pleased he was that she never partook. With her sense of humour always ready with a quick one-liner, she said, "The only bad habit I have is food." Doug responded in his slow drawl, with a twinkle in his eye, "There ain't nothing wrong with having a healthy appetite."

Over a meal of liver and onions at the diner between Kamloops and Clinton, Linda and Doug became smitten with each other. After the meal, they set up their next date, and in doing so, the rest of their lives together.

Those who live in the Cariboo do so primarily because they were born and raised there. Those who move to the Cariboo are referred to as city slickers and are attracted to the land and the privacy—endless views of mother nature with no need to worry about the business of city lights and sounds and neighbours on your doorstep.

The Cariboo is a land of dry heat in the summer and biting cold winters with quiet and pristine snowdrifts. But it is the bright-blue skies all year round that give the sensation that only God could have created such a remarkable place. Coupled with hard physical work on the many ranches, fresh air, and endless opportunities to connect with nature, the Cariboo is loved by all who pass through or choose to live there.

After a few short months, Linda Bonner and Doug Brown started to talk about moving in together. But first, Linda felt that she needed a second opinion.

Uncle Hank and Auntie Leona became surrogate parents to Linda after her father died. She had taken to visiting them every two or three months. They moved away from their beautiful Blind Bay home shortly after Auntie Leona suffered a stroke. Uncle Hank wanted them to be closer to a hospital, so they moved to Salmon Arm.

Their six daughters, Linda's cousins, were all very close to their parents, and their entire family gave Linda and her siblings many fond memories of visits from long ago.

During the 1950s, '60s, and '70s, they delighted in Uncle Hank's various farms and properties. Auntie Leona's cooking and Uncle Hank's garden combined could be formed on the tastebuds of the mind while daydreaming about what would be set on the kitchen table. Fresh sweet corn, massive, juicy, vine-ripe tomatoes, and delicious, freshly dug potatoes complemented Leona's soups, stews, and fresh-baked bread. Most memorable were her fruit pies with flaky and tender homemade pie crust.

Card games were played around the kitchen table late into the evening while everyone listened to Uncle Vince's stories. His antics and well-known laugh that originated deep in his chest always provoked laughter in others, whether his jokes were funny or not. Everything about him was contagious.

They had all admired Uncle Vince tremendously. After his passing, the relatives were unsure how Auntie Fran might be faring. Everyone tried to understand her, even when she had taken to calling them in the middle of the night. Her tone was unlike the aunt they knew and loved, and her rants were, time after time, confusing and unrecognizable.

Without speaking about it, Linda, Doug, Ken, and Karen had hoped their mother's unbalanced behaviour was falling under the radar of their dear cousins and the aunt and uncle who were all family members but also friends.

Shortly into their dating, Linda and Doug took a drive to visit Uncle Hank and Auntie Leona. Ultimately, they both approved and welcomed Doug into the family with open arms.

Salmon Arm is a city in the Columbia Shuswap District of the Southern Interior of the Canadian province of British Columbia. Salmon Arm is located within the traditional territory of the Secwepemc First Nations. The Canadian Pacific Railway brought miners and settlers in 1885. The area became known for its fruit harvest, which became a leading product for export around the nation as the town grew to city status.

In 1951, Princess Elizabeth, Duchess of Edinburgh and Prince Phillip, Duke of Edinburgh, visited Salmon Arm while on a royal tour of Canada.

Another memorable occasion took place on August 8, 1982, while Prime Minister Pierre Elliot Trudeau and his sons passed through Salmon Arm on the train. They were confronted by three demonstrators protesting high unemployment and how the Prime Minister was handling the economy. Trudeau infamously gave the protestors the finger. His gesture was caught on a television camera. After the incident, T-shirts that depicted Trudeau's caricature leaning out of a train with his middle finger raised were produced and sold to Salmon Arms citizens.

Linda's heart ached for her dad, and she was pleased that Doug had the chance to meet him, as unbeknownst to Linda, Doug had met Vince on numerous occasions before they were dating. Small towns are like that. They had a lot in common and had gotten along well. Every small town has a diner, convenience store, hardware store, and gas station. So, every time Linda's dad visited, he coincidently ran into Doug. Some may call it kismet; Linda and Doug called it destiny.

And now, only her mom was left. Linda had a hard time dealing with her mother's changes and had decided to give it some time before allowing Doug to see her as the loose cannon she had become. She hoped and prayed for just the right opportunity.

Meanwhile, back at home, Frances had set herself up with a job. Since her twenties, she had not officially worked in the outside world, living instead as a housewife, homemaker, and mother, doing the bookkeeping for her husband's bulldozing business, and driving the kids around— these were her stay-at-home professions.

The family was initially surprised and somewhat concerned when their newly widowed mother became a 7-11 employee working the graveyard shift. At the same time, they concluded that she was happy, keeping busy, and meeting people. Each in their own way, the siblings were tending to their mom, who was living alone and renting an apartment at Third and Chesterfield in North Vancouver, entirely by herself.

Karen was expecting a baby while her husband Dale was renovating the log home in Stave Falls, and both were looking forward to raising their family there. Ken visited their mom regularly, taking her out to bingo and watching old movies and game shows on television, while eldest brother Doug took care of business, helping with the death certificate and finalizing such matters. As a health-conscious eater, he took to bringing his mother salads and concocted blender drinks whenever he stopped by.

All the children loved their mom, aside from her difficulties. In turn, she enjoyed them immensely, as individual as they were, even though she could never come up with the words to tell them.

Frances missed Vince very much but told no one. On the nights she could not sleep, she thought of the instant coffee and Coffee-Mate he regularly served her. When various customers came into the 7-11, Frances wondered how Vince would have welcomed them; perhaps a pleasant hello and a funny story, she figured. When thinking of getting a cat, she remembered Vince with the farm animals...and so on it would go. He was never far from her mind, and for that reason, she never entertained the idea of going on a date. She knew that no man would or could ever measure up.

Frances was 67, with a lot of life left in her. She often stated that she was not interested in taking care of a man at this point in the game, even though she had many offers.

Instead, she would work, visit with her children, and nervously welcome the new grandchild. She would sleep on her down days, and on her energetic days, she would dazzle and entertain the customers at the store. Younger co-workers marvelled at her outgoing and fun personality, never knowing that anything was amiss or that her brain was either spinning out of control or hiding in the shadows.

Eventually, Frances quit her job and left North Vancouver. She was agitated with how everything had changed. People had died or moved away. Others were busy. She never once thought that maybe her extreme moods caused people to wonder. Her usual demure personality from fifteen years prior was gone. The new Frances rarely slept and frequently spoke up. She called people out on things and gave money away to strangers.

She boldly stated, "One can never go back." With that being said, she packed up and moved to Maple Ridge to be closer to her children. Frances landed a job at another 7-11 on Dewdney Trunk Road and continued to entertain customers and strangers while once again falling into a deep, dark stupor on her days off.

As for Linda, it was her time to shine. Her relationship with Doug was moving quickly and splendidly. So much so that they decided to move in together. However, before making the big step, Linda thought it a good idea if they went on a road trip together.

They chose Reno, Nevada, as their destination. After all, they both enjoyed driving long distances, playing bingo, and winning big. And boy, did they ever win big! Plus, Reno had the charm of the Old West through and through.

Reno, Nevada, "The Biggest Little City in The World" is as Western as they come and filled with history. In the early 1800s, prospectors took the west by storm with hopes and dreams of making it rich by mining gold and silver. Nevada was being overrun with these men, and though they worked hard during the day, they played even harder at night.

The first significant silver deposit found in the United States was called The Comstock Lode, which turned Nevada into a boozy, brawling, brotherly town almost overnight. The miners had the gambling bug, and they could be found every night in the saloons playing games and betting their hard-earned money while drinking the night away. This led to many different problems with the law, from fighting to much, much worse. In 1860, the governor of the Nevada territory took a stand against gambling. By 1861, gambling had been banned, and anyone caught gambling was penalized.

Reno was officially established in 1868. In 1869, the lawmakers decided to give in a little and legalized some forms of gambling. These laws were enough for the time and remained unchanged for another forty years. Reno became a quickie divorce destination in the early 1900s.

In 1909 there was a big push for all types of gambling to be legalized. Nickel slot machines became popular, followed by card games, which eventually made Reno the world's gambling capital.

By 1930 all gambling was legal. This meant the games played in the rundown shacks and backrooms could be moved into the casinos and be played on the main floor.

Reno was a front runner in creating the model of a destination holiday with hotel and casino gambling, a model that has been replicated throughout the world. In 1937 a businessman by the name of William Fish Harrah opened the first bingo hall. He also founded Harrah's Entertainment, which became Caesars Entertainment, which would grow to be the headquarters for many casinos worldwide.

On their first trip together, Doug and Linda left Clinton bright and early in the morning, and by noon, they were in Red Deer, with the plan to visit Doug's brother Cecil. He was enamoured with Linda right off the bat, which sealed the deal for Doug.

Linda was amazed at how fast the drive had gone, as she and Doug talked all the way. They eventually turned off the radio because it was getting in the way of their conversation. By the time they reached the Alberta border, they were finishing each other's sentences.

Doug always preferred staying in motels as opposed to hotels. He liked having a door directly to the outside, and he felt better knowing he could back his pickup truck right outside the window of their room. Not knowing Doug's preference of where to stay at the time, Linda had made arrangements for them to stay at a quaint little bed and breakfast for the sake of romance, and Doug agreed. Pulling up to the place, upon first sight, they could not help but notice how the stately manor resembled the house from the horror movie *Psycho*.

As a teenager, Linda had gone to the local movie theatre in Lynn Valley, called the Cedar V Theatre. In 1960 there was a buzz that the Alfred Hitchcock movie *Psycho* would be a blockbuster hit. The film stars were Anthony Perkins, Janet Leigh, Vera Miles, John Gavin, and Martin Balsam. The plot centred on an encounter between on-the-run embezzler Marion Crane and shy motel proprietor Norman Bates and its horrific aftermath. A private investigator, who was Marion's lover, Sam, and her sister Lila investigated the cause of her disappearance.

The film was initially considered controversial and received mixed reviews. *Psycho* was nominated for four Academy Awards, including Best Supporting Actress for Leigh and Best Director for Hitchcock.

At the age of thirteen, Linda had never shrieked so loud in her life. The famed shower curtain stabbing scene would be etched in her mind forever. In unison with the tense on-screen violence and her screaming, Linda threw her popcorn in the air with the bucket's contents emptying everywhere. Consequently, the empty container landed on the girl's head who was sitting directly in front of Linda, which startled the unsuspecting girl just as much as the movie did. Linda vowed never to see another scary movie again as long as she lived.

Now here they were at a similar house to that of Norman Bates's creepy mother. When Linda and Doug checked in, a tall, slender, quiet man took their information. He had an odd way of averting his eyes, not looking the couple directly in the eyes, giving him a dishonest appearance. Linda and Doug grimaced to one another.

Upon checking into their room, they noticed how shabby and unkempt it was. Linda was afraid to go into the bathroom, and they both got the eerie feeling they were being watched. Just like finishing each other's sentences, they also finished each other's thoughts, and it was then that they both decided to check out and drive a few more miles to the nearest motel. They had a good laugh about the possible *Psycho* movie re-enactment, with peepholes and a sinister front desk man. Both were thankful they left and that neither of them had used the shower in the scummy bath.

They checked into a motel in Reno and headed out for dinner. Reno was famous for its buffet-style dining. Linda and Doug agreed it was the best way to enjoy a meal with so much variety—all you could eat seafood, prime rib, lasagna, scalloped potatoes, and salads galore and the dessert table could not be missed. After their fine meal, they went to the Nugget Casino for some bingo.

Shortly after sitting down to play, Linda won fifty dollars. At the next game, Doug won $50.00, and at the very end was the blackout game, which was a full-card, and the caller would call fifty-one numbers. Linda won on the fiftieth number called: the grand prize of $2,000. They laughed and cheered at the fun they had and their incredible luck.

Unfortunately, being Canadian, before they could receive their winnings, calculations were made on every dollar for tax purposes, which meant $600.00 was deducted from Linda's total winnings.

The following day was a ninety-nine-cent breakfast before a day of shopping—bacon and eggs, pancakes and waffles, hash browns and toast. Ever since Linda's wine and egg diet of many years earlier, she abhorred eggs entirely, so she passed hers onto Doug's plate and shared his bacon as a replacement. Doug marvelled at Linda's healthy appetite, and both were not wasteful, always determined to get their money's worth by cleaning their plates, being full and satisfied as a result.

Linda adored costume jewelry and Reno had the market on earrings, necklaces, and brooches. She was excited to add a few pieces to her collection. Doug was patient and kindly followed Linda's lead. He strolled behind her if she was on a shopping blitz with a bee in her bonnet or held her hand if they were meandering and gazing through store windows. He highly regarded everything about her and did not want to be anywhere else, and the feeling was mutual.

On the drive back home to Canada, they chose a different route via Snohomish, Washington. After pulling over for lunch at the Snohomish Bingo Hall, they decided to play a few games. Doug won $450.00. All in all, they chalked it up to a fun, romantic, profitable holiday all the way around.

Independence could have been Linda's middle name. Between looking after children, shopping for seniors, playing crib and bingo, coupon sorting, and now dating Doug, Linda still found time to ride with her friend Jesse.

Her weight had crept up since her surgery, as it would have been impossible for her to keep up such a strict eating regime. Besides, she had finally concluded that dieting made everything boring, and there was nothing pleasurable about it. Now that she and Doug were travelling four to five times a year, it was impractical to find food at truck stops and diners that fit into a diet plan. Furthermore, Linda's mental energy felt wasted with calorie counting, point taking, weighing food, and reading packages. For so long, she had taken pride in saying no to desserts and spent equally the same amount of time worrying about weight gain.

She knew in her heart of hearts that there were certain myths about being thin and that her problems would not go away. She also knew that loneliness was a key component to her overindulging.

Linda was no longer lonely. She decided that she had never been happier, and with Doug, she was living her best life in her body that *he* professed to love. She had a new lease on life and finally felt loved for who she was.

To her, Doug was the most handsome man she had ever dated, with David being a faded, distant memory. Doug was a hard worker and was fit without exercising, never watching or worrying about his food intake, which reminded Linda so much of her father.

They moved in together and took to driving three times a year to Reno, to Red Deer to see his family, and to another place called Bonners Ferry in Idaho for more family. Everyone in Doug's clan cherished everything about Linda—all except his stepchildren. Linda could not pinpoint why they were reluctant to accept her, especially since she knew all of them from around town before she and Doug got together. At that time, they were fine with her, pleasant and friendly. However, Doug's brother was different. He marvelled at how Doug could find love again and how well-suited Linda and Doug were.

Bingo became their go-to activity. They never lost money; luck was to follow them to Marysville, Washington, the Tulalip Casino, Mt. Vernon, and the local church bingo places close to home. They had other favourite routines in among their beloved game. Every

Saturday, while Doug watched the rodeos that were broadcast from all over the world on television, Linda rode horses with her dear friend Jesse at the Cut Off Valley Riding Club. Or she would sit at the table doing her coupon sorting and bar code collecting.

They entertained friends in their small home and followed the rodeo circuit throughout the Cariboo. Among their many social activities, there was one minor hairline fracture. One part of their relationship bothered Linda, and it was something she could never tell Doug about.

Doug was good friends with her ex-boyfriend Dale. Since Doug did not drink, when Dale came over for cards, he did not drink either. She felt bad not telling Doug certain parts about her past, so when Dale came over, Linda rarely said much and let the two men have their friendship. Linda was reminded of Dale's good, caring nature, and she thanked God regularly that Doug did not drink. Besides, living in such a tight-knit community, Linda realized it was unlikely that the two men would not know each other.

Eventually, Linda introduced Doug to her family. His gentle nature and sense of humour were a perfect match for Frances and her outlandish behaviour. When Linda and her mother did not see eye to eye or Frances's moods were unbearable, Doug could find something positive or humorous about the whole scenario. Or he would simply steer Linda away from the pandemonium that came with Frances like a package deal. Being an avid card player, Linda's mom and Doug could find some semblance of order and fun when sitting across the table from one another playing cards.

Unperceived to pretty much everyone, including herself, there were many things about Linda that Frances admired. Not being able to voice or even show her admiration, Frances displayed her love in ways other than a hug or saying *I love you.*

She enjoyed playing bingo with her eldest daughter and shared their frugal ways of collecting coupons. Contests, mail-in codes, and box tops made for somewhat of a game but one that resulted in financial wins that were prudent and thrifty.

Frances still had fond memories of her firstborn and her loving husband together, when it was just the three of them before the other children had been born and the wires in her brain had become crossed. She cherished her memories of hopping on the streetcar in Vancouver, trips to the Okanagan and watching Linda ride horses, the fun they had attending the horse races at the Vancouver Race Course, and picnics at Jericho Beach in the early days.

Now that Linda was grown and the years had picked up speed, Frances wore her Freedom Fashions sequined tops, velour pantsuits, and jewel-studded flowing capes with enthusiasm and pride. But she knew that she was not as close to her daughter as a mother should be. Having never been demonstrative with her feelings, Frances struggled to express herself in the ways that Linda had longed for a mother to do. So, they would continue with the relationship they had.

By 1995, Doug and Linda shared everything from their interest in cards and bingo to their taste in everything Western. They enjoyed the simple things, specifically, well-liked television shows including *The Commish*; *Walker, Texas Ranger*; *Dr. Quinn Medicine Woman*; *Matlock*; and *Murder She Wrote* with Angela Lansbury.

Six years into their union, they were settling in quite nicely, as couples do. At times they felt cast in the same mould, on the same wavelength, and knew in their hearts they were soul mates. That said, there were also many ways in which they were comfortably different. Their personalities completed each other. Doug was cool and calm, and Linda was warm and excitable.

The tables would be turned when they would unexpectedly be faced with some terrible news. When good health abruptly shifts into bad health, not just one person is affected. When we love a person so profoundly, we, too, are afflicted when things go wrong for them.

In between joy and gratitude, which both Linda and Doug had buckets of, they were about to be tested when extreme ill-health came knocking, and Linda would soon be taking the lead.

Doug and Linda's pride and joy, 1980 GMC

Linda at Bonner's ferry

Doug Brown and Linda

Lucky Winner!

Lynne Benner is shown above with Charles from the Central Market in Clinton. She was a $1000 winner of the No Name groceries draw in Vancouver. Lynne shops at Central market and says she only had one entry. Both she and Charles were delighted a Clintonite won.

Linda shaking store owners hand celebrating her $1000 grocery prize win

CHAPTER EIGHTEEN

Joy and Gratitude

*"Gratitude makes sense of our past, brings peace for
today, and creates a vision for tomorrow."*

-Melody Beatie

In August of 1995, shortly after Doug's afternoon shift began at
the mill, he suffered a minor heart attack that no one saw coming.

After being sent home from work and coming through the
kitchen door of their small bungalow, Linda gasped at the sight of
him. His skin was of a grey pallor, and his familiar, friendly face
was void of expression. His usual broad-shouldered stance was
heavy and rounded. Doug did not appear well.

He shuffled slowly across the kitchen floor. Linda helped
him to their bedroom and into bed, not knowing if he was sick,
rundown, or just under the weather. She barely slept all night
as Doug fell into a deep, motionless sleep beside her. Close to
morning, Doug shot out of bed and began stamping his feet on the
floor. Linda instinctively and urgently called the doctor.

Dr. Campbell was the local doctor who had once been a city
slicker from the coast, a term the locals created for him and
snickered at under their breath. For reasons unknown to Clinton's

community, he left his thriving practice in Vancouver, bought a property, and became a country doctor.

Linda had gone to see him once, but he was quite disdainful towards her, telling her that he would not treat her unless she were to lose an abundance of weight first. This rattled Linda, and she chose never to go back.

Occasionally she would see Dr. Campbell at the Cut Off Valley Riding Club. The first time they bumped into one another, Linda greeted him with a big smile of acknowledgement. He, in turn, snubbed her. She persisted, making a point to say *hello, lovely day, enjoy your ride, bye for now,* each time she saw him. In response, he looked right through her as if she were invisible.

To locals, he sometimes appeared brusque and condescending. He acted a little bit better than everyone and seemed to lack respect for rural people and their lifestyle. However, Dr. Campbell was Doug's family doctor, so Linda made the call regardless of the doctor's feelings (or lack thereof) towards her.

It was an emergency of the most significant kind. He instructed Linda to take Doug immediately to the hospital in Ashcroft. There it was detected that he'd had a heart attack. Doug was then sent to the hospital in Kamloops.

The Kamloops hospital was not in Doctor Campbell's jurisdiction, so he did not have privileges there, but he still popped in and visited Doug. He was very pleasant with Doug and yet, did not receive Linda.

Linda continued to be friendly just the same.

Further testing indicated that Doug was in the early stages of kidney disease. The liver and kidneys help the body digest food, absorb nutrients, and eliminate toxic substances. In extreme cases, when the disease is evident, a person needs dialysis. This is the process of removing excess water, solutes, and toxins from the blood in people whose kidneys can no longer perform these functions naturally. This is referred to as renal replacement therapy.

Dialysis will make the person feel better and help them live longer. The process is time-consuming and can have serious side effects, including low blood pressure, infection, muscle cramps, itchy skin, and blood clots. The most common side effects are blood sugar changes, potassium imbalances, and weight gain.

Doug needed treatment as soon as possible, and it was a no-brainer for everyone involved, especially Linda.

Immediately she was to become his number one support system, cheerleader, chauffeur, nurse, and health advocate. This new turn of events meant travelling seventy-five miles three times a week into Kamloops to the hospital's Renal Unit. It turned out to be a time that was daunting and frightening but also proved to be life-changing for Linda and life-saving for Doug.

As her father had done years ago on the prairie when there was little or nothing to do, Linda made the four-hour, three times weekly visit to the hospital into an enjoyable adventure for Doug, the nurses, and many other patients. Linda and Doug made fast friends with the other patients. Linda taught them all the backwards name game and entertained them with knock-knock jokes, stories, and innocent, flirtatious fun.

Some of the single dialysis patients arrived alone and spent their four hours feeling withdrawn, tired, and grumpy. Linda did everything in her power to be a bright ray of light. She made her rounds and sat with as many patients as she could.

A fellow by the name of Stuart showed up for his treatments in his full-on Western gear, from his old, worn cowboy hat to his weathered cowboy boots. It was plain to see that he had lived a hard, rugged life. On their first meeting, Stuart did not take a shine to Linda. He was downright rude and commented to her about her weight.

Without even batting an eye, Linda said, "You better watch out, Stuart, or I will be stealing your cowboy hat while you are hooked up to the dialysis machines."

To her friendly banter, he only scowled.

When Stuart was near the end of his life, Linda visited him in hospice. On his first morning, after he woke from a fitful sleep, Linda was at his bedside holding his hand. He asked her why she was there, as he knew he had not treated her kindly.

Linda responded that her husband Doug said that no one should die alone. "Besides, I am your friend, and I wanted to make sure no one else got your cowboy hat," she said with a warm smile and a wink.

With tears streaming down his face, the craggy old cowboy thanked Linda and apologized for his behaviour. She just smiled and said, "I knew you didn't mean it and were only flirting with me."

The true meaning of "What goes around, comes around" became Linda's mantra to live by. All the years she had withstood negative remarks, unkind comments, and remained kind and cheerful to those who had wronged her was coming to fruition, enlightening everyone around her. It felt right to be kind, and somehow it healed Linda down deep into the very depths of her being.

Dialysis patients often have symptoms of headaches, nausea, cramping, and feeling washed out. However, Linda found that being around tired and exhausted people at the hospital only recharged her. She was up for the challenge three times a week and once again had that old sink-or-swim mentality. To every appointment with Doug, she brought her game face, energy, and enthusiasm to help others.

After eighteen months of driving back and forth from Clinton to Kamloops, Linda and Doug had begun to feel weary. The straw that broke the camel's back was when they had a rear tire blowout by Deadman's Creek. Their lives were saved that day, as Doug knew precisely how to steer the car.

They were cruising along at the speed limit on their way to Doug's dialysis session when the back tire burst like a sniper's gunshot coming from the middle of nowhere. Except they were somewhere, on a sharp curve on the part of the highway near Deadman's Creek, an appropriate location, because this was not the first time something like this had happened there, especially to an exhausted traveller.

In split-second timing, the car was airborne, careening off the road and landing on sagebrush at the bottom of the embankment. Doug prevented the vehicle from rolling by gripping the steering wheel with both hands and steering until the car came to a grinding halt. They found out later that everything underneath the car had been ripped right off, and it was a miracle they hadn't flipped sideways or, as Doug explained it later, "careened ass over tea kettle" or far worse, been engulfed in flames.

When their 1980 Cadillac finally skidded to a stop, Linda looked over at Doug behind the wheel and said, "Smokey and the Bandit ride again!"

Shook up, but still needing to get to the hospital for Doug's dialysis treatment, they scrambled their way back up to the highway on foot. Doug was taking Linda's hand and guiding her and sometimes pushing her from behind. She stumbled, and time seemed to slow down. She wanted to sit down to try and make some sense of what just happened, but instead, she reached out for Doug. He was there. He was always there for her. And then she briefly panicked, knowing that one day, maybe soon, he would be gone.

Doug handled the situation differently. He needed to busy himself so as to appear indifferent to what was happening. Therefore, they made it to the top because of Doug's determination, both looking dishevelled and dazed from the incident.

Their shock and trauma from the recent crash forged them upward and away from what used to be their beautiful car—and what could have been their deathbeds. Back up on the side of the highway, they came face to face with two women peering over the now-flattened guardrail. Both were middle-aged, and Linda thought they looked like they might be going to a bingo game.

A small crowd had gathered, confident the car's inhabitants would indeed be badly injured or deceased. There appeared to be quite a fuss over Doug and Linda. People were flurrying around them, asking if they were OK. One woman said, "How the hell did that fat woman climb up that embankment? It is not humanly possible!"

Completely unscathed, other than being shaken up, they had only one thing on their minds, and that was Doug's life-altering appointment. The caring and concerned middle-aged women insisted on driving Doug and Linda to the hospital to get checked over. Linda blurted out, "Fantastic, because we were going there anyway!"

It turned out they were fine, and as Doug was hooked up to the dialysis machine, Linda called Jimmy, and he came to pick them up after Doug's treatment. On the drive back to Clinton that afternoon, Jimmy was annoyed, not because he had to pick them up, but because they were in an accident. He knew they could no longer continue making the drive. He said, "Lynn, something's gotta change."

That night Linda dreamed there was a FOR SALE sign on their house. She took the dream as a premonition. The following day, she called the realtor and asked if he could come over and put a real SOLD sign on their home so she could take a Polaroid photo of it and place it under her pillow for good luck.

Within days, their house had been sold, and they purchased a mobile home in Kamloops, with only ten days to move in. Jimmy and his friends packed them up, moved them in, and unpacked them again, in what seemed like one fell swoop. The trailer park was located only a few short miles from the hospital, making it no longer necessary for them to drive the seventy-five miles from Clinton to Kamloops.

With more time on her hands and knowing the doctors, nurses, and patients, Linda took her giving nature to the next level when she met a woman by the name of Barb. Barb was a volunteer for the Kidney Foundation. She was approachable and amiable. Barb explained everything in layman's terms, not the usual medical jargon that was difficult to understand. They instantly hit it off, and Linda took over for Barb as an official Kidney Foundation volunteer.

While Doug was in treatment 8:00–11:30 a.m. Monday, Wednesday, and Friday, Linda began her most impressive volunteering effort by opening the Kidney Table in the Royal Inland Hospital entrance hall. Linda sold T-shirts, gave out information on dialysis, and shared the importance of becoming an organ donor. Her conversations were often one-on-one, gentle, kind, and informative.

The T-shirts came in fifty-five colours and were made with recycled fabric. On the front it said, *RECYCLE YOURSELF,* and on the back it said, *DON'T TAKE YOUR ORGANS TO HEAVEN, AS WE NEED THEM HERE!* All the proceeds went to the Kidney Foundation.

After her time spent at the volunteer table, Linda still had time to visit with all of the other patients.

Linda also began the bottles and cans recycling campaign in the hospital. She picked up, drained, and sorted, long before they had recycling receptacles. The proceeds went to the pediatrics unit of the Kamloops Hospital to purchase toys and books for the kids.

Soon enough, word got out about Linda and all the good she was doing, volunteering her time, raising awareness and money, and offering empathy, knowledge, and goodwill towards others. She was asked to speak on the Kamloops news channel CFJC and at various other events throughout the city.

Linda spoke compassionately as a family member to someone who had kidney disease. She explained the medical side, followed by general information for the public. She represented recipients, families, and friends who were affected by kidney disease. Doug beamed with pride.

When asked to speak at a TOPS (Take Off Pounds Sensibly) meeting, her weight was at an all-time high of two-hundred and ninety-five pounds. Her special diets, weighing food, and lap-band surgery protocols were a thing of the past.

TOPS is a non-profit, non-commercial network of weight-loss support groups and wellness education organizations. TOPS offers tools and programs for healthy living and weight management with exceptional group fellowship and recognition.

Before it was her turn to speak, Linda sat through the organization's usual weight loss meeting. She was mesmerized by the format and how the session was run. There was lots of sharing the highs and lows and joys and sorrows of being obese. People were congratulated for their successes and told, "Better luck next time," if they happened to gain weight. There was no shaming or belittling.

Linda learned that the difference between TOPS and Weight Watchers was that elected peers lead the meetings, whereas Weight Watchers group leaders were paid employees. She felt that another important difference was that TOPS was significantly less expensive than Weight Watchers.

When invited up to the podium, Linda did her speech in her usual enthusiastic way and answered questions. As she was wrapping up, she asked if she could join the TOPS group. She was given a standing ovation.

She knew that the life span for someone on dialysis was five to ten years, and she wanted to be as healthy as she could be to take care of Doug and live out his last days with him to the best of her ability. Linda came to enjoy and look forward to her weekly TOPS meetings, which helped her lose one hundred pounds and, almost more importantly, became her support group.

This was not the first time she had lost one hundred pounds, but she hoped it would be the last time. This time though, she did things differently, natural and healthy, no gimmicks, shakes, or powders and completely without strict regimes or guilt-tripping sales pitches.

Linda prepared and followed Doug's meal plan to a T. She found that his restrictions helped her find balance with hers. Once a hearty eater and never a complainer, Doug had lost his appetite and was often disappointed that his favourite foods had become taboo for him—potatoes, bacon, deli meats, bananas, and chocolate.

Renal dietitians encourage most people on hemodialysis to eat high-quality protein because it produces less waste for removal during dialysis. High-quality protein comes from meat, poultry, fish, and eggs. Processed meats such as hot dogs and canned food should be avoided because of the high sodium and phosphorus levels. Because of her years of dieting, Linda could relate to his heartache when it came to going without his favourite foods. On and off again, food deprivation was well known to Linda.

As a couple, they rarely talked about life without the other. It felt wrong to Linda since she was so happy. *Why dampen the mood?* she often thought. Eventually the inevitable grew near, and Linda could no longer avoid it.

Four and half years on dialysis had taken a toll, and Doug's heart had become weaker and weaker. Doug had been admitted to the hospital on January 7 and pulled off dialysis three days before he passed away. Linda went faithfully to the hospital and spent her days at Doug's bedside. She chatted about their years together and how much fun they had.

She was calm and leaned in to pay close attention to her dying soul mate. Choosing her words with care, she reflected on her deepest self. She loved reliving their backstory and how they met, how bold she was at knocking on his door with muffins in hand. And how smitten he was with her. It truly felt like love at first sight for both of them. Deep down inside, she knew that she was pushing past her fear and ignoring her pain.

At 6:00 p.m. on January 14, Linda drove home to quickly eat and grab the stuffed animal cow she had bought for Doug. They both got quite a charge of the farm animal dressed in full-on Western wear, and when a button was pressed, it belted out the country-rock tune "Ghost Riders in the Sky," always inspiring Doug's familiar chuckle. The song was written by Stan Jones but was later made popular by Johnny Cash. It was an old-time favourite of many cowpokes, ranch hands, and especially rodeo-loving Doug.

Only minutes after she arrived home, the hospital called and urged Linda to return as soon as possible. Doug's time was drawing near. The weather had shifted, and the bitter winds had picked up speed, combining with a heavy dumping of snow. Linda did not care and felt fearless. Grabbing the singing cow, she fled back to the hospital, making her way in the thick snow to be at Doug's bedside.

While holding his hand as he slept, she tipped her head back and closed her eyes, noticing that her heart was full of thankfulness. Linda was grateful and appreciative of their life together.

She pressed the button to allow their silly little cow friend to bellow out the words, "An old cowboy went ridin' out one dark and windy day...Yippie I oh, yippie I ay, ghost riders in the sky..."

Gently laying her head on his chest, she listened to his faint, weak breathing as the cow repeated its sing-song rendition. Taking his face in her hands, she gave him one last look at her radiant smile. Simultaneously, Doug took his last breath at the end of the song, and with an emotion-rich voice, Linda cleared her throat and said goodbye. She whispered, "Say hi to my dad for me; I know you will both get along great." Sadly, her best friend and the love of her life died on January 14, 2000.

Linda had so many friends from her past and her present that she no longer felt lonely. They filled her home with food, cards, and condolences. The long-lasting relationships, the warmth of a small town, and her volunteer efforts helped Linda to cope during this sad and dark time.

After Doug's passing, Barb, her Kidney Foundation friend and mentor, called Linda to give her condolences and tell her the Catholic Church wanted to provide her with an award for all of her volunteering. Linda went to the church. It was Mass at 5:00 p.m. on Saturday, the evening after Doug had died.

The place was chock-full of parishioners and many people who were not Catholic, whom Linda knew from the community. As small towns go, it was not unusual to recognize people at every street corner, gas station, store, dude ranch, hospital, and church.

The priest prayed, giving thanks for Linda and all that she had done for the Renal Unit patients and the Kidney Foundation. The overflowing room of supportive people all bowed their heads in unison.

After receiving the award, Barb and Linda went out for dinner at Denny's. Linda realized that she still had Doug's wallet in her purse, so she opened it after ordering. She noticed there was $40.00 inside, next to a photo of herself. With that, Barb and Linda toasted Doug with their diet Cokes, and he paid for their dinner of liver and onions that night. Linda knew that Doug would be pleased and smile in agreement to picking up the tab.

The mobile home trailer park was in a peaceful, tranquil setting not far from the raging Thompson River. It had been decided that Linda would hold a memorial for Doug in the cabana, a common area that could be booked for occasions and was shared by all who lived there.

"Cabana" reminded Linda of travel, a shanty by the sea, or a summer house in the desert. It sounded festive and summery on the bitterly cold January day in Kamloops, far from the dusty heat of Reno, Nevada, where she had shared many moments with Doug.

Frances, Doug, Ken, and Karen all wanted to attend Doug's memorial. However, a terrible snowstorm had hit, the roads were a mess, and all radio stations were warning against travel. Her brother Doug insisted that Ken and he at least try to get there.

He was pretty adamant when he suggested that Karen, her six-month-old baby, Mackenzie, and their mom stay behind. He did not want to be responsible if they were to get stranded, or worse, get into a car accident.

Linda had no idea that any of her family members would be there, so she almost collapsed when she looked up from a table strewn with cookies, sandwiches, and empty coffee cups, to see her two siblings, Ken and Doug.

The past week had been a whirlwind of emotions. For quite some time, Linda had been dealing with anticipatory grief, inwardly grappling with Doug's loss even before it happened. She had not been able to emote her grief to any of their friends and all the people she helped at the hospital, primarily for fear of upsetting them or causing anyone to lose hope, especially others who were getting dialysis treatment. Consequently, she was still feeling somewhat detached from Doug's death.

However, being surprised by her two brothers brought tears to her eyes, and she felt overwhelmed with love for both of them. "Family has a way of doing that," she said, laughing through her tears as they all embraced. Linda was beholden and felt truly loved.

She had hardly recognized the oldest of her two brothers, who usually wore his hair long, with a full beard. He had gone and cut his hair and shaved his beard clean off. Her brother Doug lightly teased her that he knew her Doug always liked the clean-cut look, so he presented his new face in honour of him. Linda beamed, and her heart swelled.

The day after the memorial service, the hospital staff booked the conference room, and over two hundred people signed the guest book. Various staff, friends, and other patients filtered in and out throughout the day to pay their respects. Linda insisted on no flowers. In exchange, for those that could, she had them fill out the paperwork to become an organ donor. Many people obliged.

She continued volunteering and fundraising for the Kidney Foundation and had become somewhat of a celebrity, with her numerous appearances on the news and at speaking engagements at conferences in both Kamloops and Vancouver.

But at night, alone in her mobile home that she had shared with Doug, everything reminded her of him. The singing cow stared blankly at her, pleading to belt out its memorable tune. Linda could not bring herself to push the button or bear hearing the song again, at least not yet.

Even more noticeable was Doug's vacant place beside her on the couch. Its emptiness now screamed at her. The indentation of his body was still there, and sometimes she deliberately sat in it, feeling closer to him in that moment. Other times she avoided it and put a throw cushion where Doug used to sit.

His soft plaid shirts that still smelled of him hung in the closet next to her outfits of varying sizes. Doug's belt buckle, worn cowboy boots, and rodeo magazines made her wish they had never met. Angry, she wanted to throw them in the garbage, but then she quickly erased those thoughts and wanted to keep all his belongings with her forever, thinking she should build a shrine as a memorial of their love.

To encapsulate her pain, Linda summarized that meeting Doug was the happiest day of her life, and she would not change a thing except to eradicate kidney disease forever with a magic wand or a secret potion.

Lying down in bed at night, Linda could still hear the slow rhythmic sound of his breathing and feel his warm body beside her. This brought comfort. Then she would remember all his pain and discomfort, which brought on visions of her dying father—two men that strongly impacted her life. Two men she would never forget. Two men she would give anything to see again. Both were now free of pain and greatly missed.

Linda had learned about the concept of heaven when she was a girl but never gave it much thought, other than childlike speculations that her horse Tosca was there prancing in meadows and fields of gold. However, after Doug's death, in the early mornings before dawn when sleep was elusive, she felt a spiritual connection to the promised land and just knew that someday she would see her beloved again.

Visions of such a paradise always brought Linda peace and a feeling of being safe and protected.

Things started to change at the hospital; policies and confidentiality kept Linda out of the Renal Unit. New rules had been set in place. She could no longer pop in and visit, which disappointed her as it brought her such joy and healing in addition to providing companionship for the many patients who sat alone through their treatment.

Never one to fret for long, Linda decided to continue volunteering, selling T-shirts, and giving out information at the Kidney Table one day a week while also volunteering elsewhere.

Having been told throughout her life that she was a natural-born friend to all, she became a greeter at Walmart. She was basically paid to smile and welcome shoppers into the store.

Pinegrove was an assisted living place that accepted Linda as a volunteer with open arms. On her first shift, she was surprised to run into Dr. Campbell, but not as surprised as he was to see her. He had suffered a stroke and no longer practised medicine, and now he lived at Pinegrove. Linda recalled the many times he had snubbed her at dances and the Cutoff Riding Stables, and now here they were together, face to face under entirely different circumstances.

Nevertheless, she jumped right on board, tending to him and displaying her usual kindness, pretending they were good as gold with each other and had always been that way. Dr. Campbell was rapidly failing and had no visitors, so Linda regularly sat by his bed and held his hand.

The doctor apologized just weeks before he passed, saying he stubbornly only liked thin ladies and how foolish he had been—and was now astonished by Linda's one-hundred-pound healthy weight loss. More than that, he admired how strong she was and what a lovely relationship she'd had with Doug. Theirs had been a union that he had many times envied.

Dr. Campbell repeatedly went on to say how sorry he was for ignoring her and asked for Linda's forgiveness. She responded considerately and said, "Why, of course. I already forgave you years ago."

For some reason, the letter D was ever-present and continuing to follow Linda. After Doug's passing, she had many callers and started casually dating again, but no one could ever hold a candle to Doug or take his place.

At first, Linda thought that Donald Jackson could be a close second. He was a successful cattle rancher, and Linda enjoyed and appreciated visits to his ranch. She would wander around the property, helping out where she could. Still having a way with animals—they were always drawn to her, and she adored them—she befriended a young cow, who perked up and took to following her everywhere she went. From the moment Linda arrived, he would run up to the fence to greet her and push his head in for some nuzzling as she was leaving. Linda nicknamed him Pet, and that's precisely what he became, her pet away from home.

Donald was a hard worker and enjoyed eating out. They always went dutch, taking turns in treating the other for meals. He was frugal and preferred eating at fast-food restaurants but suggested that Linda take them somewhere more luxurious when it was her turn. She found this comical and often teased him about it but never complained.

Even though they were good company for one another, Donald broke up with Linda because he said she was a gold digger and only after him for his money, which was the furthest thing from the truth. On their last date together, he insisted she pay him back twenty-five cents for missing his phone call. He had begun to tell others that she owed him money. Linda gave him the quarter and happily went on her way.

Still missing Doug, Linda delved into her volunteering and chose to make friends, not lovers, from then on in. On one of her shifts, another volunteer brought Linda a token of appreciation.

As she handed a gift-wrapped bag to Linda, she said, "This gift is because you give more than you receive."

With tears in her eyes, Linda opened the bag, and after removing the brightly coloured tissue, she pulled out a white Beanie Baby bear with gold angel wings. Turning the plush collector toy over in her hands, she noticed a tag that read, *Date of birth, January 14, 2000.* Covering her mouth with her hand, Linda was shocked and then elated to read the cute little angel bear was born on the date of Doug's death.

Linda has become a beacon of hope for the elderly and personifies the comfort of compassion for the dying. She has carried on with her father's theory that laughter is the best medicine.

Not always seeing eye to eye with her mother, she has long since forgiven her for the darkness and unpredictable mood swings that consumed her. Linda now has a better understanding of what her mother must have been going through. Memories of her manic behaviour give Linda the desire to find balance in her own life due to her mother's imbalance.

Looking back, Linda has fond early childhood memories of growing up in a loving family in Vancouver and North Vancouver in the 1950s and '60s. She is happy that her independence brought her Cariboo adventures in the 1970s and '80s, helping her to find true love in the '90s.

Underneath the trials and successes, heartache and jubilation, there has always been a firm foundation of love.

Linda has gone on to win awards for her humanitarian actions and the generous giving of her time and for bringing awareness to The Kidney Foundation and The Organ Donor Association. She is a friend to all and takes pride in raising money, writing letters, developing campaigns, volunteering, and focusing on others' quality of life.

She still sometimes wonders why bad things happen to good people but then reminds herself and others of her favourite quote, "Anyone can have a once-upon-a-time or a happily-ever-after, but it's the journey between that makes the story worth telling."

Ken and mom being silly

Barb and Linda B.C. Transplant Games

Linda after losing 100 pounds on the stairs
of her and Doug's trailer

Handsome brother Doug before
surprising Linda at the memorial

Linda's 100-pound weight loss standing next to 100 pounds of potatoes

Linda and mom showing off Linda's weight loss standing next to mom

Ken and Linda

Linda and Doug happy as can be

Linda working the kidney foundation table

Doug, Linda, Ken, Karen, Mackenzie, Keith, Paul in Kamloops
for the Kidney walk in honour of Doug Brown

Congratulations

Linda Volunteering

Family reunion in Maple Ridge, Erika, Jessica, Emma, Paul, Karen
Marjorie (top row) Terrina, Doug, Mackenzie, Ken, Tanya and Linda

"Love recognizes no barriers."

-Maya Angelou

EPILOGUE

Linda now resides at RiverBend Seniors Community, on Mayfair Street in Kamloops, British Columbia, and refers to it as her forever home. On June 5, 2016, she moved from her trailer that she shared with Doug. She has often volunteered at the front desk, played crib and bingo with other residents, and read to her fellow seniors. Linda continues to share her jokes and stories to cheer up and spread joy to those around her.

Linda is now in her seventies. We live far from one another, but we talk on the telephone every Sunday afternoon. She has filled in many gaps and told me things that I did not know about herself and our family long before I came on board. Throughout our many telephone conversations, Linda has shared her life story with me, most of which I did not know.

Both of our parents have passed away. We talk about them too. We have discovered that our recollections differ, and we find our differences fascinating, sometimes comical, and other times heartbreaking.

Linda's number one priority is her dear friend Margaret LeBlanc, also a resident at RiverBend Manor—someone who is picked up by Handy Dart three times a week and taken for dialysis. Margaret would tell you of her friendship with Linda and how valuable her knowledge and support have been. Linda knows that Margaret's days are hard and is always ready to listen to her experiences. Linda ensures that Margaret is safely on the bus and is waiting for her when she returns in the late afternoon after her treatments to welcome her home.

Through many conversations, Linda and Margaret learned that they share their love for anything Western and had some of the same friends and maybe even crossed paths years prior. There was a time when Margaret dated Alcide, at which they smile and laugh at how they both dodged a bullet in not marrying him.

Linda suffered a setback in 2012 when Interior Health required her Kidney Table service to be shut down due to privacy issues newly recognized by the Federal Government. It was at this time that she became depressed and had a hard time coping. The pain of past hurts, and the closure of her passion project all came on at once and brought her down.

This sudden change brought the memories of her beloved Doug front and centre to her mind.

She remembered how proud he was of her for helping his fellow patients. He said it was important for the Renal Unit patients to have an "average person" to talk to, as the professionals just did not have the time. Doug wished that someone like Linda had offered him the same kind of exchange when he first began his dialysis treatment.

Linda continues to fundraise, sell T-shirts, and bring awareness to the Kidney Foundation and the importance of becoming an organ donor.

She has come to terms with her past and forgiven most of her tormentors. But not all. Some memories are still painful and have taught Linda a few things about trust and the sad truth that not everyone has your best interests or safety at the top of their list. She reflects on living one day at a time and tries not to sweat the small stuff. Finding balance in her relationships with family and friends, volunteering, healthy eating and living a life with no regrets are all aspects of living her beautiful life. Her sense of humour is just as evident as it ever was and still helps her out of the occasional sticky situation.

Linda's advice: "Live your life to the fullest, always follow your dreams, and never worry what others might be thinking. Help those that need it whenever you can. Be proud, stand tall, and always trust your gut instincts. By connecting your heart and brain, you can never go wrong."

The following remarks are given by a fourteen-year-old Grade 9 student for a speech at a Rotary meeting:

"I would like to talk about a special lady. She is a person who is there to assist anyone in need. Her name is Linda Bonner. Linda volunteers in many ways in our community, but I know Linda from a place called Overlander Extended Care Hospital, where she goes to be with our elderly in their time of need. Linda cares for my grandmother, who is in Overlander, and she has assisted our family in many, many ways over the years. We call her "Our Angel."

Linda volunteers much of her time at Royal Inland Hospital, promoting organ donation, assisting patients in the Renal Unit, and collecting bottles for the pediatric ward. There is always a big, huge smile on Linda's face, which assures me she loves what she does in her volunteering duties. Thousands of dollars are collected by Linda for donations to the Kidney Foundation. Over $100,000 was raised in BC, just by pulling the (aluminum) tabs, which were sent to the Foundation, who uses the funds raised to send children with kidney disease to "Camp Dialysun."

Linda also promotes organ donation. During the week, Linda goes from room to room at the hospital collecting plastic pop bottles, water bottles, and other recyclable items. All the proceeds go to support the pediatric department with new toys, video/DVD machines, TVs, games and many other items to keep children entertained and happy during their stay at the hospital."

-Grade 9 student

Linda has been the recipient of many awards and commendations for her volunteer efforts. However, this story is not about accolades. It's about the courageous and loving heart of a woman who just won't quit.

She keeps in touch with all three of her siblings—Doug, Ken, and Karen—and talks on the phone with them weekly.

Linda and her dearest friend Margaret LeBlanc

Linda, still smiling 2021

LIST OF AWARDS
AND ACCOMPLISHMENTS

October 1998: BC Transplant Award
July 1999: Kidney Foundation Organ Donor Program
August 1999: Ranching and Farming
Division & R.I.H. Crib Craze 99
November 1999: Kidney Foundation Organ Donor Award
December 1999: Catholic Women's League
Certificate of Appreciation
March 2000: New Century Ranching Division
May 2002: Top Award, Kidney Foundation, Vancouver BC
May 2002: Vintage Car Club of Canada
April 2008: Kidney Foundation, BC
Branch, Patient Services Award
May 2010: Kidney Foundation, BC
Branch, World Kidney Day Award
May 2013: Kidney Foundation, BC
Branch, Kidney Walk Award
July 2013: Pine Grove Volunteer Extraordinaire
July 2014: Pine Grove Volunteer Extraordinaire

In 2013, MLA Cathy McLeod presented comments
regarding Linda in the House of Commons Award
for her dedication to the Kidney Foundation.
While living in Riverbend, Linda has also received
two certificates of achievement from the Kidney

Foundation for her fundraising during the Kidney
Walk for Kamloops Brand of Foundation.
Also, Linda has achieved the ultimate in Cribbage
scores—a "29" hand in the 1970s and the second one in
the 1980s. She has pins on her walker to prove it!

The End

P.S

The singing cow still belts out "Ghost Riders in
the Sky," and the angel bear stays close.

Love, Pain, and Courage.

My sister's story is unique to who she was and who she has become. We all have a story worth telling. Below are the stories of three special people, who in different parts of the world have become a force to be reckoned with. They, too, have made it through trials and tribulations and have displayed love, pain, and courage in the face of adversity and sometimes danger.

That is why I have chosen to highlight the following short stories, and I ask that you keep them in mind. You may come across them again somewhere in a more complete format because every story is truly worth telling.

The upcoming accounts are about three remarkable women who have experienced kidnapping, severe bullying, and the struggles of immigrating to a new country. Their stories are also unique to who they are and who they have become. You will feel inspired and connected to these women as you read about their extraordinary journeys.

Anne Fletcher Dion

Melina Mertens

Shahnaz Qayumi

The retelling of these stories
by Karen Harmon and the three who lived them.

Anne's Story

"When you judge others, you do not define them; you define yourself."

Anne Margaret Fletcher-Dion, born in 1957 in Vancouver, British Columbia, has a secret that is not a secret at all.

It appears to be classified and taboo information simply because people choose to look the other way. Even worse, they sweep it under the table or the carpet and pretend it does not exist at all.

The NIMBY attitude, "Not in my backyard," is more prevalent than ever before.

Many choose to peer straight ahead when driving down city streets that are littered with broken souls and poverty—lives that have been damaged and lost, showing the wreckage and tragedy on the faces of those who dwell on and hide in the shadows of the streets. No notice is taken of the deaths that occur there daily.

It is a scavenger's existence, a relentless hunt for shelter, food, cash, and safety. It triggers fear and constant fatigue, living in the numbing cold. It causes these lost ones to do things they would never have dreamed of doing, just so they can survive, exist.

They are caught in a vicious circle of the middlemen, the keepers of the law, the bureaucrats, and the politicians who seemingly have joined hands to impose poverty.

The bottom line is survival.

Derogatory terms are often used to describe a street person. These terms dehumanize victims of circumstance, terms like hippies, hobos, beggars, druggies, panhandlers, and bag ladies. In reality, the homeless people are our sisters and brothers, mothers, fathers, and children. On the rise are little people as young as ten years old—some from a good upbringing, others from abusive homes.

They are vulnerable women and mentally ill individuals—people of all ages and socio-economic backgrounds, all co-existing, the fragmented helping the wounded. Sleep can come on a park bench, in an alleyway, behind a store, or in a shelter if there is room. Women are the most vulnerable and often find no sleep at all, just to stay safe and alive.

The politicians, police, detectives, health care professionals, shelters, and the media keep this secret under wraps and wonder who will blow the whistle on it next.

Anne is an advocate and has made it her mission to soothe the weary, love the heartbroken, and bring attention to a growing issue of great concern. Her past experiences have graced her with a comforting familiarity regarding another's torment and pain.

The recurring memories of Anne's thirty-year-old incident tear through her brain, and she knows that it is the nature of trauma and grief that she may never be able to shake off or get past. She repeatedly wonders how she is still living in it, engrossed in the memory that ripped her family apart and took her down when someone she loved was torn from her.

Anne lives day to day, mending and repairing what she can.

Her perception of what is safe and protected, right and wrong, is forever skewed. She knows where evil lives and therefore seeks out goodness.

Where there is a culprit, there is always a victim.

North Vancouver, British Columbia, is brilliant for its deep, lush forests and mountains to the north. It was once a small community, now grown larger, nestled directly underneath their towering beauty. The vast Pacific Ocean is to the west and south, and looking to the east, on a clear day high atop the familiar mountains, one can see as far as the Fraser Valley, to the mighty Fraser River and acres and acres of farmland.

Anne grew up in the quaint community of North Vancouver with parents who adored her. In a safe, clean neighbourhood, she went to school, had friends and enjoyed a *Father Knows Best* and *Leave it to Beaver* childhood.

As a little girl, a blanket of comfort over Anne was the familiar scent of Old Spice cologne and the aroma of fresh-cut grass, reminiscent of her father, who has long since passed. Memories of newly laundered sheets, a pot roast in the oven, and neighbouring children laughing bring happy thoughts of days gone by.

Anne, always sweet, was raised to be a good girl.

She married shortly after leaving home, had a great job, made new adult friends and looked forward to the rest of her life with the man she admired and loved. Anne anticipated the whole kit and kaboodle—the white picket fence, laughing, exuberant children, birthday parties, camping trips, and family dinners.

As life carries on and weaves its way, we recognize the passing of time and how it ebbs and flows. The unpredictability of what comes next is written in the stars but is not always evident in our minds. Nevertheless, we maneuver forward, seeking, wishing, hoping, and praying.

In retrospect, we do our best. But through trial and error, we discover that our best is sometimes not enough.

Thirty years ago, Anne made headlines. Her actions were on the front page of local newspapers. She was interviewed many times on various news programs. When Hollywood came knocking, a Lifetime movie was made about the tragic event in Anne's life, starring movie actress Lindsey Wagner.

It was on a night like any other in December 1992 when an event took place that still haunts Anne to this day. It was also on this night that she began her advocacy journey.

Her daughter, then fifteen years old, was late coming home. She had been going through some usual teenage angst, but nothing unmanageable. However, this particular night was different. Anne's maternal radar was on high alert. Her gut instinctively knew that her daughter was in danger.

All Anne could do was sit by the telephone. Waiting with shaking hands and a pounding heart, she remained still. She was suspended in time until the loud ticking of the hall clock told her it was past midnight. She worried and waited some more.

Out of the silence, the telephone rang. Before the second ring had a chance to shrill, Anne picked up the receiver. After a short pause, a young man's voice said, "Your daughter is being held against her will at the Surrey Travel Lodge," followed by a loud click. The caller abruptly hung up.

Without wasting any time, Anne contacted her friend Dawn, and together they jumped in Anne's 1979 red Trans Am and headed for Surrey.

Not aware, or even caring for a moment how beautiful she was, blonde hair blowing up from her shoulders, clad in a black leather jacket and her usual faded blue jeans, Anne took off like a bat out of hell, a mama bear to the rescue. Everyone knows that mother bears protecting their cubs are dangerous.

There was a frenzy and petulance welling up as they roared down the highway to a neighbouring community forty-five minutes away.

Rain lashed against the windshield, and Anne drove over the speed limit. The highway was barren, which gave the two women free rein. The sound of the engine changed as Anne went faster. Her hands gripped the steering wheel, giving her a sense of balance. She controlled the vehicle and inwardly praised it for its efficiency.

When they arrived, they found the motel parking lot, and the sound of wheels crunching on loose gravel seemed magnified in the deafening silence. Coming to a grinding halt, Anne turned off the engine and dimmed the lights.

In the early morning darkness, parked outside the seedy motel, there was a peculiar sense of quiet expectancy.

Dawn jumped out of the vehicle and ran to the motel office. A middle-aged, balding man watching a small black-and-white television looked up from behind the front desk with his glasses partway down his nose and a layer of sweat on his forehead. He offered no help and waved off Anne's friend. Engulfed by a stench of body odour and feelings of frustration, Dawn ran back to the car and climbed in next to Anne, in a state of indignation.

Perplexed and rattled, they sat and waited in anticipation of something, anything, a clue, an indication that Anne's daughter was somewhere on the premises.

Within minutes, they saw them walking across the parking lot—a man in his 20s, smartly dressed and considerably attractive, like a sparkly fishing lure meant to attract the unsuspecting, and he had with him a twenty-something young woman.

Following behind the couple was a man in his 50s, average build, looking for all the world like a father with kids, maybe looking forward to an early morning basketball practice, or maybe to having breakfast with a wife, balancing their budget while drinking coffee and making a grocery list. Behind him was an even older man in his 60s, a truck driver. His gleaming eighteen-wheeler stood in wait. His noticeable protruding belly, whisker stubble, greasy, slicked-back hair caused the bile to creep into Anne's throat. His gait was slower than the others. Anyone watching could tell he had done this before.

The young frontman led the wayward ensemble like the pied piper, coaxing and guiding Anne's daughter and another underage girl along. It was obvious the girls were being misled and coerced.

The men eyed the girls' backsides with a look of casual anticipation of the eventual reward and purchase that would be well spent.

In Anne's panic, she opened the car door and fiercely called out her daughter's name. Looking up, the younger man proceeded to hustle the girls and men towards the second floor of the motel, with Anne now chasing after them. She bounded up the stairs behind them as the door to the motel room closed in front of her.

Anne hollered out with a racing heart and adrenaline pumping as she began kicking the door with all the brute force her body could expel. She desperately banged, screamed, and kicked.

Silence momentarily shrouded the room as the door broke free from its hinges and landed directly at the feet of the men.

Pandemonium erupted.

Before any rescuing could occur, one of the men pulled out a .357 Magnum.

"Not so fast," Anne shouted, as she pulled out a .22 revolver that her friend had shoved in her purse as a "just in case" measure of protection they hoped to not need.

Once again, time was suspended; everyone froze.

Within seconds, sirens filled the parking lot's dead calm, loud footsteps were thudding up the dilapidated motel staircase, and police were everywhere.

Anne's daughter had been kidnapped and was being lured into the sex trade industry, and with Anne's fierce mama bear instincts, true grit, and love, she rescued her daughter and blew the story wide open.

Recruiting, transporting, or holding victims to exploit them is human trafficking. It doesn't have to involve shipping containers or crossing borders. It's happening in communities across Canada. Anne was able to save her daughter and others that night from human trafficking.

Some days the bright sunshine is our friend, and the dark, rainy nights our foe. But it is in the darkness if we squint our eyes and will it to happen, that light can be found.

Anne is that lightness who expects no praise or accolades. She is fighting the good fight and wants safety and justice for those who fall prey to drugs, alcohol, the sex trade, and life on the streets.

She is an advocate, a voice, and a force to reckon with. Her heart is for the lost—the ones who were supposed to be our future, who once trusted us, formerly babies in our arms and now presently living lost and unnoticed on the streets.

Three purple hearts are a code Anne started in 2016. The colour purple represents the people she calls warriors. She herself humbly holds the nickname "Warrior Mama," given to her by people in jail, the homeless, and those addicted or in recovery.

Anne has received many messages from mothers who have lost their sons and daughters to the downtown core that is infested with corruption and harm.

Through Anne's advocacy, she has reached out and shared her story. Sadly, her daughter is still struggling, stemming from the abduction in the early '90s.

In turn, parents reach out to Anne, hoping for her wisdom and advocacy to comfort them. She has a kinship with the broken and grieving. Their stories are heavy on Anne's soul. To help her cope, Anne built a Zen garden, where she finds peace and calmness—a place to meditate and pray, to be present and still.

In her garden, she places candles, stones, and beads: a variety of objects that have meaning in their presence, keepsakes and mementos that are special and relevant to Anne.

She has taught many despairing and grief-stricken mothers how to create their personal Zen garden, a place to be with their child.

Anne has gone on to study crystals and stones, the energy they bring, and their purpose. In particular, it is the amethyst she uses to make bracelets, its colour purple representing the warrior. The bracelets are gifts to those who need to be reminded or taught of their inner strength and warrior self. She sells some to those who want to give back, with all the proceeds unabashedly donated to shelters and group homes.

Anne is a truth-teller. Some refer to her as strong, independent, and fearless. In reality, she is an empath, someone with a big heart who takes on other people's pain.

I would call Anne a fierce, angelic survivor who knows her mind and has extreme empathy for others.

Anne's life mission is to help. She is busy, primarily joyful, and in a constant state of healing. Her two adult children, three grandchildren, four great-grandchildren, friends, and all the people she offers unconditional love to, are the ones who propel her forward. Their love and support remind Anne of a quote she once heard and now lives by, "One word frees us of all the weight and pain of life; that word is love."

My recounting of Anne's story is just an introduction.

Anne's life has been remarkable, inspirational, and sometimes heart-wrenching. The expanded version will be available in her memoir—a book we all need to read.

If you would like more information about helping others, purchasing one of Anne's bracelets or reaching out to Anne, please contact me, Karen Harmon at, karmon70@gmail.com

Melina's Story

"Believe in yourself. You are braver than you think, more talented than you know, and capable of more than you can imagine."

–Roy T. Bennet

Melina Mertens was born in August 1998 in Haltern am See, Germany. She is the only child of her loving and devoted parents, Martina and Dirk.

Growing up in Germany, Melina enjoyed a picture-perfect childhood filled with family and friends. She delighted in the pristine beauty of cobblestone streets, canals, rolling landscapes, vineyards, lush forests, castles, and remarkable architecture— all bringing to mind storybook visions and distinguishing, picturesque backdrops.

Fond memories for Melina include day trips to medieval castles, the zoo, and touring around neighbouring towns and communities. There were hours of outside play and creative indoor crafts, drawing, and playing instruments. By the time Melina was five years old, she had already taught herself how to read.

Life was easy and breezy. Even with her father travelling for work, Melina felt safe, loved, and special.

However, when Melina turned eleven years old, everything drastically changed, seemingly for no apparent reason.

It was like any other day. With books and a lunch bag in hand, Melina made her way to school. Upon entering the building, one of her classmates, a boy she barely knew, shouted out and made some disrespectful comments about her appearance.

Melina responded stoically by not responding at all. After this, the name-calling increased. She was called an ugly freak and anything else nasty that the tormentors could come up with. One student suggested she put a paper bag over her head.

Simultaneously, her friend Elena was also bullied in another class. It became a known fact that Melina and Elena were the two

342

victims of the school. Elena was often emotional and showed her pain, crying and begging her parents to bring her home. Melina tried to stay strong and not show her pain. Either way, the other students continued harassing both girls.

It was difficult not to wonder if it were true what the other students were saying about them. Their self-esteem plummeted, and many phases of depressive thoughts began.

At home, she could be herself again, helpful to her mother, joking with her father, and cheerful most of the time. Even when she went to bed in the quiet confines of her room, she chose not to cry. She held back her tears, which only wedged her despair down deeper. She was plagued with heartache and sorrow but tried not to show it.

Melina dreaded each day at school when the bullies would be out in full force. It began to spread—people that did not know her started to join in chanting horrible things as Melina walked past.

Over and over again, her mind tried to understand and figure out a plan. She knew she had done nothing to provoke this behaviour, and she wondered why no one was sticking up for her or coming to her aide.

Melina tried talking to the schoolmaster, and her mom confronted the leading bully's parents, but nothing changed. She was so thankful to have her best friend, Elena.

In Grade 7, Melina joined the choir and instantly loved it. She became enamoured with Justin Bieber in a schoolgirl crush sort of way and joined a Justin Bieber fan club Facebook page. These two actions instantly enabled Melina to cope with the day-to-day tyrants that would not leave her alone.

She loved to sing and therefore excelled at choir, and the friends she made on the Facebook fan page all began to share their stories on being victimized by bullies. Melina was able to communicate with strangers about her pain and get comfort from her new internet friends. Singing in the choir gave her complete joy. And listening to Justin Bieber's music gave her hope. Sharing her struggles with like-minded teenagers was healing.

Unfortunately, the bullying followed Melina into high school. Still, she had Elena, her choir friends, and many buddies on Facebook. Together they supported one another and learned how to ignore and maneuver around the oppressors and their harassment.

At one point, Melina wrote a beautiful letter and posted it on the school's Facebook page. She explained what bullying does to people and how it makes them feel. She personalized it as an open letter to all the people who had mistreated her. Disastrously it was like adding fuel to the fire, and she was labelled an attention seeker.

Very hurt by this, Melina knew their claims were not valid. Seeking attention was not her intention at all.

In Grade 10, the worst tragedy possible occurred. Melina's closest friend Elena was killed in an airplane crash, along with a number of other students from the school.

When Melina and the other students first heard of the plane crash, there was an announcement over the school's loudspeakers. The headmaster said the whole student body could go home after the sixth period. It was a confusing time, students were crying, and many were racing home. Everyone was in shock. Melina searched out her choir friends, none of them knowing if there were any survivors. Collectively they tried calling their friends who had been on the plane, and when their calls did not seem to be going through, they began to speculate the worst.

Sixteen students, some teachers, other travellers, and the flight crew all perished. Everyone had been expected home that evening. The deaths were senseless and due to pilot error.

Melina feverishly watched the news, hoping for a better outcome than the rumours were depicting. News footage showed where the plane had crashed and what was left of it—almost nothing. She could not fathom the loss of her dearest friend, the girl who brought a smile to her face; the hopes and dreams Elena and Melina shared were shattered. The pain of never seeing her friend again was incomprehensible.

It was the week before Easter break. Students still attended school, but the time was spent sitting together with their teachers.

They each talked about their feelings and how they were coping. At this time, through grieving sessions and counsel, Melina realized there were more significant problems than a math exam or homework and her years of being victimized. The students were encouraged to talk and cry and therefore grieve.

The townspeople came to the school throughout the week. Everyone brought candles, photos, and stuffed animals and laid them on the stairs of the school's entrance. In the auditorium, there were photos, candles, and posters created by the students. The church offered commemorations every evening.

A few weeks later, the funerals followed. Melina's teachers were supportive and kind, and everyone was there for each other. Some of her peers met at a park when the weather was pleasant, and they talked about the crash. They imagined their dear friends who tragically passed, now in heaven, happy and not feeling any pain. This helped them all work through the tremendous loss.

Melina felt numb, but she could feel the stirrings of healing and mending. She was able to recognize and be mindful of the importance of being alive. It was a turning point in how she viewed herself and others.

A year later, the headmaster organized a voluntary trip to Le Vernet, where the plane crashed. Melina went and found the beauty of the countryside to be remarkable. The landscape seemed incredibly surreal and breathtaking. She had never been to the mountains before and felt peaceful, thinking of her friend and the others. They hiked every day, and Melina felt close to Elena.

The people of Le Vernet were sympathetic, considerate, and hospitable. When they gathered, the residents told the young people that they must go on living; their smiles were the future.

Melina has never forgotten these wise words from a town of loving strangers. Every year since the crash, there is a commemoration, and afterwards, students, families, and friends bring flowers to the graves.

Melina's healing process developed over time.

*

First, she had to acknowledge the pain. The years of being victimized and the sudden death of her friend were almost unbearable. She mastered practical coping skills and figured out that she needed to do what felt right at the time: sleep, talk to someone, exercise, or listen to music. In retrospect, she knows that crying would have been a great release for her, but now she understands the importance of letting go.

Melina acquired information about the people who spoke badly about her; the horrible things they said about her showed who they were, not who she was.

She never stops dreaming and thinking about her future and is currently attending university in Germany, studying art, drama, and film history. The techniques on preparing for a role and creating a balance between her body perception and spatial perception are crucial tools that she can use on and off set. Melina feels that the best part of the learning process is listening, living in the moment, and accepting diversity.

Looking back, she felt safest in her choir practices, where she was never judged, and everyone felt like a close-knit family. If a friend were to describe Melina, they would say she is reliable, ambitious, loyal, open-minded, strong, passionate, enthusiastic, a good listener, and a stand-out in the crowd.

Melina's advice

"I want to encourage others to be proud of themselves and to follow their dreams. Cherish bad experiences as well as good ones because you can learn and grow from them both. Do not let anyone's judgement control how you live and how you see yourself. At the end of the day, you are unique, special, and wonderfully made. Take control of your life, as it is your happiness that counts.

I want to honour Elena Bless, who died in the plane crash 4U9525 in 2015. We were bullied separately, but we were united and came together because of it. She was the most kind-hearted and forgiving person I have ever known. My memories and love for her will live on.

*There have been many people over the years who have
touched my life. People who have given:*

*Desiree Boese, Fenja Maron, Leonie Manitz, Jana Buecker, Rebekka
Taplick, Natascha Mueller, Celina Joensson, Megan Thanheiser,
Soufjan Ibrahim, Kai Willmes, Sarah Koehler and Elena Bless
for touching my life and making a meaningful impact.*

*Zita Albrecht, my choir teacher, you came into my life for a reason. You taught me the
joy and healing that only music and singing your heart out can bring. Thank you."*

Melina has a bright future ahead of her and a past that she
keeps close to her heart, primarily to remember the pain and
sorrow. To never forget and to never give up. But to also reach out
to those who have struggled. She remains empathetic, strong and
hopeful. She is an advocate for inclusion and acceptance for all
human beings.

Shahnaz's Story

*Hope * Resilience * Perseverance * Education*

Shahnaz Qayumi was born in Kabul, Afghanistan. Her father was a doctor, and her mother, a loving wife and caregiver to Shahnaz and her sister. They had a wonderful childhood and grew up in a happy home.

After graduating from high school, Shahnaz went to Kyiv, Ukraine, to study, where she obtained a master's degree in developmental psychology and pedagogy. She returned to Afghanistan when the communist regime had taken power in Kabul. There she worked as an assistant professor at Kabul University in the psychology department.

However, the brutal communist regime forced Shahnaz to flee Pakistan. From there, she escaped with her family and immigrated to Vancouver, Canada, in 1983. Shahnaz had hope for a safer life and the resilience to start over.

In Canada, she faced many challenges, such as learning a new language, a different culture, and education barriers. She and her family were immigrants with no connections or friends, but through perseverance and drive, Shahnaz was able to establish herself in the Canadian academic community.

In addition to her previous education in Afghanistan, Shahnaz went on to obtain an MA in developmental psychology, a master's certificate from Harvard in global mental health: trauma and recovery, and a teaching certificate in early childhood education.

She became a member of the Vancouver Society of Immigrant & Visible Minority Women, as well as a mentor for those who were in leadership roles in Canadian society through the National Organization of Immigrant and Visible Minority Women of Canada, NOIVMWC. She has helped to organize the Afghan Cultural Heritage Day in Vancouver.

Currently, Shahnaz teaches early childhood education at Langara College in Vancouver, BC.

As a human rights activist and a teacher, Shahnaz is also an accomplished published author. Therefore, she brings her gift of writing and her reverence for children's health and well-being into her stories.

Shahnaz's books are for children and express the diversity of human rights, the magic of giving, and the challenges of escaping an original birthplace out of necessity. She also brings an awareness of women's rights, a child's right to an education, and improved mental health.

Her well-received children and young adult books are inspiring and beneficial to all. *Like You and Me*, *Afsana Seesana*, and *Run Away from Home Like a Gingerbread Man*, by Shahnaz Qaumi. Her fourth book for young adults, *Far Away From Home*, will be out soon.

Her books are for sale and available on Amazon.ca

They make great gifts for a classroom teacher, someone new to the country, and just about anyone who enjoys learning.

Shahnaz is a strong, caring woman with her heart and mind set on making changes for women and children worldwide.

Karen Harmon is a third-time author born in North Vancouver, British Columbia, where she resides today. Educated and employed as a Special Needs Teaching Assistant for the School District of West Vancouver, Karen can also be found teaching various exercise classes as a BCRPA fitness instructor in both North and West Vancouver. Karen takes health, family and fitness seriously, but can find humour in almost any situation.

Karen was raised in the 1960s and '70s with a bipolar mother and an extroverted, doting father. Even though her childhood was unique and eclectic, she would not change a thing.

As a mother of three adult children, Jessica, Emma and Mackenzie, Karen shares her co-parenting with her husband of twenty-five years, Paul.

In addition to writing, Karen's other main hobby has been cycling with her bike-trip friends yearly since 1993 all over British Columbia and parts of the United States.

Karen has over 10,000 followers on her social media platforms combined and over 120 ratings and reviews on Amazon and Goodreads.

She has enjoyed travelling to Belgium, Germany, Holland, Paris, Singapore, Thailand, and Indonesia to host events and speak to her many supporters. She offers an inspirational message of hope and how to find a successful balance with health, family, friends, education, work and play.

Karen Harmon writes passionately in her three memoirs: Looking for Normal, Where is My Happy Ending? A Journey of No Regrets, and Fat and Beautiful: My Sister's Story.

Looking for Normal is based on Karen's recollections of her parents meeting in 1945 at the Cave Supper Club in Vancouver, B.C., and her personal experiences of growing up in the 1960s, taking the reader on a memorable journey from 1930 to 1978.

"With poverty, addiction, mental illness and family relationships being current topics of discussion, Karen Harmon has tapped into a story that everyone can relate to. I am looking forward to sharing her upbringing with my students".

— Cathy Sieben, Secondary Teacher, Gibsons, B.C.

Where is My Happy Ending? A Journey of No Regrets is a follow-up to her first memoir, but can be read independently. After graduation, the story follows Karen into an unknown world of disco dancing and meeting unsavoury characters as a naïve seventeen-year-old. Navigating through the 1970s, '80s and '90s, searching for Mr. Right, she often makes mistakes and seemingly bad choices. Karen's story will remind many women of simpler times and the pitfalls they faced along the way.

"Quite like Karen's first book, it pained me to put this one down, and when I finished it, I was so sad it was over. I thoroughly enjoyed getting swept away in Karen's exceptional storytelling once again. I smiled and laughed often and sometimes cried too. I found myself rooting for Karen, from one adventure to another. I couldn't wait to see where her story went next. I could relate so much to Karen, from her low self-esteem issues, many second-guessing decisions, her high hopes, dreams, people-pleasing, grief, and so on. She's funny, intelligent, vulnerable, inspiring, wise, and unique with words. There are so many lessons to learn here. This book is a gift.

— Author Nadine Sands.

Karen's third book, Fat and Beautiful: My Sister's Story, dives into the extreme bullying her sister received and endured in the 1950s and onward. At the young age of six, Linda began fighting back with wit and humour. Following Karen's unique writing style, Fat and Beautiful: My Sister's Story, will once again intrigue, educate and enamour the reader as done in Karen's first two books.

All three of Karen's books are bittersweet memoirs and cover diversity, historical events, music, and each era's life and times. With the obsolete recognition of mental health, addiction and a family trying to succeed amongst society's trappings in Western British Columbia, Canada.

Made in the USA
Monee, IL
01 October 2021

79164216R00215